PARISWALKS

PARISWALKS

SIXTH EDITION

Sonia, Alison, and
Rebecca Landes

An Owl Book

Henry Holt and Company • New York

Owl Books
Henry Holt and Company, LLC
Publishers since 1866
175 Fifth Avenue
New York, New York 10010
www.henryholt.com

Library of Congress Cataloging-in-Publication Data
Landes, Sonia, 1925–
    Pariswalks / Sonia, Alison, and Rebecca Landes.—6th ed.
        p.   cm.
    Rev. ed. of Pariswalks / Alison Landes. 1999.
    "An Owl book."
    ISBN-13: 978-0-8050-7786-5
    ISBN-10: 0-8050-7786-3
    1. Paris (France)—Tours.   2. Walking—France—Paris—Guidebooks.
    I. Title: Paris walks.   II. Landes, Alison, 1953– Pariswalks.
    III. Landes, Rebecca.   IV. Title.
    DC707.L28 2005
    914.4'3610484—dc22   2004060733

First published in 1975 by the New Republic Book Company
First Owl Books Edition 1981
Sixth Edition 2005

Maps by Jeffrey L. Ward

Printed in the United States of America

1   3   5   7   9   10   8   6   4   2

To David, *père de famille,*
and to Nicholas and Elana

Contents

MONTMART[RE]
CEMETERY

PLACE PIGALLE

PARC MONCEAU

GARE ST. LAZARE

PLACE CHARLES DE GAULLE
(ETOILE)

BLVD. HAUSSMANN

RUE DU FAUBOURG ST. HONORE

AVE. FOCH

Arc de Triomphe

PLACE
MADELAINE

Opéra

AVE. DES CHAMPS-ELYSEES

AVE. DE L'OPERA

ROND POINT
DES CHAMPS-ELYSEES

WALK 7

PLACE
VENDOME

PLACE DU TROCADERO

PLACE DE LA CONCORDE

RUE DE RIVOLI

JARDINS DU
TROCADERO

JARDIN DES
TUILERIES

Palais
Chaillot

Seine

Louvre

Tour Eiffel

PARC DU CHAMP DE MARS

Hôtel des
Invalides

WALK 3

ST. GERMA[IN]
DES PRES

BLVD. RASPAIL

BLVD.

M

RUE DE RENNES

ODEON

JARDINS DU
LUXEMBOUR[G]

RUE DE VAUGIRARD

M MONTPARNASSE

GARE
MONTPARNASSE

MONTPARNASSE
CEMETERY

BLVD. ST.

WALKS AND MAIN SIGHTS

Central Paris

Walk 1: St. Julien le Pauvre

Walk 2: La Huchette

Walk 3: St. Germain des Prés

Walk 4: Place des Vosges

Walk 5: Rue des Francs-Bourgeois

Walk 6: Bastille to Eglise Saint-Gervais

Walk 7: Les Grandes Trois: Concorde, Madeleine, Vendôme

PLACE DENFERT-
ROCHEREAU

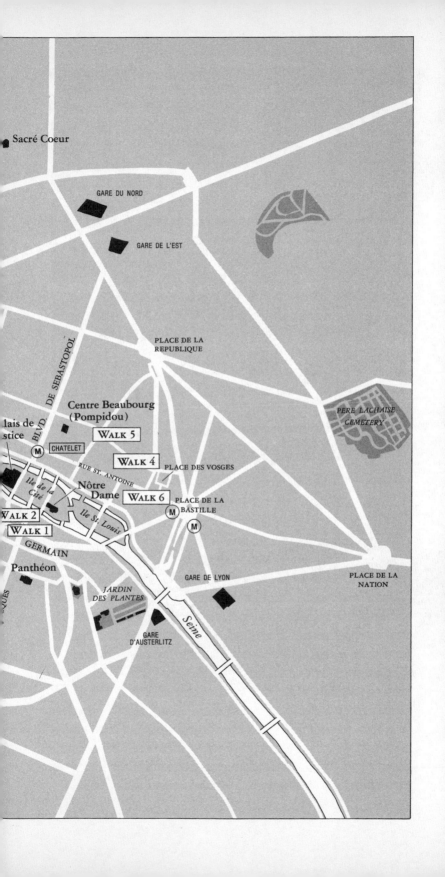

Preface

It all started thirty-two years ago, in 1972. Sonia was in Paris with her husband, David, who was on sabbatical from the history department at Harvard. Alison was a sophomore at Sarah Lawrence College, studying in Paris. We (mother and daughter) were excited about our plans for a project to write a short guide for our friends who were always asking us what to see and do in the famous city. In less than a week, we knew there was more out there than a pamphlet. There was a book.

Another book about Paris? How could ours be different? Since we are fairly (all right, very) fanatical about food, we thought at first that we'd combine a gourmet lunch followed by a walk in the neighborhood—a good idea, but we found it too confining.

Instead, we were seduced by the streets where we lived. We realized that another way to see Paris was an intimate look at a few choice blocks—"close-up tourism." The first two walks grew out of our old neighborhood. We were living on the quai Saint-Michel, opposite Notre-Dame, in the first settlement on the Left Bank. The area was so rich in history and architecture one could read the past by walking down the street.

We felt eminently qualified: we had lived in Paris on and off for many years; the children had gone to school there; one had even been born there. We had first gone as a family in 1948 because David, the *père de famille,* was writing his thesis in French history. That was when Pierrette, a French Breton lady, came to live with us. She still does, keeping the French feeling alive in the household. Since then, the pleasures of Paris and friends, David's research, our desire to educate the grandchildren in French schools for a term each, and revising this book have brought us back countless times.

It is now 2004, more than thirty years and six editions later, and we are still adding and subtracting, learning and changing. The "we" is now a mother, daughter, and granddaughter team. Sonia slowed down, and Rebecca, Alison's daughter, grew up to help Alison research, walk, and write. It was a natural transition that Rebecca should work with her mother as Alison had worked with Sonia. We all love one another's company, and Paris is our special bond. Now we are three.

Introduction

In this book, we offer you step-by-step tours of seven of the oldest and most fascinating neighborhoods of Paris. On the Left Bank, Saint-Julien-le-Pauvre, La Huchette, and Saint-Germain-des-Prés. On the Right Bank, the Marais, including the place des Vosges, the rue des Francs-Bourgeois, and the Bastille to Saint-Gervais, and to the west, the neighborhood that includes three *places:* Concorde, Madeleine, and Vendôme.

These morning or afternoon walks, which cover no more than about a mile each, will make you a connoisseur of these areas. What is hidden to the casual observer becomes the key to Paris. Through the signs and stories of the past, the architectural details, and the life of today, the city unveils itself. This knowledge makes you a friend and possessor of the *quartier* forever.

We feel that this book represents a significantly different approach to travel. After seeing Paris in the large—the obligatory monuments and sights—you must see Paris in its details to be, even for a short time, a part of the city. Our approach, which we call "close-up tourism," allows you to get to know a piece of the city intimately, house by house, shop by shop.

So what we have done is take the reader by the hand to walk

the streets, looking at each building and sign that tells a story. There is no hopping about the city, no seeing sights out of context, no having to choose what to see next. There are no long stretches of irrelevant streets or *métro* rides to take that interrupt the sightseeing. Paris has something to show you at every step, and we have found it for you.

We have chosen for this purpose *quartiers* where many of the streets are still the narrow, irregular, meandering paths of medieval and early modern times. These seven neighborhoods have, in part, been preserved by the accidents of history, though repeatedly threatened by the hammers and shovels of urban planners and boulevard builders.

No matter how often we research our walks, we never fail to make new discoveries, even for this, the sixth edition of *Pariswalks*. One friend who used previous editions said she would never walk down a Paris street in the same way again. We expect this to happen to you, and we would be pleased to hear about your discoveries.

On these walks you may sit, stand, snack, lunch, or dine. Eating places have been carefully chosen for their interest as well as their cuisine. Aside from eating and shopping, the walks are free. They are designed to be comfortable and fun. Most of the people in the area know us well, and if you show them your copy of *Pariswalks,* they will be happy to speak with you. Our maps and directions should guide you without difficulty.

It is wise to read each walk before setting out, in order to plan your day more effectively. We advise morning walking: more courtyards are open for mail and deliveries. You will not be disturbing anyone by walking quietly into courtyards or by peering through windows. Paris is for everyone. Press the main button on the door keypad to enter. Not all are locked. If you run into residents or a *gardien* (caretaker) inside, just smile and say hello; they will most likely ignore you.

Wear comfortable shoes (Paris streets are hard on the feet), and have a wonderful time!

Brief Chronology
of Paris

B.C.E. 52	Roman invasion of Lutetia
C.E. 360	City receives the name of Paris
481–511	Reign of Clovis, who makes Paris the capital
511–588	Reign of Childebert I, son of Clovis
768–814	Reign of Charlemagne
885	Norman invasion of the capital
1000	Church of Saint-Germain-des-Prés begun
1180–1223	Reign of Philippe Auguste; built the wall around Paris
1226–1270	Reign of Saint Louis; Sorbonne founded
1337–1453	The Hundred Years' War
1380–1422	Reign of Charles VI
1420s	Paris under English occupation
1515–1547	Reign of Francis the First, the Renaissance king; the era of the chateaus on the Loire River
1547–1559	Reign of Henri II and Catherine de Médicis; he was killed in a jousting tournament
1572	Massacre of Protestants on Saint Bartholomew's Day
1574–1589	Reign of Henri III, Henri II and Catherine's son
1589–1610	Reign of Henri IV, married to "*chère* Margot," his cousin Marguerite de Valois, sister of Henri III; then, in 1600, to Marie de Médicis. Henri was killed by a madman, Ravaillac.
1605	Place des Vosges started
1610–1643	Reign of Louis XIII, following the murder of Henri IV by a mad cleric. Place des Vosges inaugurated April 5,

	6, and 7, 1612. Richelieu was Louis's first minister, from 1624 to 1642.
1643–1715	Reign of Louis XIV, called *le Roi Soleil* (the Sun King). He reigned for seventy-two years and is remembered for the epigram *L'état, c'est moi* (I am the state). He turned a hunting lodge into the palace at Versailles. His eight children by Mme de Montespan were tutored by Mme de Maintenon, whom Louis secretly married after the death of his wife, Queen Marie-Thérèse (1683).
1715–1774	Reign of Louis XV left France almost bankrupt. He was known for saying *Après moi, le déluge* (after me, the flood).
1774–1792	Reign of Louis XVI, with Marie Antoinette
1789–1799	French Revolution. The revolutionary government guillotined Louis and Marie Antoinette in the place de la Concorde in 1793.
1793–1794	The Terror. In 421 days, 2,669 people were condemned and executed. Robespierre, revolutionary leader and member of the Committee of Public Safety, was chiefly responsible.
1795–1799	Directory, a government made up of senators and representatives. The military suppression of the royalists and Jacobins led to the rise of Napoléon.
1799–1804	Consulate under Napoléon Bonaparte
1804–1814	Empire, with Napoléon as emperor. He conquered much of Europe but was finally defeated by the British Wellington at Waterloo. He died in exile at Saint Helena in 1821.
1852–1870	Reign of Napoléon III. Georges Haussmann was his city planner, who changed the appearance of Paris.
1910	Great Paris flood
1914–1918	World War I
1939–1945	World War II. German occupation from 1940
1962	Malraux law decrees Paris buildings must be cleaned every twelve years.
1968	*Evénements de mai* (events of May): serious student riots in Paris, calling for wide-ranging educational reform
1977–1994	A period of historical building in Paris: the Centre Pompidou, the Louvre Pyramid, the Grande Arche de la Défense, the Musée d'Orsay, the Opéra-Bastille, the Très Grande Bibliothèque (the French National Library)
1981	François Mitterrand begins his first term as president of the French Republic.
1992	The date of the realization of the European Economic Community. The Common Market becomes a single unit, and European internal borders become irrelevant.
1995	Jacques Chirac elected president of the Republic
1999	The common currency, the euro, is introduced.

Tips

MONEY

- Use your bank's ATM card (not your credit card) to get euros from the automatic teller machines. They all take any American bank card. You will get the bank exchange rate of the day with only a small transaction service charge. Forget the traveler's checks. There are ATMs at the airport, so don't bother buying euros in the United States before you go.
- Many credit cards add an additional exchange fee for all charges made in currencies other than U.S. dollars. Consider paying cash for purchases abroad.
- Beware of pickpockets on the *métro* and at any crowded, tourist-packed area. They look for people who seem distracted or confused. Do not carry your passport around with you. The only time you might need it is to file for duty-free discounts. Carry a photocopy of the relevant page instead. Carry only the credit card you need and don't keep your important things in one place.
- Duty-free discounts in the form of a refund can be obtained only for purchases totaling more than €175 spent in one store in one day. Many stores require your passport number for the form. Ask the store to credit your credit card with the refund, and it will usually

appear on your statement a month after the initial charge. The store will give you the papers that you must present along with the duty-free items at the airport's *détaxe* desk when you leave the country. This means that you must take care of this before you check your luggage, unless your items are in your carry-on luggage.

- Students (carry your ID card; it is helpful to have an international student ID, which can be purchased at STA Travel, a student travel organization, for about $5) and senior citizens should inquire about reduced fees at museums and movies.

TRANSPORTATION

- Taxis charge an initial €2 to pick you up and often take no more than three persons at a time. A charge of €2.60 will be levied for a fourth adult, if there is room in the cab. Tariff A is used within the city limits from 7 A.M. to 7 P.M. and costs €0.62 per kilometer. Tariff B, €1.06 per kilometer, is used outside of Paris and in the city between 7 P.M. and 7 A.M. If you are outside the city during night hours, the rate switches to Tariff C, €1.24 per kilometer. If you order a taxi to come get you, you will be charged for the time it took for the cab to arrive from its original starting point. Taxis are plentiful, except at night, after the subway has stopped running. The subway lines post the time of their last train; if you are far from home, it is wise to begin your return trip before the last train.
- Buy a *carnet* (booklet) of ten *métro* and/or bus tickets at a time to save money (€10.50). Or look into passes for travel and museum entrances. Information on passes is available on the Internet at www.RATP.fr. Bring some passport-size black-and-white photos for *métro* passes. If you don't get a pass, be sure to have tickets for the bus before you get on; there is a surcharge if you buy your ticket from the driver. Keep your ticket handy, as there are occasional checks by RATP police for scofflaws. Also, when using the RER, the suburban line that operates into Paris from the airport, hold on to your cancelled ticket. You will need it to exit at your destination.

FOOD

- To save money, order the *menu conseillé* (recommended menu) at restaurants. You will be offered sparkling or flat water. It is also acceptable to drink tap water, which is free. Just ask for *une carafe d'eau.*

- Dinner is served from 7:30 P.M. on. If you are a nonsmoker, dine on the early side. There will be fewer people at the restaurant. The French consider anything before 8:30 P.M. to be early.

- If cigarette smoke bothers you, be sure to pack some Febreeze to deodorize your clothing and Visine for your eyes. Smoking is considered a god-given right for the French, and nonsmoking sections, though available, are rarely enforced. Check smokefreeplaces.net/en/FR/75/75000 for a list of restaurants that are smoke-free or provide non-smoking areas.

- Reserve at least a month in advance at famous restaurants and always reconfirm. Reserve about a week ahead for trendy places. Call the same day for other restaurants.

- The French do not do doggie bags. If you can't finish your meal, forget it. The only exception to this is at very expensive restaurants, where they will wrap up a dessert or let you take the petits fours home with you.

- A 15 percent service charge is already included on your restaurant bill. You may leave small change. Check on service charges at your hotel.

- A good *café crème* tastes better than our latte, although the French generally drink it only in the morning. Don't be shy, however, about ordering it whenever you want. Or try a *noisette* (literally, a hazelnut), an espresso with a touch of milk. Starbucks has come to Paris, and young French people adore it. The shop on the avenue de l'Opéra is always packed.

- Bring plastic plates and utensils and a corkscrew, and buy some of your meals to eat at a park or in your hotel room. *Charcuteries* (delicatessens) sell prepared dishes. It is not on our walks in this edition, but the food hall at the Bon Marché department store (*métro* Sèvres Babylone) is the foodie's heaven.

COMMUNICATIONS

- Buy a *télécarte* (phone card) from the post office, a newspaper store, or a *tabac* (a café that sells cigarettes) for use in public telephones. To call the United States, dial 001 and the number. Try to have the person you want to reach in the United States call you at your hotel. It's much less expensive to call from the United States. They dial 011-331 and your number. Pay phones are becoming rarer in Paris because everyone owns a cell phone.

- It is possible to rent a mobile phone, and it is convenient if you will be in the area for several days. In Europe the rule is "caller pays." If you call someone from your mobile, you will pay. However, when others call you, *they* pay. We use our cell phones to make a short call to the United States, and then get called back. The international long-distance rate in France to call a mobile phone is slightly higher than to call a land line. The details of cell phone rental and use are complicated. For more information go to www.paris.org.

- If someone in the United States will be calling you regularly while you travel, it is worth adding an international calling plan (about $5/month) to their phone service. The rate for calls to France drops from over $1/minute to less than 10¢/minute, depending on your service.

- If you have a laptop with 802.11b wireless capability, you can find cafés with wireless Internet. Open a browser window to register on the network. As little as $10–$20 will buy unlimited access for twenty-four hours.

- Buy the *International Herald Tribune* every day, even though it costs €1.85. Buy *Pariscope,* the activities-of-the-week booklet with an English section. It comes out on Wednesdays. In the movie listings, "v.o." means the movie is shown in its original language.

MISCELLANEOUS

- For house-call doctors, call S.O.S., at 01 47 07 77 77. The cost is about $60. Pharmacists also are very helpful and can sell over-the-counter medications that are stronger than American versions.

- McDonald's has the best public bathrooms in Paris. The public toilets on the streets are also a good choice. They are automatically disinfected after every use and are a somewhat safer bet than the toilets in the basements of cafés.

- Always dress in layers. The weather can change very quickly in Paris; what starts as a miserable day can often turn sunny by the afternoon. Carry a small umbrella. Wear comfortable shoes, since you will want to walk for hours. Heels are dangerous—they slip on wet pavement, and even the comfortable ones will cause blisters by the end of the day. Even if they make you look like a tourist, sneakers are often the best way to go. Also, keep an eye out for dog droppings.

- Always smile and say hello when you enter a small store. You will be seen as a rude American if you go in only to browse and never make contact with the shop owner. You don't have to buy; you just need to acknowledge the shopkeeper.

- Department stores have boutiques for virtually every designer. You can shop in one place and see everything. Galeries Lafayette has a weekly free fashion show. Go to www.galerieslafayette.com for details and reservations.

Walk · 1

Saint-Julien-le-Pauvre

Shakespeare and Co. Kilometer Zero Paris.
—Bookstamp at Shakespeare and Company

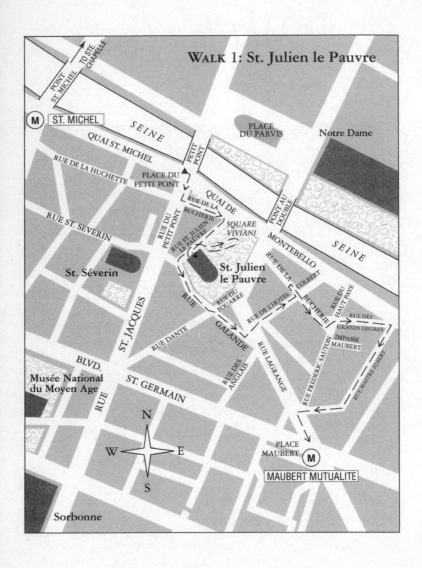

Starting Point: The corner of the Petit Pont and the quai de Montebello, 5th arrondissement
Métro: Saint-Michel, RER
Buses: 24, 47 on the Petit Pont; 21, 27, 38, 85, 96 at place Saint-Michel

Here you are in the heart of Paris, looking at Notre-Dame on the Ile de la Cité, where the Parisii, the tribe for whom the city was named, originally settled long before Caesar came here in 52 B.C.E. (The Romans stayed four hundred years.) At that time there were eight or nine islands in this region of the Seine, but as the water receded, the number was reduced to only two—this one and, behind it, the Ile Saint-Louis.

Walk to the large square, the place du Parvis, and look at Notre-Dame, glowing after its recent cleaning. About twenty feet from the portals look on the ground for a brass octagonal marker. It says, POINT 0 DES ROUTES DE FRANCE. It is said that if you stand on it and turn three times, your wish will come true. This spot marks the official center of France; stone markers along the French roadside mark the number of kilometers to this spot. This walk will not take you beyond 0 KILOMETERS PARIS, but there is much to see.

The Seine in prehistoric times was a wide, slow-flowing river more than a hundred feet higher than it is today. The river meandered all over the area between Mont Sainte-Geneviève, to the south (take a look about five blocks down and you will see the hill), and Montmartre, one mile away to the north.

Even Parisians forget that the river was once so wide, but in 1910 an extraordinary flood in the month of January reminded them of the tributaries of the Seine still flowing underground. The subterranean waters welled to the surface and swept through the city. From the present course of the river to the place de l'Opéra and from the Gare Saint-Lazare to the suburbs of the north, the secret Seine emerged from hiding and took possession of the city once again.

Postcards depicting the flood show men and women rowing around Paris at the level of street signs. A great many important historical records were lost, including those from some of the major libraries and banks. Deep cellars in this area are still cemented in mud from the flood, and excavations regularly unearth buried architecture and artifacts.

For ancient Paris, this sprawling river, whose waters were sweet and clean enough to drink, was a boon. Because of it, the Parisii felt safe from surprise attacks; an enemy would have to cross large stretches of swamp to reach the island. The river was also an excellent highway for trade, as it still is today. By Gallic times the Seine had already dug its present channel, but the banks to either side, especially the Right Bank, remained swampy and uninhabitable.

The first part of the mainland to be settled was the south, or Left Bank, where the ground rose more sharply than on the marshy Right Bank, called the Marais (marsh). (See Walk 4.) If you look up the rue du Petit Pont with your back to the bridge, you will see, about two hundred yards away and beyond what is now the rue des Ecoles, the Collège de France on the left side and the observatory tower of the Sorbonne on the right.

Two thousand years ago, Roman baths stood on these sites, for it was on this hill that the ancient residents finally got far enough above the water line to build important structures. The remains of the baths still exist under the Collège de France. Other ruins close by, unearthed as recently as 1946, can be seen in the garden of the Musée National du Moyen Age. The area between this high-water line and the river—the area you are visiting today—was settled much later.

The site of the present church of Saint-Séverin, the back of which you can see down the rue du Petit Pont on the right, was a small, dry hillock where a hermit chose to settle in the fifth century. Later, as the Seine continued to dig itself a deeper channel, the area between high ground and the river filled with houses and narrow paths.

Even as late as the Middle Ages, the street level was thirty feet (three stories) lower than it is today. This is why three levels of cellar still exist in the seventeenth-century buildings you see in the area. Until the middle of the nineteenth century the streets and alleys of the *quartier* ran steeply down to the river's edge.

The present ground-floor shops are on what was once the second floor of these buildings. Notice the thirty-foot embankment that rises from the Seine; where that stands, houses once stood.

The first bridge connecting the Ile de la Cité to the mainland, the present Petit Pont, was built here because at this point the island is closest to the Left Bank. A little fortress, the Petit Châtelet, which doubled as a tollhouse, stood at the end of the bridge on the spot where you are now. It was the custom then, as it is today on some bridges, to pay a toll in order to pass in and out of the city.

Another, larger, fortress, the Grand Châtelet, stood on the right bank of this part of the Seine, at the Pont Saint-Michel. Both these bastions were used as prisons during the French Revolution. With the help of underground passageways to many points in the vicinity, prison affairs could easily be carried on in secret.

The Petit Pont was not only a passageway; two- and three-story houses and shops lined either side of it, making it the busiest street in town. In the Middle Ages the picturesque aspect of this bridge—really a street thrown across the river—was enlivened by philosophers offering their intellectual wares and by jugglers, singers, and dog and bear trainers. During the day it was a paradise for cutpurses, at night for cutthroats. The bridge was rebuilt after fire, flood, and attack more times than the French care to count. Fire was the most common cause of its destruction until the eighteenth century, when the bridge was finally rebuilt in stone.

In the Middle Ages people believed that the bodies of those drowned in the Seine could be located by setting a votive candle on a wooden disc afloat in the river and noting where it stopped or went out. It was especially important to find drowned bodies before the authorities did, because a huge fee of 101 *écus,* the equivalent of a year's pay for a manual laborer, is said to have been charged for the delivery of a loved one from the morgue at the Châtelet.

One story about this bridge and its fires has it that a poor old widow whose son had drowned set a candle afloat in hopes of finding his body. The candle floated close to a straw-laden barge, setting it on fire. The barge touched the wooden scaffolding of a pillar of the bridge, and from there the flames spread to the bridge itself. In three days, the raging fire destroyed the bridge and the houses on it.

If you like, climb down the steps on the island side of the channel near the Petit Pont, or on the Left Bank toward the Pont au Double, and look at the Seine close up. You will be in the company of fishermen who catch live, though small, fish; of *clochards* (tramps) who find this spot slightly warmer and more private for sleeping than the streets; and of lovers of all ages expressing varying degrees of affection.

The quai de Montebello, the street that runs along the riverside in front of you and is packed with cars (we say this with absolute confidence after having watched the street over an entire year at all hours of the day and night), was built by Baron Georges Haussmann. He was the famous city planner of Napoléon III who, in the 1850s and 1860s, built most of the avenues and boulevards that have fortunately and unfortunately saved Paris for the automobile.

Cross the *quai* with the light (watch for turning cars). The small strip of park before you was once covered by the Petit Châtelet. Later, an annex of the Hôtel Dieu hospital was located here. The park was finally cleared in the early 1920s. This little park with benches and the park of Saint-Julien-le-Pauvre, to your left (with your back to the river), are the only pieces of green along the Seine, the only spots in Paris as far downstream as the Eiffel Tower that the French have allowed to lie fallow. This pocket-size park, which once belonged to vagrants and *boule* (bocce) players, has now been redesigned and discourages lingering.

Place du Petit Pont

The street that leads out from the bridge is called the **place du Petit Pont**. At the next crossing its name changes to the rue du Petit Pont. In both places, the street is the same width. If you look closely at the buildings on either side of the rue du Petit Pont, you will probably be able to work out why the *rue* is as wide as the *place*.

The apartment houses on the left side of the street were built in the seventeenth century. They are straight buildings with slim, rectangular windows free of ornamentation except for iron grillwork on the windows. On the right side of the street are nineteenth-century buildings heavy with curves, carvings, protuberances, and balconies. They stand on ground cleared when the street was widened and rebuilt in 1857.

The rue du Petit Pont lasts one short block, then becomes the rue Saint-Jacques. From prehistoric times this road, which climbs straight up the gentle hill in front of you, was the main road from Paris to the south.

When the Romans first came to Lutetia, which was what Paris was then called, they came this way. Soon after, they transformed the dirt road into a paved road nine meters (twenty-nine feet) wide. Two huge stones from this construction were found below the road's surface in 1926; you will see them later in the parvis of Saint-Julien-le-Pauvre. Elephant remains have also turned up, which will give you an appreciation of how the Romans thought big and built big, and why we still speak with admiration and awe of Roman roads.

As early as 1230 the rue Saint-Jacques was given its present name because the famous pilgrimage to the shrine of Saint Jacques (Saint James) of Compostela traveled south along it. The route to Santiago (Spanish for Saint James) de Compostela followed the north Spanish coast before turning inland, and the pilgrims were quick to gather and bring back scallop shells (*coquilles*) as proof of their voyage and their devotion. The pilgrims displayed the shells whenever and wherever possible, and as a result the shells have come to be a common symbol even to this day. Shell Oil uses its name to signify its role as a refueling stop for us on our modern pilgrimages; we eat coquilles Saint Jacques; and shell designs are common as a decoration on buildings and churches, and in wood on furniture.

Rue de la Bûcherie

Turn left into the **rue de la Bûcherie**, the street facing the small park, and pass the café, **Le Petit Pont**, a good place for a light lunch and a most pleasant spot on a sunny day. A *bûcherie* is a storehouse for wood. It was on this street that barges loaded with logs for heating deposited their goods. There used to be a restaurant here called La Bûcherie, which remembered its past not only in its name but with a wood fire, which burned on a hearth in the center of the room. Regrettably, today there is a tourist-oriented café in this spot.

The house next door, **no. 39**, is very special. The houses we have been looking at are mostly seventeenth-century; this one was built in the early sixteenth. It is a small two-story wooden structure, the kind that was typical five hundred years ago and can still be seen in towns like Riquewihr, in Alsace, or Conques, in southern France, but that has almost vanished from most European cities. The building once served as an inn and was hidden from sight for most of its long history. Le Petit Châtelet, as the inn was called—after the fortress it stood behind and to whose employees it gave meat and drink over the centuries—was tucked away until 1909, when the ground was cleared between the rue de la Bûcherie and the river. It is again a very small, intimate restaurant with a fireplace to cook *brochettes*.

The little building is architecturally interesting for several

George Whitman and his daughter, Sylvia, in front of their famous bookstore

reasons. Almost no wooden structures in Paris have survived; the big enemy has been fire, as evidenced by the history of the Petit Pont. Note the large dormer windows that jut out from the steep roofline and the smaller windows on the attic floor above. Step back and look at the exposed side of the building on its right, and you will see, coming out from the exterior wall, the ends of the framing beams used in its construction hundreds of years ago. These are the wooden joists, half of which one sometimes sees as exposed rafters in a ceiling.

Now look at the exposed side of the half-timbered remains on the left of the building. There you will see one of only three open staircases (*escaliers à claire voie*) left in Paris. This was the typical staircase of the sixteenth century; it was replaced in the seventeenth by the closed *escalier à vis* (corkscrew staircase).

Immediately to the left is **Shakespeare and Company**. You will get a hint of the store's uniqueness from the amusing announcements on the notice board outside. George Whitman and his lovely daughter, Sylvia, like to sell especially to people who like to read. The ground floor is devoted mainly to books-for-sale of all kinds—old and new, almost all in English. Whitman owns the house next door and keeps his own library and an antiquarian bookshop there. The walls are covered with books he does not sell, including a first edition of James Joyce's *Ulysses*. This is where one gets a feeling of Whitman's unusual personality.

The shop itself is a treasure trove of books and people, and if you nose around long enough and look interested, Whitman might invite you to tea. The front room was once a stone court-yard; into it Whitman has set fragments of marble friezes, tiled borders, and brass plaques. The narrow, one-person-at-a-time staircase at the very back of the store leads to a maze of book-lined rooms filled with chairs, couches, and beds. You can read the books in these rooms, meet people, even take a nap if you wish, and go to Whitman's famous tea parties, on Sundays at 4 P.M.

More than a bookseller, Whitman takes in travelers, espe-cially serious writers—a vanishing breed, he feels. If an author notifies him ahead of time, he or she may stay in one of Whit-man's rooms free or in exchange for working in the shop for a week or so, until other quarters are found.

Shakespeare and Company has always promoted the liter-ary avant-garde. When the publishing house of the same name was originally founded by Sylvia Beach (the source of Whit-man's daughter's name), it was the only house that would pub-lish James Joyce's *Ulysses*. Now Whitman gives young writers a chance to be published in his review and to be heard at poetry readings in his library, every Monday night at eight.

Give this store some browsing time. It is generally open from noon to midnight, or one to one. If you want a souvenir of Paris, buy a book and get it stamped here. The inscription around the head of William reads SHAKESPEARE AND CO. KILOME-TER ZERO PARIS.

Outside the shop, notice the small green fountain consist-ing of a base and four women holding a crown from which a stream of water flows down. In 1842, a British gentleman named Sir Richard Wallace visited Paris and was unable to ob-tain a glass of water from a local restaurant. On his return to En-gland, he purchased more than one hundred of these water fountains and had them installed all over Paris, where they be-came a main source of drinking water. Drinking cups were sus-pended from the hooks below the women's feet. In love with

Paris, Wallace also offered his collection of paintings to the city, which turned him down. It became instead the famous Wallace collection in London.

After World War II, most of the Wallace fountains were stolen and modern copies were made. The original fountains had four different women; in the copies the women all have the same face, the same eyes and lips. Other differences are the positioning of their feet, the ruffles on the bodices of their dresses, and the way the folds of their dresses fall. This one is not an original, but look for other Wallace fountains as you walk around the city.

Rue Saint-Julien-le-Pauvre

Go around the corner to the right, into the **rue Saint-Julien-le-Pauvre. Nos. 4–8**, on your right, are all owned by the same people. The **Esmeralda Hotel, no. 4**, is a hotel named for Victor Hugo's heroine in *The Hunchback of Notre-Dame*. The hotel also achieved some fame in another book, *Linnea in Monet's Garden,* a children's book written by Christina Björk and illustrated by Lena Anderson. For connoisseurs of the neighborhood, the details in the book's watercolors will be impressively authentic. The owner of the Esmeralda is, herself, a character for a book. She came to Paris from the provinces and thought that the city was especially beautiful from the Seine. She and her husband went into partnership with a financial backer and, with one decrepit boat, started the Bateaux-Mouches sightseeing boats on the Seine. On their first day out, their boat malfunctioned, going only in circles. Today, however, this pleasure boat line is a hugely successful tourist attraction—though as a result of her divorce, the owner of the Esmeralda no longer has any connection to the line.

The owner never intended to run a hotel but somehow acquired the building. It had only one bath and was occupied by women who had lived there for forty years and hardly paid any rent. She had to wait for changes in the law before she could evict them, restore the building's seventeenth-century details, and put in all the necessary bathrooms. Today the small rooms are each

11

uniquely decorated with antiques and will fulfill all your dreams of a truly "Left Bank" experience of Paris. Book well in advance.

Notice from across the street the soft-beige stone building, **no. 10**, and in particular the apartment's elegant windows on the French first floor (what Americans would call the second floor), which are taller than the others. The tall, multipanel windows are much more elegant than the plain French-door style windows on the floor above. At each floor the windows are progressively smaller, denoting lower ceilings in the apartments. At the very top, almost out of view, the tiny mansard windows (named after their inventor, the architect François Mansart) that peep out from the sloping roof are reduced to one small pane. The tallest windows of the ground floor mean, of course, higher ceilings, a mark of distinction still dear to the French, especially in old, nonstandardized apartments.

The exterior decoration tells the same story. Thus, the iron railings on the protruding sills of the two balconies on this first floor are finer than those on the floor above, after which there are no more balconies or grillwork at all. (Look at other examples of handwrought iron decoration on nineteenth-century houses as well as those of the seventeenth century as you walk around the city.)

It is clear that the first floor above the street was once the coveted apartment, *appartement noble*. The ground floor, called the *rez-de-chaussée*, which means "even with the road," was reserved for the concierge's one or two rooms, the courtyards, and the rubbish. The wealthy nobles and bankers stepped up one flight; the middle-class professionals and shopkeepers climbed two or three; the servants and workers trudged to the top. Apartment buildings, therefore, in all but the poorest neighborhoods, were microcosms of French society.

The advent of the elevator, however, turned this arrangement upside down and also made possible the one-class highrise building. Today the servants' rooms—often used as workshops or extra bedrooms, sleep-in servants being hard to come by—are located on the ground floor, alongside the concierge; apartments cost more the higher you go, and the prize residence is a sunlit, glass-enclosed, terraced retreat at the top, as far as possible from the city's noise and dirt. There

No. 10, rue Saint-Julien-le-Pauvre: Before the advent of the elevator, the best apartment was on the French first floor.

are relatively few of these newer apartment buildings on the Left Bank, but the next time you visit the bourgeois neighborhoods of western Paris (the seventh, eighth, and sixteenth arrondissements), take a look at the imposing, prosperous buildings with cut-stone façades and follow the lines of balconies up to the elegant penthouses at the top.

A very important person lives upstairs in the house at **no. 12**: the architect Claude Frémin. He is responsible for some of the most remarkable restorations in the area. Frémin's latest project has been the restoration of the street: the wide brick pavements have been returned to their original medieval width.

The **Tea Caddy**, at **no. 14**, is one of the nicer tea shops in Paris. A stop at this cozy shop is wonderful. Light meals (mainly eggs in various forms), pastries made on the premises, and a wide variety of teas are served. The Tea Caddy was founded in 1928 by Miss Kinklin, an English governess to a Rothschild offspring. The tea shop, which she had always dreamed of, was the family's retirement gift to her.

The Tea Caddy was formerly the stables of the building next door. The entrance of no. 14 is an impressive stone gateway with massive wooden doors. Look above at the pediment where Themis, the Greek goddess of justice in all its relations to men, sits. She is represented as a dignified and commanding prophetess holding the scales of justice and surrounded by olive branches of peace, while a cherub holds an hourglass.

The symbolism of this sculpture was carefully chosen in the early seventeenth century, when this entry was added to the official residence of Isaac de Laffémas, prefect of police of the Châtelet under Cardinal Richelieu. The prefect was, among other things, the king's prosecutor, and we have cause to wonder how wisely he used those scales. While he and his family lived comfortably above ground, three levels of cellars below were used as a prison. The cellars date from the fourteenth century and were originally used to house the monks from the church of Saint-Julien-le-Pauvre, across the street. This prison eventually fell into disuse in the seventeenth century, but 150 years later, in 1793, the Revolution created such an overflow of prisoners in the Petit and Grand Châtelets and everywhere else that these cells were restored to use.

Themis, the Greek goddess of justice, at no. 14 rue Saint-Julien-le-Pauvre

We have it on good authority that some rusty instruments of torture remained in the lowest basement until recently. Hélène, an excellent hairdresser whose salon was just down the street, saw two of them when she and her husband were on the trail of a damaged water pipe: a rack and a devilish seat with a hole in it to allow the heat from boiling oil to cook a bound and helpless victim—in the name of justice, of course.

The house has been converted into apartments whose owners keep the front door locked. This is unfortunate because the interior restoration was beautifully done and is a perfect example of how modern additions and restoration can enhance an original fifteenth-century structure. Look over the wall at the façade of the building. It is merely façade. Concealed underneath this trompe l'oeil of plaster cut to look like stone is a fifteenth-century half-timbered wall.

Visit the odd **church of Saint-Julien-le-Pauvre**. Before you is a truncated edifice with a lopsided pediment crowning a flat, improvised façade, the remains of a thirteenth-century pillar, and an iron-caged well flanking the front portal. There is much to tell about Saint Julien himself, so you may wish to sit inside the church (cool in summer, warm in winter) and read his story, which supposedly took place in the first century. The story has been told by Flaubert in his *Trois Contes*.

Julien, the son of a noble family, was an avid hunter. One day he was having excellent luck in the forest. He had killed a doe and her fawn and was about to shoot the stag when the animal turned and spoke to him. "How darest thou kill my family and pursue me. Thou who wilt one day kill thine own father and mother!" Julien was staggered by these words and swore a sacred oath that he would never hunt again. To prevent the fulfillment of the prediction, he left his parents' castle and went off to serve the king.

In the course of his duty Julien traveled to distant lands, where he fought so valiantly that the king knighted him and rewarded him with a castle and the hand in marriage of the widow of a rich lord. The couple lived together very happily, except for Julien's irrepressible passion for the hunt. One morning his wife encouraged him to go into the forest, saying that he had abstained long enough and, besides, it could in no way affect his parents. Julien succumbed and set out to hunt. But though he imagined game in every thicket he could kill nothing.

In Julien's absence an old and travel-weary couple arrived at his castle. His wife took them in and, as they conversed, discovered that they were Julien's parents, who had searched for him everywhere since his unexplained departure. She welcomed them heartily and invited them to stay, offering them her own bed.

When Julien returned from the hunt, tired and frustrated, he went straight to the bedroom to rest. Opening the door he perceived two figures in his bed and flew into a rage. "This is the reason my wife encouraged me to hunt," he said to himself, and he drew his sword and slew the sleeping figures. At that, his wife came to tell him the good news of his parents' arrival. When Julien realized what he had done, he wept bitterly. "What will become of me, most unfortunate man? It is my dear parents I have killed. I have fulfilled the promise of the stag on the very day that I broke my vow never to hunt again. I will enjoy no rest until I know God has accepted my repentance."

With these words he resolved to abandon his estate and fortune in order to do penance. His wife would not let him leave

Julien and his wife ferrying a beggar across the Seine

alone, and so the two settled on the shores of a large river, ferrying people across the water and offering them lodgings in the small guest house that they built there.

One bleak winter night, when Julien had gone to bed exhausted, there was a knock at the door. A hideous stranger, half-frozen and half-dead, stood there asking first for hospitality and then to be rowed across the river. Julien brought him into his own bed and treated him with care. Later, as he was ferrying him across the river, the stranger, who had looked so hideous moments before, was suddenly transformed into a radiant angel. He said, "Julien, the Lord sent me to tell thee that thy repentance hath been accepted and that thy wife and thyself will soon be able to rest in God."

Julien's story is depicted in a remarkable fourteenth-century stone relief, which is now fixed onto the façade of a modern cinema around the corner, at no. 42 rue Galande, which we shall see later.

Not only was the large river where Julien and his wife settled the Seine, but the site of their guest house later became the

17

junction of the two main Roman roads from Paris to the south: the rue Saint-Jacques led to Orléans, and the rue Galande led to Lyons and Italy. Actual proof of the existence of an oratory and hostelry on this spot dates from the sixth century, when Bishop Gregory of Tours visited the area, and the church of Saint-Julien in particular. Records have been found showing that Gregory preached a midnight mass here in 587.

Both the hostelry and oratory were destroyed in 866 by Norman invaders. The church was rebuilt much later, between 1170 and 1240. Much of that structure remains today, making Saint-Julien the oldest church in Paris. Although Notre-Dame was started a few years earlier, in 1163, it was not completed until 1330. Parts of the church of Saint-Germain-des-Prés—the bell tower, the bases of two towers, and part of the nave—are older, but at the time it was built, the church was outside the city walls, so it doesn't count for strict antiquarians. Saint-Julien-le-Pauvre is a poor church in comparison with the other two. It has neither bell tower nor transept, but it does have lots of pillars.

What the church lacks in appearance it makes up for in colorful history. The original center of learning in Paris was Notre-Dame, on the Ile de la Cité. It was Peter Abelard, the famous and infamous theologian-philosopher, who broke with established doctrine there at the beginning of the twelfth century and led a massive student exodus to Saint-Julien-le-Pauvre, on the Left Bank. Three thousand rebels went along with him, thereby creating what became known as the Latin Quarter, that is, the quarter of Latin-speaking clerics.

Saint-Julien-le-Pauvre became the official seat of the newly chartered Université de Paris and enjoyed the privilege of being the site of the election of the *rector magnificus* and of a sermon every two years restating the rights of students and teachers. The church grew rich and built a network of underground cells to house more than a hundred monks. In time, however, the center of instruction shifted south, and by 1449 the monks had been reduced to a lonely three.

In 1524 the church was almost destroyed; the next year it was decided that elections would never be held there again. Students, unhappy over the election of a new rector, proceeded to break chairs, windows, furniture, and statues, forcing the church to close. With closure came neglect. An appraiser in 1640 noted that the rain and weather penetrated the building "as if it were open countryside."

This is why the present entrance stands far back from the original front of the church, which stood about where the street runs now. The whole entrance hall was on the point of collapse and had to be removed in the middle of the seventeenth century. All that is left are the ravaged thirteenth-century pillar with thin colonettes above, on the left side, and the twelfth-century flowering well, on the right. Beside the well lies a huge slab of stone that dates from the fourth century but was unearthed only in 1926. Stones like this one formed part of the famous Roman road that became the rue Saint-Jacques.

After its long period of abandonment, the church and its land were ceded in 1655 to the Hôtel Dieu, the city hospital. The hospital restored the remains of the church sufficiently for it to serve as the hospital's chapel as well. During the French Revolution, however, more than a hundred years later, the chapel, along with so many other churches, was shut down.

Saint-Julien continued to suffer ignominy and was used alternatively as a salt storehouse, as fairgrounds for wool merchants, and as a flour granary. Photographs from the nineteenth century show barrels of goods piled on the parvis, the area in front of the entrance. Houses and stores leaned against the church, glad to use its wall as one of their own.

Sometime after the Hôtel Dieu took over Saint-Julien and its property, it built two wide three-story annexes on the Left Bank facing the river, between the Petit Pont and the Pont au Double. These massive additions blocked the view of the river and darkened the streets in this area. Photographs taken from the front of the church looking toward the Seine show a street that looks like a dead end. The buildings were finally taken down in 1877, when the hospital confined itself to its historic location on the Ile de la Cité, next to Notre-Dame. The city fathers decided then that no structure would ever again be built on this spot. That is why we are fortunate enough today to have two green pockets on the banks of the Seine on the quai de Montebello.

It was not a disaster for those squat sick wards to have been demolished. Hospital care in those days was to be avoided like the plague; prayer was said to account for much of what healing did take place. But it would have been a disaster to tear down Saint-Julien itself. That intention seems scarcely credible, but in fact an extension of the rue Monge (what is now the rue Lagrange) was planned that would have cut into this area and gone right through the church and to the rue Saint-Jacques. At the last minute, as is so often the case when it comes to saving historical monuments, the plans were revoked, and Saint-Julien and the small neighborhood remained intact.

Look at the uncomplicated interior of the church. You may be surprised to see the painted rood screen (iconostasis) with three doors and six rows of icons in front of the altar. There is a simple explanation for these unexpected objects. In 1889 the unused church was given by the archdiocese of Paris to the Eastern Catholic community, the Melchites. Their service, sung in Greek, can be heard on Sunday mornings.

Most striking is the tremendous number of twelfth-century columns, especially in such a small area. The capitals, like those in Notre-Dame, are decorated with leaf and fern patterns, except for one on the right-hand side, nearest the screen. From that one, four harpies—birdlike women with wings—peer down at you, warning perhaps of the wages of sin. Storytelling on capitals was typical of the earlier Romanesque style of architecture, used for the benefit of the illiterate masses. Notice also, to your left, the large arabesque iron music stand that faces the screen.

Outside again (with your back to the church entrance), look to your left at the back of a seventeenth-century building covered with fake timbering, nailed on forty years ago to give the appearance of great age, as though three hundred years were not enough. (Contrast this with the genuine article, the Petit Châtelet on the rue de la Bûcherie.)

The blood-red door belongs to the **Caveau des Oubliettes**. The entrance is now around the corner, on the rue Galande. It is an underground jazz club installed in what the owners claim was once a prison. *Oubliettes,* from the French word meaning "to forget," were cells where prisoners were put away in solitary holes and left there with nothing but a grate above for food to go in and waste to go out. Turnover of occupants was rapid.

Ownership is new since we were last here, but we hope the new owners will be willing to show you the old prison holes with the messages scratched by the dying, as well as the other items in the prison: the guillotine, the chastity belt, and the barbaric instruments of torture they claim their establishment still contains. We're skeptical. In fact, our research indicates that the cells of the Caveau were used not for prisoners but for monks, while the real *oubliettes* are those we speak about earlier, on the right side of the rue Saint-Julien-le-Pauvre. The jazz club is open every night from 9:30 P.M. to 2 A.M. Jazz starts at 10 P.M.

Before turning into the rue Galande go into the garden next to Saint-Julien. This is the square René-Viviani, the loveliest park on the banks of the Seine. Eight hundred years ago it was the scene of boisterous, bustling student activity and dormitories. Later it became the site of one of the annexes of the Hôtel Dieu. Forty years ago it was the untended backyard of Saint-Julien. Today it is an oasis amid the concrete, stone, and asphalt of some of the busiest streets in Paris. Here you will find tired tourists and passersby, couples, mothers and children, and an occasional vagrant. The French frequently do not allow anyone to walk or play on the grass. But you can in the square René-Viviani, because everyone is more relaxed in this part of town.

Paris is filled with parks and small squares, but this one has more to offer than most. It has the great distinction of affording from its benches what may well be the finest view of Notre-Dame. After peering through the trees and changing your seat several times, turn and look at pieces of church sculpture in the park itself. These odd fragments of broken statuary, worn down by time and weather, were once a part of the Abbé de Cluny. When pieces of sculpture decorating churches decay beyond recognition, they are moved to parks and replaced by whole new copies made in restoration workshops behind Notre-Dame.

What passes for the oldest tree in Paris stands in this park, but not without the help of stone buttresses. The acacia, known as a false acacia (*Robinia pseudoacacia*), which still blooms every spring (a miracle of tenacity), was planted in 1680 by a Mr. Robin, who brought it from Guyana. Two kinds of props hold it up: the modern straight-lined, buttress-like crutch and the older imitation trunk of ridged stone.

A fascinating sculpture and fountain by Georges Jeanclos, dated 1995, present Saint Julien in all his compassion and caring. He is entwined on a triangular pyramid surrounded by sufferers while water pours from the heads of three stags above. Jeanclos says, "I wanted to express the action of supporting and carrying the bodies of others in an act of love, tenderness, and compassion." Take time to examine the faces carefully and then take a moment to appreciate the recently replanted flower gardens.

Return to the church and continue walking around it until you reach a sealed window, which is in a lower garden. Directly behind this window is the apse of Saint-Julien; in front of the window there once was a well, believed to cure the crippled and the sick. The window in the apse of the church was turned into a door for easy access to the well, and the sick were charged for its use. One day, the church decided to give the water away free of charge. Suddenly it cured no one. The door was walled over.

Go up the stairs and cross the square to what is now the **rue Lagrange** (named after the great mathematician and astronomer who helped invent the metric system during the French Revolution), which starts at the *quai* and then bends toward the place Maubert. The *rue,* from the *quai* to the bend, adjacent to the park, has swallowed what was once the rue du Fouarre, of which only a little leg is left, connecting the rue Lagrange and the rue Dante. In the Middle Ages this was a narrow way, lined solid with student housing, and its animation and intellectual activity made it one of the most famous streets in Europe. Classes were held in the open air, with the students sitting on the ground and not on benches, in order that, as a document of Pope Urban V in 1366 put it, "occasion for haughty pride be kept away from youth." The ground was always filthy and often damp, so the students spread straw to sit on. The Old French word for straw is *feurre* or *fouarre,* close to the English word *forage.* Hence the name of the street, originally named the rue des Ecoliers, after the students.

Classes were taught by such notables as Peter Abelard and Albertus Magnus. At a later date, Dante Alighieri, whose street begins where the present rue du Fouarre ends, studied here. In his *Paradiso,* Dante refers to the *vico degli strami* (road of straws) (10:137) and speaks of the violent discussions he shared in and listened to there.

When the rue du Fouarre was in effect the campus of the Université de Paris, the students lived in dormitories called *collèges* in the square René-Viviani. Each dormitory represented a different "nation," and collectively they constituted the College of Nations. In the thirteenth century these were Normandy, Picardy, France, and England. In time these proliferated, and all European and even some Asian countries were represented in Paris. Thousands of students and hangers-on filled this area.

Vagabonds sleeping on the students' beds during the day and high life among the students and their clashes with the citizens gave the street a bad reputation. In 1358, Charles V, then regent, was forced to chain the street at both ends to keep it closed at night. Today the old road is a wide thoroughfare, and the rush of cars crossing from the Left Bank to the Ile de la Cité is continuous.

Rue Galande

Recross the park, where the *collèges* stood, and leave it by the gate through which you entered. Go left, past the church, to the corner of the **rue Galande** and the rue Saint-Julien-le-Pauvre. This place marks the beginning of the road that led to Lyons and Rome. In 1202 the street took the name Garlande, later Galande, after the name of a family who owned a large enclosure of land here. This was the road that students and teachers took to go from the Ile, or from Saint-Julien, to the rue du Fouarre, and it remained as important as the latter. In 1672 the street was widened to all of eight meters (twenty-six feet) and became one of the best addresses in Paris, a place where families of the nobility lived. After the Revolution though, things went downhill, and by 1900 the guidebooks were advertising Galande as one of the seamiest streets in the city. Much restoration, some of the best in the area, has taken place on this street, and we will be able to see several of the magically transformed buildings.

Watch for two tiny houses tucked in between existing walls or roofs, an economical way to build. **No. 75** is a wooden house, a rarity, above a restaurant. **No. 77** is a french fry place from which you can carry off your lunch and eat in the square René-Viviani.

The **Trois Mailletz**, at **no. 56**, has a long history. The stone-masons who were building Notre-Dame came here for drinks and food. After World War II it became known for a series of jazz clubs housed there and for the torture instruments in the *oubliettes* in the cellar, the same cellar as 14 rue Saint-Julien-le-Pauvre. In the early 1980s the club was sold to a group of young people, who remodeled the building and threw out the torture instruments. When they couldn't pay the rent, they too were thrown out. Today there is an excellent fifties-style classic jazz club on the spot, with food and music until 3 A.M.

At the door of **no. 52** a stone pillar has been uncovered. Curious caryatids adorn the corners of every window of this house, front and back; the neighbors say the figure is Quasimodo. This is the entrance of the Caveau des Oubliettes. Visit **Le Chat-Huant**, **nos. 50–52**, a friendly shop with Asian calligraphy supplies, jewelry, and clothes. This shop has survived for decades, and its attractive and reasonably priced merchandise is the reason.

Cybele, at **no. 65 bis**, is a gallery, bookstore, and archaeological treasure trove. The paintings are modern, featured in changing exhibits in the restored, vaulted twelfth-century cellar, while upstairs there is a fine collection of books on the ancient civilizations of Egypt, Greece, and Rome, along with authentic archaeological artifacts in a restored seventeenth-century building.

If you can get into the courtyard of **no. 48**, try to find, toward the center back, an oval stone, the entry to an underground cellar. A square stone under the planter on the left covers the entrance to a corkscrew staircase descending to the first basement.

No. 65, now restored, was built in the sixteenth century

Sixteenth-century frieze at no. 65 rue Galande

and was occupied by the noble family of Châtillon. The restoration here was undertaken by the City of Paris. The residents moved out during the work period but were given the option to return to this now magnificent building. The rents are low, and the tenants have the right to pass their apartments on to their children.

Above the doorway notice the recently discovered frieze of a woman's head surrounded by garlands of roses and oak leaves. When we were working on the first edition of this book, in 1973, we were the first to get a glimpse of her. One day, as we were studying the building, something fell at our feet from above the doorway. It was a blackened piece of nineteenth-century plaster of Paris, which had covered the original sixteenth-century stone garland carving. It made us feel as though this was "our" discovery, and the carving became a symbol of the hidden Paris we were uncovering for our readers.

Garlands of acorn and oak appear above the French first-floor windows, rolling waves above the next bank of windows, and rosettes above the next. Garlands of flowers are a fitting decoration for this street, rue Galande. The two-windowed, rounded gabled roof is crowned by a double ledge extending from the roofline. This sort of gable-front house, with the roof at a right angle to the street, was declared illegal in the sixteenth century because rainwater collected between the buildings. From that time on, rooflines had to be parallel with the street so that the rain would drain into gutters instead of falling on passersby. About thirty gable-front houses still exist in Paris, on a street that we will pass later. The stone sculpture of garlands and an urn above the entry were also uncovered by the restoration work on the building.

Nos. 61 and **59** look like one building on the outside but hold surprises on the inside; these were not revealed to us until we had walked the street dozens of times. The flowing tresses of a lovely Art Nouveau lady crown the entrance to both buildings here. She is three hundred years younger than the lady to your right, at no. 65. No. 59, as it says in the stone, was built in 1910, and it and no. 57 are examples of the brick construction that Paris has used for low-cost houses. Rich and not-so-rich Parisians insist on buildings with cut-stone façades.

Notice that the building is set back about ten feet from its neighbor. This is an example of the fond hope the city had of moving back the building line in order eventually to widen the entire street. As each building was torn down, its replacement had to be set back at this prescribed distance. Fortunately, few buildings do come down in Paris, and that explains the ins and outs of Paris sidewalks.

Except for the woman's head, this part of the building is not exceptional. The door here is usually locked, but give it a try. The hall is divided in two; the left side leads to apartments, but

Twentieth-century frieze at no. 59 rue Galande

down the corridor on the right side you will find an iron-grille door that opens to an old and beautifully restored house, no. 61.

The stairway and stairwell beyond the iron grille are an example of the care taken to bring the building back to its original shape. When Martin Granel and his family bought the place, it was almost impossible to get inside. The wall to the right of the staircase bellied out so far that the pillar of the house on the ground floor had to be reset. The brick-and-wood stairs were redone with old wood that came from the south of France. The banister behind the pillar dates from the time of Louis XIII. The stones on the ground in the courtyard to the left of the staircase came from a former printing establishment next door, and black print and designs, in reverse, were almost legible on the portions of the floor that were not frequently walked on. A once-open staircase, now enclosed behind a wide expanse of beautiful windows, looked down on a green courtyard with a stone fountain.

In 1198 some of this land on the odd-numbered side of the rue Galande was given to the Jews for a burial ground. It had earlier served as a cemetery in Gallo-Roman times, from 270 to 360. In the twelfth century, the Jews returned from a sixteen-year exile imposed by King Philippe Auguste, one of the many exiles they suffered in different countries during those years of crusading fervor and intolerance. They came back, of course, to their old neighborhoods at the Petit Pont and rue de la Harpe, where they had previously had a cemetery on the far side of what is now the boulevard Saint-Germain at the level of the rue de la Harpe. This site was not initially permitted for their use, so they turned what had been a vineyard on the rue Galande into their burial ground.

When Philippe III became king, in 1270, he declared that the Jews of Paris could have only one synagogue and only one cemetery, so the one on rue Galande was abandoned in favor of the one near Saint-Germain, which, by then, had been reopened. In 1306 Philippe le Bel expelled the Jews once again, and closed this second cemetery.

The absence of any trace of tombstones suggests that the Galande ground may have been used by Jews of modest means. The engraved tombstones found in 1849, however, under no.

79 boulevard Saint-Germain, have generated passionate Hebraic studies.

No. 46 was once the **Auberge des Deux Signes**, a restaurant that was a masterpiece of discovery and restoration. We include this building's story to give you a flavor of what kind of historical remains hide in these buildings, even though, unfortunately, you can no longer visit them. The building belonged to M. and Mme Dhulster. M. Dhulster's father, who came from Auvergne, had a coal and wood business, which he combined, as was customary, with a restaurant-bar to serve the needs of his workers. Because there was no central heating in those days, each apartment needed its own fuel; because there were no elevators, haulers had to climb a lot of stairs to deliver these goods. By the time they returned to the coal depot, they required nourishment.

The coal and wood business turned into a restaurant. The uncovering began when the municipality planned to realign the street and remove part of the building, which dates from the sixteenth century. Because the construction of the house was superior to that of many around it, the owners received permission to let it stand and to restore it. Among their most successful efforts was the cleaning of coat after coat of plaster from the large beige stone pillars in front. These are now separated by sections of plate glass, but, earlier, these spaces were filled with many smaller panes, and originally there may have been only shutters, open for trade in the daytime and closed at night.

The big surprises lay hidden in the back of the house, where construction from the fourteenth century was uncovered. Not afraid of hard work, Dhulster decided, in 1962, to dig out a lower level of his basement. Like all the basements in the area, his had been flooded and filled with mud in 1910, and undoubtedly during previous inundations as well.

A few steps down, he began to unearth vaulted arches built six hundred years ago. With the help of his son, Dhulster carried out twelve thousand coal sacks of dirt and gravel over a period of two years, finally revealing a large vaulted room that had served as a dormitory for a hundred monks from Saint-Julien-le-Pauvre.

In 1969, while the family was redoing the bedrooms on the French first and second floors in the back part of the house, a pickaxe hit some iron, and the unveiling of an entire fifteenth-century Gothic window began. Part of Saint-Julien-le-Pauvre, the chapel of Saint Blaise, the saint for masons and carpenters, once stood here. It was demolished in 1770, obviously not completely, and in 1812 a house was built over and around the wall that remained standing.

This window, a stone *pignon ogival* (pointed gable), had to be completely dismantled (each piece weighed about five hundred pounds) because the floor and ceiling rafters attached to it had pulled it out of shape. The enormous yet fragile puzzle was then pieced together and returned to its original position. Jacques Chirac, then mayor of Paris, awarded M. Dhulster the National Order of Merit for the realization of this building.

In a tiny alley that was once outside the chapel's wall was a well. Exploring this was Dhulster's final project. Not only was its border in perfect condition, but the well still had water in it, beautifully limpid. Dhulster let himself down this deep well and, as usual, made another discovery. Some of the stones moved on pivots; which meant that there was still another buried cellar, farther down. Since M. Dhulster is no longer here, it will probably never be explored.

You can still eat directly across the street, at **no. 57**, a well-run restaurant, **La Rôtisserie Galande**. The owners use two huge rotisseries, one for meats and one for fish. We had slices of rare roast beef and roasted potatoes smothered in garlicky green beans. Plain but delicious and reasonably priced.

Outside, on the wall of **no. 42**, find the sculptured stone rectangle depicting Saint Julien and his wife rowing their charges across the river. It is the oldest standard (shop sign) in Paris and mentioned as early as 1380.

At the corner to the right, at **no. 4 rue Dante**, is **Galerie Bosser**, a collector's find if you want vintage comic books, a figurine of Tintin and other comic characters, or old movie posters. Also at no. 4 is the **Librairie Gourmande**. This is one of the two cookbook stores in Paris. The proprietor, Mme Geneviève Baudon, was a *bouquiniste* (bookseller) on the Seine for more than thirty years with her husband. When she reached three thousand books, she had to make a decision: open a bookstore or a restaurant. Now in her bookstore, she advises some of the best chefs in France and sells to "foodies," collectors, and the rest of us. The walls, tables, and even the floor are covered with books old and new; the valuable ones are in a glass case at the back of the store. A picture of her dear friend Julia Child hangs on the wall next to her desk.

Continue down the rue Galande with the rue Dante on your right. At **nos. 29** and **31** you can see fine examples of medieval gabled roofs. Notice the room tucked in between the sloping gabled roof and the straight wall of the house next door. The restoration of these buildings, like most restorations here, took place about thirty years ago under the careful surveillance of the Monuments Historiques, a group that watches over all historic renovations in Paris.

Rue de l'Hôtel Colbert

Across the rue Lagrange, at the corner of the **rue de l'Hôtel Colbert**, is the **Hippopotamus**, where at all hours of the day you can get grilled steak or hamburger—without the roll. Remember, however, this is a chain—do not count on a great meal.

On the other corner, across from the Hippo, be sure to look at where the plaster has been neatly chipped away to show you the original stones underneath. Walk down a bit, past the first two windows, and you will come to a rounded one, probably once an entrance. If you have the good fortune to find the curtain pulled back, look in and you will see an extraordinary blend of old and new—a huge stone fireplace to the left, a modern sunken kitchen at the back, a spiral staircase to the right. A few steps farther and you can enter the apartment building (remember that you might have to press a button in order to be admitted, and again to leave) and look through an iron grille to an interior garden. Tall French windows look out onto a raised grassy section dotted with trees.

At **no. 12**, a sixteenth-century house, is the restaurant **Les Bouchons**, once used by the homeless as an *asile de nuit* (night shelter), where they'd sleep *à la corde* (on the rope). A rope would be stretched across the room, and for a sou, men could stand and rest their arms and heads on it. At dawn the rope would be dropped, and all the men, brutally awakened, would fall to the floor. Notice the wooden doors, beams, and stone spiral staircase. François Clerc serves excellent southwestern cuisine here, ranging from reasonable to fairly expensive. Wine is sold at the store price. Reserve.

The **Hôtel Colbert, no. 7**, is a superb recent copy from a seventeenth-century plan found in the archives of the Ecole des Beaux-Arts. This is an elegant but personal small hotel and a lovely place to stay. Its *salon de thé,* decorated with large upholstered chairs, is perfect for relaxing after a long day of "Pariswalking." The rooms have all been redone, and they are now air-conditioned. An apartment for four under the eaves with a view of Notre-Dame and the rooftops of Paris through a skylight just might fulfill your most romantic dreams.

Look to the left, across the street at the corner building. Above the street sign on the wall, at **no. 8**, you will find the old name of the street cut into the stone, RUE DES RATS (street of rats). An old resident assures us that the name was fitting, that just a short time ago, rats abounded here. The name of the street was originally rue d'Arras because a college from the diocese of Arras was founded here in 1320. A poet rhymed it with rats, and it wasn't long before the new name took hold and was inscribed as such when street names were cut in stone. In 1829 the inhabitants of the street petitioned for something more elegant, and the city authorities took the name from an important *hôtel* (a grand private residence) that once stood on the street. Why the house was called the Hôtel Colbert no one knows, because Colbert never lived there. In any event, the original building was demolished when the rue Lagrange was cut through, in 1887.

The wall into which this street sign has been carved is the side of the Amphithéâtre Winslow, part of the old Faculté de Médecine. Look up at the round decorated window, called a bull's-eye (*oeil-de-boeuf*), which you will soon see inside. The entry is just around the corner to the left, on the **rue de la Bûcherie**.

When you get there, notice the ironwork on the 1909 grille inside the courtyard, on the right-hand wall. Enter the building, which is now an information center on city benefits—from vacations to jobs—for government employees. Take a comfortable seat to the left and read the history.

The Faculté de Médecine was created by King Philippe VI in 1331. Before this, in the Middle Ages, only monks studied medicine, necessarily limiting medical care to men. (Given the ignorance of the medical profession, women were lucky to be neglected.) In 1131, however, an ordinance forbade men of the church to study medicine, a prohibition confirmed in 1163 by the Council of Tours and thereafter enforced by excommunication.

Thus, there were no trained doctors in France until 1220, when several small schools were opened; these subsequently merged into the Faculté de Médecine more than a hundred years later. At first, classes were held with the other schools on the rue du Fouarre, and exams were given in the masters' houses. It was not until 1472 that the present buildings were started. They were subsequently enlarged on several occasions, and they flourished until the Revolution, when the Faculté de Médecine, like all the other schools, was abolished. In 1808 the buildings passed into private hands and in the next century knew a wide variety of uses: as a laundry, an inn, an apartment building, even a brothel. In 1909 the structures were finally rescued, restored, and classified by the city as historic monuments.

In Jacques Hillairet's *Dictionnaire Historique des Rues de Paris,* there is a marvelous description of the kind of medicine that was taught by this school in the fourteenth and fifteenth centuries:

The prescribed remedies were, for a long time, limited to a choice of three: laxatives, enemas, and bleeding. It was in this tradition that Charles Bouvard, Louis XIII's doctor, administered to the king in one year 47 bleedings, 212 enemas, and 215 purgatives, total: 474 treatments, after which the doctor was ennobled. Richelieu submitted in the same year to 54 bleedings and 202 purgations. As to Ambroise Paré, he bled 27 times in four days a 28-year-old young man, that is, a bloodletting every 4 hours for 4 days, and in 1609 Le Moyne took 225 pints of blood in 15 months from a young girl.

There were, however, other treatments. A treatise on medicine that appeared in 1539 affirms that the blood of a hare cures gallstones; the droppings of mice, bladder stones; the excrement of dogs, sore throats; boiled wood louse, scrofula. It is also written that lung of fox washed in wine cures asthma; earthworms washed in white wine, jaundice; kittens finely chopped with goose and salt, gout; the excrement of a red-headed man, weak eyes. The wax from your ears applied to the nostrils promotes sleep. Montaigne wrote that a man's saliva will kill a serpent. In 1540 André Fournier, professor at the Faculté de Médecine, gave this recipe to make hair grow again: boil three hundred slugs, skim off the grease, add three tablespoons of olive oil and one tablespoon of honey, and anoint your skull with the mixture. One of his colleagues in this same period recommended the following remedy to get rid of fleas: take the heads of many red herrings, tie them with a string, place this in your mattress, and the fleas will flee.

From the Faculté de Médecine's reception room, enter the room to your left, where people are being helped, and turn left again into the rotunda. This is the Amphithéâtre Winslow, built in 1744. The floor of the amphitheater is inlaid with rosewood in a pattern representing the sun. The balconies are embellished with wrought iron and friezes of roosters and pelicans, supported by eight Doric columns. It is said that this room was used for medical demonstrations. We wonder what one could see from the balconies.

Rue de la Bûcherie

Turn right into the **rue de la Bûcherie** to **Galerie Urubamba**, at **no. 4**, which was formerly a butcher shop. Find the marble slabs that served as counters and the meat hooks above the window. Today, the shop has a fascinating collection of native North and South American arts, including fabulous feathered headdresses and silver-and-turquoise jewelry.

Across the street, at **no. 3**, is **Le Rouvray**, one of the first shops to brighten up this once dark and dreary neighborhood. Run by an American, Diane de Obaldia, a connoisseur of

American patchwork quilts, the shop is the center for this art in Europe. Le Rouvray offers classes, equipment, and books for instruction.

At **no. 2 rue du Haut Pavé**, don't miss **Tapisseries de la Bûcherie**, the showroom for exquisite tapestry and embroidered creations. Mme Dominique Sarl has written a book on medieval tapestry, recognized by its field of "the thousand flowers" on the cover—the flowers symbolize the fields in medieval tapestries. She gives courses and lectures here, as well as at the Musée National du Moyen Age and the Louvre and all over France. She hopes to make this corner a center for embroidery and tapestry.

Rue des Grands Degrés

Cross the small square to the **rue des Grands Degrés**. The street was called Saint-Bernard in the fourteenth century, but in the eighteenth it got its present name for the stone steps (*degrés*) that descended to the Seine. In this street in 1714, Voltaire toiled as a clerk for a lawyer, M. Alain. As a twenty-year-old, Voltaire had made brilliant law studies but was leading a loose life in The Hague. His father had obtained an appointment for him as the personal secretary to the Marquis de Chateauneuf, but Voltaire was more interested in the attentions of a certain Mlle du Noyer, an "adventuress." As a result, his father was more than slightly peeved and had an order for his arrest issued if Voltaire did not return to the law.

Open the door to **no. 7**, on the left, to see a lovely small house. The door is unlocked because there is a doctor's office in the building.

Le Reminet, at **no. 3**, is a tiny restaurant with two tables outside (in good weather). It is a nice spot to enjoy a delicious, not too expensive meal. Rebecca and Alison shared an appetizer of lobster-stuffed ravioli that instantly brought forth smiles of contentment. The chef's wife, who is the hostess, speaks excellent English.

At the corner, look up at the third floor (in the American system) of **no. 1** to see the signs painted on the walls. These were old shop signs, and although the paint is peeling, they are still lovely and classified as historical.

Continuing the food theme, take a break at **Dammann's** ice cream store. This shop carries about thirty delicious handmade flavors, including Bulgarian yogurt, caramel with sea salt, and chocolate-orange, all made with natural ingredients.

Around the corner is one of the most serious restaurants in the neighborhood. **Atelier Maître Albert**, at **no. 1 rue Maître Albert**, used to be a heavily decorated spot for romantics, complete with swings in the bar. In 2004 noted chef Guy Savoy reopened the restaurant with a modern but comfortable décor. The front rooms are a smoking lounge and handsome bar, while the back is a dining room bracketed with a fireplace on one side and a huge rotisserie on the other. Savoy concentrates on the food of his childhood, so this is a good choice to experience excellent French food without the esoteric ingredients that predominate at starred restaurants.

The street is named for the medieval teacher and Dominican, Albertus Magnus. Magnus taught philosophy, theology, and natural sciences at the bottom of the street in the **place Maubert**, where there is a large open food market every Tuesday. In the thirteenth century, the square was famous for its outdoor classes.

Diane Johnson's delicious novel *Le Divorce,* about the ins and outs of French-American intimacy, takes place on these few streets near place Maubert. If you have read it, you will be walking familiar territory—always a delight.

If you are energetic enough at this point, visit one or more of the spectacular monuments in the area, such as Notre-Dame, La Sainte-Chapelle on the Ile de la Cité, the Sorbonne, or the Musée National du Moyen Age, all within easy walking distance.

Walk · 2

La Huchette

Voici la rue de la Huchette, mais prends bien garde à ta Pochette.

This is the rue de la Huchette, but better watch out for your wallet.

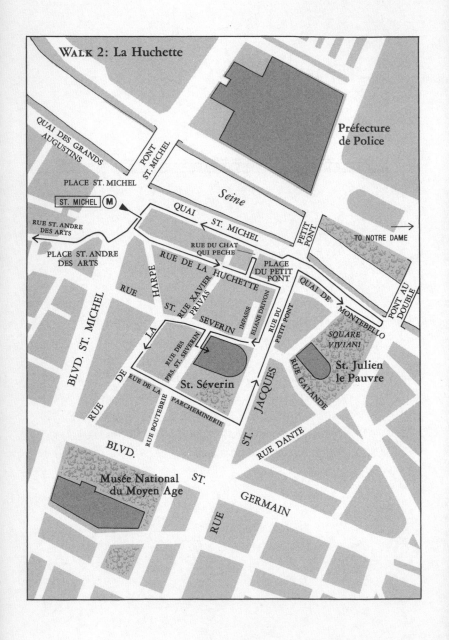

WALK 2: La Huchette

Préfecture de Police

QUAI DES GRANDS AUGUSTINS

PONT ST. MICHEL

ST. MICHEL

PLACE ST. MICHEL

ST. MICHEL Ⓜ

Seine

QUAI ST. MICHEL

RUE ST. ANDRE DES ARTS

PLACE ST. ANDRE DES ARTS

PETIT PONT

TO NOTRE DAME

RUE DU CHAT QUI PECHE

RUE DE LA HUCHETTE

RUE DE LA HARPE

PLACE DU PETIT PONT

QUAI DE MONTEBELLO

PONT AU DOUBLE

RUE XAVIER PRIVAS

ST. SEVERIN

INPASSE

ELIANE DRIVON

RUE DU PETIT PONT

SQUARE VIVIANI

BLVD. ST. MICHEL

RUE DES PRS. ST. SEVERIN

LA

DE

RUE DE LA PARCHEMINERIE

St. Séverin

RUE GALANDE

St. Julien le Pauvre

RUE

ST. JACQUES

RUE BOUTEBRIE

BLVD.

ST.

RUE DANTE

Musée National du Moyen Age

ST.

GERMAIN

RUE

Starting Point: Place Saint-Michel, 5th arrondissement
Métro: Saint-Michel, RER
Buses: 21, 24, 27, 38, 85, 96

When you leave the boulevard Saint-Michel and turn left into the **rue de la Huchette**, imagine yourself back in the crowded and dirty Middle Ages. This neighborhood of tangled streets and narrow houses looks in many ways the same as it did hundreds of years ago. Aside from the contour of the land—which then sloped down to the water's edge instead of rising to the level of the present embankments of the Seine—this quarter is the same maze it was in the twelfth century, although the houses date from the seventeenth.

Baron Georges Haussmann, Napoléon III's famous city planner, cut wide swaths of boulevards (Saint-Germain, Saint-Michel, Saint-Jacques) all around this neighborhood but was stopped from touching the interior. He did, however, widen the western entrance to Huchette, which is why the houses from Saint-Michel to the Hôtel du Mont Blanc are nineteenth century.

The **Hôtel du Mont Blanc**, on the left, marks the spot

World War II commemorative plaque on the rue de la Huchette

where the street once narrowed. The hotel has had its ups and downs, going from country-style inn to badly run down. Now it is on the upswing again, and half of the ground floor has been converted into a French restaurant. The hotel is reasonable, and all the rooms have been redone and include direct-dial phones and double windows.

It was in one of the back rooms of this hotel that Elliot Paul started his nostalgic, intimate account of life on the rue de la Huchette, *The Last Time I Saw Paris*. The title was taken from the song of the same name, which recalls the happiness and sweetness of Paris before the German occupation.

To the right of the door, against the wall that juts out and narrows the street, you will see a plaque commemorating an event from World War II. Before the Allies entered Paris, street fighting broke out all over this area and barricades were erected at each end of Huchette. Just across the Seine, Parisians liberated the Prefecture of Police from Nazi control and used the spot as a vantage point for shots at the enemy. One of the tragedies of the fighting on the rue de la Huchette was recorded on this plaque: HERE FELL JEAN ALBERT VOUILLARD, DEAD IN THE COURSE OF DUTY, KILLED BY THE GESTAPO THE 17TH OF MAY 1944, AT 20 HOURS. RAINBOW. "Rainbow" was the name of his cell of resistance fighters. The bullets that were sprayed into the wall have been plastered over.

The irony here is that the width of the street at the top was the unfinished work of Haussmann. His intention was to widen all these narrow pathways so that revolutionaries would be unable to barricade the streets as they did in the Revolution. At the end of the German occupation of the Second World War, however, it was the resistance fighters' ability to do this that permitted them to defend Paris against the Germans at this spot.

Across and down the street, at **no. 23**, you will find the smallest theater in Paris. It used to perform only Ionesco—*The Bald Soprano* and *The Lesson*—the same plays since the mid-fifties. A third avant-garde play—one that changes and is not one of Ionesco's—has been added to the repertoire.

The plays are performed at 7, 8, and 9 P.M. You can buy tickets for one, two, or three of the performances. The theater holds eighty-five persons, seated straight across the room, no aisle. If you visit after five in the afternoon, try the door to the box office, then smile at the lady who sells the tickets, open the inside door, accustom your eyes to the dark, and get a glimpse of this tiny theater. At one point the son of the founder wanted to turn this into yet another restaurant (!) but fortunately he was stopped by the government. Attend a performance if you can; Ionesco's French is easy to understand, and the plays are pure fun. The intermission is almost as good as the play; this street is really a night street. Turn to the right for some Tunisian delights before going back to see the rest of the play.

In the fourteenth and fifteenth centuries Huchette was called the rue des Rôtisseurs, the street of roasters. Whole sheep and oxen were turned on spits over open wood fires, and beggars held up their bread to soak up the smoke and the aroma. A papal delegate called it "verily stupendous."

Today Greek and Tunisian restaurants have returned the street to its old activity, and the roasting goes on. Starting at 11 A.M., the lambs and pigs turn and crackle on spits, a sight that

The Ionesco Theater

takes some getting used to. The schwarma (lamb on a spit) and the stacks of kebabs ready for the grill wait for your order.

Rue Xavier Privas

You are now at the crossing of **rue Xavier Privas** and Huchette. Xavier Privas was a singer from Montmartre who was famous in the 1920s, and although that is not particularly interesting, the previous names for the street are. At first this part, from Huchette to Saint-Séverin (to your right), was known as Sac à Lie (bag of lees). Lees are the dregs of wine, which, when dried, were used to prepare and clean leather hides and parchment. This was in the days when streets were known by their activities. Since few people could read, written street names were not displayed until 1729. With time and the disappearance of the sacks of lees, the street name changed from Sac à Lie to Saqualie. This was finally engraved into no. 19, at the far end of the street, as "Zacharie" in the seventeenth century, and so it remained for almost three hundred years.

The opposite end of Xavier Privas, which runs from Huchette to the *quai,* used to run downhill, not up, to the Seine: it was filled with the life and business of fishing scows, which were moored at the bottom of the street. Owing to many unpleasant incidents and the general filth, the street was gated in during the first half of the seventeenth century. Recently, when the Paris sanitation men went on strike, the street rivaled its medieval reputation. You will notice that there are no entry doors on this small section of the street, between Huchette and the river. No one's territory, so everyone's dump. One morning the pile reached over six feet high, and the army was forced to come down and shovel away the mountain of rubbish.

Each morning, however, the pedestrian walkways (no cars) take on the most picturesque and old-fashioned appearance. The shop- and innkeepers are outside in their white aprons washing their windows and their walks; the residents stop and talk or hurry about with their baskets of bread and meat (which, however, they now are forced to buy five blocks away, at the place Maubert). Huchette once boasted a butcher, a baker, and even a candlemaker; in fact, rue Xavier Privas, from the rue de la Huchette to the *quai,* was once called the "street of three candlemakers."

Look across Huchette to **no. 14**, a five-windows-wide seventeenth-century building. The ironwork of the balconies is hand-wrought, made to order for the original owner. He had his initials, D.C., laced into the decoration, except for two windows on the French first floor, which have a *Y* in wrought iron in a circle. There is still another *Y* to be found. You can see it on the stone space between the two windows—a framed circle with a graceful *Y* incised in its center. What is this all about? Shoppers two hundred and fifty years ago understood. The letter *Y* (called a Greek *i* in French: *i grec,* pronounced ē-grek) advertised the wares of the shop below. The shop was a *mercerie* (sewing shop), famous for its needles and sewing materials. There was also an important article of clothing sold here—a garter that tied a man's breeches to his leggings. The tie was a *lie* (as in the word *liaison*) and breeches were *gregues*. One of fableist La Fontaine's rabbits has a pair; in a moment of danger he "*tire ses gregues*" (hitches up his breeches) and runs away. When you put the tie and the breeches together (the *lies* and the *gregues*) you hear *i grec*. Now look once more at the incised *Y* on the wall between the windows—it looks like a garter. There are more of these amusing plays on words, called *calembours* (rebuses), left in Paris, one close by, on Saint-Séverin. Among the best of them was a sign with six circles, *O*s, which when spoken (seez-ō) sounded like *ciseaux* (scissors). It represented a scissors and knife shop on the rue du Dragon.

Rue du Chat qui Pêche

Look down the alley to the left at one of the most nondescript but oft-described streets in Paris, the **rue du Chat qui Pêche** (street of the fishing cat). It took its name from a sign that hung above a shop, no doubt a fish shop, though no source actually says it was. Before the street took its present name, it was called the rue des Etuves (street of steam baths). There were half a dozen such streets and alleys in the Paris of the late thirteenth century, and some twenty-six bathing establishments. Every morning the crier was out on the street calling to prospective clients: "*Li bains sont chaut, c'est sanz mentir!*" (The baths are hot—no fooling!) They were hot in more ways than one. Many of them provided mixed bathing and supplementary services. One preacher warned his flock, "Ladies, do not go to the baths, and don't do you-know-what there." The combination of clerical disfavor and public harassment reduced the number of these establishments to two by the early seventeenth century. The result was a malodorous population. Those who could afford to doused themselves with perfume; the others—well, people's noses must have been tougher then.

This narrowest street in Paris was, contrary to what you might expect, wider in the sixteenth century. The six-foot-wide alley, with its gutter of water (and urine) running down its middle, looks and sometimes smells like a medieval street. Walk up the alley, away from Huchette. The alley suddenly widens, brightens, and then opens onto the Seine and, to the right, a surprise view of Notre-Dame. In the sixteenth century this street, like Xavier Privas, tumbled down into the Seine. It too was gated in at night, though no sign of the gate can be seen in the stone.

Return to the rue de la Huchette. **No. 12**, on the corner of Huchette and Chat qui Pêche, was built at a later date than its neighbor and is the reason why Chat qui Pêche is narrower today than it once was. **No. 10**, next door, is the "corner" house where Bonaparte lived in his poorer days, in a room at the back, facing the Seine. He was reputedly dying of hunger when Paul Barras, later important in the Directory (France's executive power between 1795 and 1799), gave him a chance to show his mettle. Bonaparte began his rise to glory when, with a "whiff of grapeshot," he dispersed the Paris mob in front of the church of Saint-Roch. Jacques Hillairet, in his superb dictionary of the streets of Paris, summarizes Bonaparte's career in a change of address: "From this point on, fortune smiled on him. When he resided once again on the banks of the Seine, it was, in 1800, at the Tuileries."

Notice the absence on Huchette of the wide doorways

(*portes cochères*) that were often built to allow a horse and carriage and later an automobile to enter a courtyard. Huchette was never a luxury street. The doors are narrow, and the halls lead back deep inside to reach the one staircase that serves both the front and back of the house. Long and narrow buildings were common in the seventeenth century because street-front property was so costly. Open any of the doors, and if a restaurant kitchen hasn't filled the space, you will find a long, dark walk to the courtyard and stairs.

At **no. 5**, the **Caveau de la Huchette**, dedicated to the jazz of the 1920s, calls itself "the celebrated cabaret of jazz where one dances." It is open every weeknight and Sunday from 10:15 P.M. to 2 A.M., and Saturdays until 4 A.M. Friends of ours spent a night of nostalgia there dancing the lindy (named after Charles Lindbergh) to tremendous applause from the young connoisseurs who frequent the club. This is a good place for singles. Although the French dance style is different from ours, you'll have fun. There is a low cover charge, but no drink minimum.

The building that houses the Caveau dates from the sixteenth century and was connected by secret passageways to the Petit Châtelet, then a prison at the Petit Pont. A publicity flyer put out by the proprietors states that the Templars, a religious military order formed during the Crusades, used the cellar as a secret meeting place in the late thirteenth century. Their riches were so great that King Philippe IV felt the need to suppress them in order to relieve them of their wealth. It was the curse the Templars laid on the king and his descendants that Maurice Druon took as the theme of his series of historical novels, *Les Rois Maudits* (The Accursed Kings).

In 1772 the Freemasons met here in secret. Then, during the Revolution, these cellars and subcellars served as tribunal, prison, and place of execution. The process was swift. A deep well in the lowest level is said to have washed away all traces of this summary "justice."

During World War II, secret resistance cells found their natural home here, while outspoken patriots filled the cafés. Jacques Yonnet, in his strange and haunting book, *Enchantement sur Paris,* describes the street as one of the ignition points of the occupied city. Perhaps the "Rainbow" resistance fighters met here.

There is also a story of the discovery of a two-thousand-year-old bracelet during excavations in the Caveau. A huge treasure, including a five-hundred-pound gold cross, is supposedly buried under these buildings, hidden during the French Revolution.

No. 4 is a large seventeenth-century building, originally with three *portes cochères,* that was redecorated in the eighteenth century. Typical of this kind of face-lifting was the placing of masks on the façade. Here, fortunately, in a black rectangle, someone has preserved an old sign reading À LA HURE D'OR (at the golden boar snout), dated 1729. Look above the awning for the sign.

Leave the narrow rue de la Huchette and enter the **rue du Petit Pont**, which becomes the rue Saint-Jacques. To the left is the *quai,* the Petit Pont, and Notre-Dame. To the right is a long avenue that stretches south toward Orléans and, for the pilgrims who went on France's most popular pilgrimage of the Middle Ages—to Santiago de Compostela in Spain (see Walk 1). The building on the south corner of the rue du Petit Pont and the rue de la Huchette looks like a seventeenth-century structure but was actually built from scratch in 1979.

Face the Seine and look to your left, to the northwest corner, where the street is renamed place du Petit Pont. Close to the ground, you will find a plaque commemorating bravery in World War II. It tells of two anonymous civilians and one soldier, Jean Dussarps, who were killed defending the little fort on the street. Below that, honor is paid to Béatrice Briant, who was the leader of a group of voluntary fighters against the Germans.

Turn around and walk south to **no. 6** rue du Petit Pont, where an old and elegant grocery finally closed after holding out for more than fifty years. The shelves of the bookstore now at this address, the Librairie Saint-Nicolas, date from the grocery.

Rue Saint Séverin

Continue walking away from the Seine down the rue du Petit Pont, and turn right into the **rue Saint-Séverin**. Countless nineteenth-century descriptions of this street and its neighbors all sound the same theme:

All these streets, as I say, are picturesque and dirty. Between Cluny and the river is a network of very old, squalid, and very interesting streets.

To some degree the same comments can still be made. If you happened to walk here in the early morning when the crowds had gone home (whenever that may be) and the rubbish remained, you would be tempted to use the same adjectives. Half of the food from the restaurants seems to have landed in the gutter. But at 7:30 the street cleaners arrive, and a new day begins.

The street was widened in 1678. If you look at the massive Gothic church on the left, it is not difficult to see why the houses on the other side of the rue Saint-Jacques were chosen for removal. The houses opposite the church date from the late seventeenth century.

The **Latin Mandarin**, at **no. 4**, is a small restaurant with a minute kitchen in the back. The restaurant may once have been a hall or a courtyard. It was started twenty-five years ago by a tiny lady, Mme Duc, who ran the restaurant with the help of her ten children. Her husband worked elsewhere, as an accountant. Vietnamese women often run small restaurants and food shops, but you rarely see Vietnamese men in the neighborhood; they work elsewhere. On the other hand, you rarely see North African or Greek women; the men run the restaurants. The present owner is a close friend of Mme Duc and he offers the same fare, with some new dishes of his own.

Impasse Salembière, now **impasse Eliane Drivon**, is a closed alleyway. Once it was an open street, notorious for its piles of rubbish and sleeping *clochards,* who found it a haven. Now that the doors are locked at night, the alley is immaculate. Take a few steps back and see how the walls of the buildings almost touch one another up above, typical of many medieval streets, to protect the pedestrian from the rain. Look at the old street name cut in stone above the street sign—RUE [BLANK] SÉVERIN—and the number 10 for the section of the city. The *Saint* was scraped out here as elsewhere during the Revolution, when the passionately anticlerical populace ravaged all things religious. Look for evidence of this on other streets named after saints. Look down through **no. 8** to see how long the corridor runs.

Notice the very low, narrow seventeenth-century door to **no. 12**. Press the top button of the keypad to the right. Push open this small, heavily carved door to a centuries-old entry that boasts rafters in the ceiling, exposed building stones on the walls, a wrought-iron gate too heavy to budge, and an iron stair rail followed by an odd hand-carved wooden one.

Turn left now and look to the entrance of the **church of Saint-Séverin**. In the sixth century, when everyone else lived on the Ile de la Cité, a hermit named Séverin found a patch of dry ground in the swampland across the river and settled there. The site was ideal for a hermit—separated from society but close enough to receive visitors. Contrary to popular belief, the main aim of a hermit was not to cut himself off from humanity but to induce it to beat a path to his solitary door. Séverin must have received many, for at his death his reputation as a good man was so widespread that an oratory was built in his memory and called Saint-Séverin. From that early date onward, several churches have been built on this site and destroyed—one by fire, one by a Viking invasion—but all have been named for the hermit Saint Séverin.

After you have looked at the massive exterior, partly cleaned, enter the church. Take a seat in one of the back rows and take in the whole of the structure. The present church represents a combination of styles that stretches across the centuries, from the thirteenth to the twentieth. There was never enough money to complete the building at any one time, so the work went on and on, and still does. Before the nineteenth century, architects and builders felt no compulsion to preserve or restore original forms. No age or style was sacred, and all construction was "of the day." As a result, the church has a parade of arches that tells the story of Gothic architecture from its primitive beginnings to its last flamboyant manifestations.

Look up the right-hand aisle. The three pillars enclosing two arches closest to the entrance are early-thirteenth-century Gothic and are among the few remains of the previous church, which was destroyed by fire. The two arches between them, though broken (or pointed), are almost round, as in the earlier

Romanesque style. The pillars are short, cut by capitals halfway up their length. On the wall above the arches and above the columns is a simple cloverleaf pattern, sculpted in stone. Look now at the next four arches, done two centuries later. The columns are tall and straight, and the arches meet at a tighter angle. The goal of Gothic architecture was to reach higher and higher into open space, up to God. Notice the arcs that radiate outward from the stone trefoils on the wall above these arches. The small semicircles turn on themselves to make new ones, and the effect is that of a flame, from which we get the term *flamboyant*. All of this is still controlled, however, in contrast with the late flamboyant pillars behind the altar.

Look at the pillars and arches surrounding the altar. Study the stonework carefully and you will notice that the basic structure of the arches is the same as that of the fifteenth-century ones just described. Why, then, do they look so different? It's a seventeenth-century story.

The famous and capricious cousin of Louis XIV known as "la Grande Mademoiselle" got into a dispute with the curé of Saint-Sulpice, her neighborhood church, and decided to change parishes. To show her pleasure with the one and annoyance with the other, she bestowed her gifts and her idea of fashion on the church of Saint-Séverin. The priest dared not, or at least did not, refuse. In the spirit of the Renaissance, la Grande Mademoiselle wrapped the pillars in red marble and rounded off the archways with the same red marble. There is more of the same stone in the shape of an altar, now in a side chapel on the left. (Formerly it was placed in the center to match its surroundings.) The lady was busy elsewhere as well. If you look at the bottoms of the early flamboyant pillars of the fifteenth century (numbers four through seven, counting from the entrance), you can see the remains of fluting that was added to the simple pillars.

Now let us go to the flamboyant pillars behind the altar. The effect is astonishing and marvelous. This spot is often called the Palm Grove; the pillars do look like trees spiraling up into palms overhead. The central twisted pillar is the prime example of French flamboyant Gothic. The spirals begin at the bottom and palm out above into so complex a network that it is almost impossible to trace their path. The grove has been called "a sanctuary of serenity," but we find this particular pillar anything but calm. It is known as "Dante's pillar"; Dante is reputed to have leaned against it often. The fact that he lived two centuries before the pillar was built did not stop the nineteenth-century chroniclers of old Paris from linking it to him!

Now, as you face the entrance, follow the outside aisle behind Dante's pillar around to the left (back toward the entrance) until you come upon a stout pillar capped by the figure of a magnificent broad-shouldered man holding up the arch and reading out a message. Half of this pillar was built in the fourteenth century and the other half in the fifteenth. It would have been simple to complete the pillar as it was begun, but here is proof that emulation of the past or any idea of unity of style was totally absent from the thinking of the time. And so it stands, fourteenth and fifteenth centuries both embodied in one pillar.

Continue up this side aisle toward the entrance and on the wall to your left you will find one of the best collections of votive tablets in Paris. This was the parish church for the Latin Quarter, and grateful students covered the walls with votive tablets that gave thanks to God for success in exams. The sexton told us that "they" planned to remove them because gratitude was no longer à la mode, but he was wrong. They remain.

Cross over to the other side aisle (on the left side, walking away from the entrance) and, in the first chapel, you will find a red porphyry marble altar. Professor Raoul Gaduyer, a venerable theologian-sociologist who knew every stone in this church, spent hours explaining and telling us stories. At the red altar, however, he hesitated, smiled, then hesitated again. We waited patiently for the smile to reappear and the story to begin. This large porphyry altar was another of the gifts of la Grande Mademoiselle. But the antiheroine of this story was Louis's mistress, Mme de Montespan. During her long liaison with the king she was concerned about his attentions to other, younger women. In her anxiety and despair she finally contrived to get the priest (Heaven help him!) of Saint-Séverin to say a black mass on the red altar to ensure Louis's fidelity. The tender hearts of two unfortunate turtledoves served as the unholy instruments of her black magic.

Bad enough, but her magical exploits continued (and here we are discussing only her black masses, not her poisoning of some of Louis's other mistresses). Another mass was said elsewhere in Paris with the same thought in mind—Louis and his love. That time the red altar was supplanted by a smaller and softer one, the naked body of Mme de Montespan. But the chalice would not stand upright, because of either her curves or her trembling. The solution was to place it securely between her thighs. All of this, as you can imagine, was done in great secrecy. Private records were kept, however, and these have recently turned up in the archives of the Prefecture of Police.

Continue down this side aisle to the chapel where the modern windows begin. The sixteenth-century painting on the wall to the right of the windows was uncovered in 1968, when the modern stained-glass windows were installed. The painting, barely visible, is a Last Judgment. The words on the right call up all saintly souls, men and women, to Heaven. On the left (*sinistre*) side, however, are those damned to eternal Hell—they are all of them women, beaten on their way by devils, all of them men. An interesting testimony to the artist-priest's view of the roles of the two sexes. Look at the nonrepresentational stained-glass windows. During World War II the fifteenth-century windows were shattered, and temporary ones took their place. In 1966, enough money was finally raised to commission an artist, Jean Bazaine, to make new ones. Bazaine is a fine colorist in abstract art who also did the mosaic at the UNESCO building in Paris. He drew his inspiration from the Bible, using quotations about fire, earth, and water. The bold primary colors of the windows set in solid shapes, one next to the other, create a striking contrast to the quiet strength of the stone.

This is a marrying church. Come any Saturday morning and you will be sure to see a wedding. Outside, go to your left and look at the freshly cleaned cloisters and garden.

Across rue Saint-Séverin, at **no. 22**, is one of the narrowest houses in Paris. It is eight feet (two windows) wide. This was the house of the Abbé Prévost, an eighteenth-century minister who wrote voluminously, though only one original manuscript remains, that of *Manon Lescaut* (1731). It is the tale of a young noble man who falls in love with a prostitute, who is ultimately arrested and deported to the New World (described as a New Orleans complete with a desert and wild Indians). We are convinced that the inspiration for his book came from his proximity to Saint-Séverin and a shocking practice the church then indulged in: each year an award was given to the five most virtuous maidens in the parish. It was not enough, however, to praise the good. To warn against immorality, the church placed the most scandalous and unvirtuous women of the parish in cages and exposed them outdoors to the scorn and not-so-tender mercies of the passersby. It was the Last Judgment—the blessed and the damned—translated from life to art.

In 1763 Abbé Prévost, then living in a suburb of Paris, succumbed to a stroke of apoplexy. An autopsy seemed in order, but when the doctor used his scalpel on the corpse, it rose up and called out. The abbé was not dead after all! A few minutes later, the abbé obligingly passed away, not of apoplexy, but of the doctor's deep cut.

The corner house, **no. 24**, is a lovely rounded building, and on the corner above the blue street sign you can still see the street name cut into the stone, as you saw earlier. It says RUE on one line and on the next line SÉVERIN. Here is another example of the removal of *Saint* from the street name. The number 18 cut into the stone refers to the old divisions of Paris.

Look through the window down the long narrow hall of **no. 30** at the plaster-and-wood construction of the walls. In the seventeenth century, walls were built of timber framing with a gravelly mixture filling the spaces between. This mixture was held together by pieces of wood and rags, just as clay bricks are held together by straw. This filler was usually covered over with white plaster, with timbers exposed, but the heavy incidence of fire in these oil-lit interiors led King Henri IV to decree that any wall with exposed timbers had to be completely plastered over. A white clay, which was found just belowground in Paris not far from here, was quarried and used widely in the area around Notre-Dame, Saint-Julien-le-Pauvre, and Saint-Séverin. "Plaster of paris" has since become the generic term for any white plaster. Many walls were so weighted down with their coat of plaster, however, that they buckled and even collapsed.

On the French first floor at **no. 13** there is a fourteenth-century *enseigne* (standard) for what was once an inn; it depicts a swan whose neck is wrapped around a cross. This is another rebus, like the *Y* on the rue de la Huchette. A swan in French is *cygne,* a homonym for *signe* (sign). Combining the *cygne* with the cross yields the "sign of the cross," the standard symbol for lodgings.

The first commercial standards were put up by taverns and hotels so that a foreigner could find a place to eat and sleep in a strange city. These standards often represented a bundle of straw, which gives a good idea of the character of the sleeping accommodation. Even today there is hardly a city in France without a hotel called the Lion d'Or (golden lion) or, in rebus form, *le lit [où] on dort* (the bed [where] one sleeps).

In the thirteenth century, the commercial standard was soon understood to be a smart way to advertise; by the fifteenth, it had become a serious problem. The standards were made from sheets of iron, cut and painted and hung on long poles to extend into the street past the large shop shutters. Like signs today, they were hung out as far as possible and made as large as possible to attract the most attention.

A *parfumerie* (perfume shop) had a standard of a glove, each finger of which could have held a three-year-old child. A dentist hung a molar that was the size of an armchair. These standards were constantly threatening to fall; one man was reputedly killed when the dentist's tooth fell on his head.

The combination of the shutters, an open sewer running down the center of the unpaved street, and huge groaning and clanking signs blocking out the sun made the streets dark and cluttered.

For reasons of safety rather than aesthetics, the government tried to pass legislation to limit the size of signs. In 1667 they said the signs could be no more than thirty-two inches wide and had to be hung at least fifteen feet above the ground, so that horsemen might ride safely in the streets. It was not until 1761 that standards were banned altogether, to be replaced by the old-style wall decoration like the Cygne de la Croix. Visit the Hôtel Carnavalet, the Museum of the History of Paris, in the Marais (Walk 5) for an exhibit of standards.

The sign of the cross, a fourteenth-century standard for an inn

Since literacy was rare, the names were more often simply visual recognition or mnemonic devices. Some were mystifying: The Bottle Tennis Court, The Small Hole, and The Cage. Other names were clearer. The Tree of Life was a surgeon's house; The Red Shop, a butcher shop (the surgeon might have used that one too); The Reaper, a bakery (another possibility for the surgeon). One common name whose symbolism was clear in the Middle Ages was the Salamander. Salamanders were at that time believed to be impervious to fire, and therefore *salamander* was the old name for asbestos, the "wood that wouldn't burn." Bakers often took this name to symbolize their clay baking ovens, and the word is still in use today for the ceramic room heaters commonly found in Europe.

Many of the names were religious, some specifically so: The Golden Cross, The White Cross, The Red Cross, The Name of Jesus, The Fat Mother of God (which was not vulgar but, rather, complimentary in the hungry Middle Ages). Some names were only vaguely religious in that they used the number three and thus invoked the Trinity. The number three was extremely popular: The Three Catfish, The Three Goddesses, The Three Pruning Knives, The Three Torches, The Three Panes (this was a bakery and not a glazier's), The Three Nuns' Coifs, The Three Doves, The Three Fish, The Three Pigeons.

No. 34 is the most elegant building of this street and was a stylish private home in the seventeenth century. One sure sign is the presence of a large coach entrance for the carriages of the proprietor. The other residents of the quarter obviously were not expected to own coaches or, if they did, were expected to keep them elsewhere. The Ministry of Cultural Affairs has classified as monuments the entrance doors, the courtyard, and the iron stair rail of no. 34. The wide and graceful courtyard is decorated with eighteenth-century *mascarons* (mask decorations) just above the ground floor. One is missing, however, as a result of fire.

Rue de la Harpe

Turn left into the **rue de la Harpe**. This was one of the great streets of Paris from Roman days until the middle of the last century. It ran parallel to the rue Saint-Jacques and wound its serpentine way from the river down toward the South of France. This long street, which was the principal north–south thoroughfare of its day, was amputated by two thirds when Haussmann laid out a new, wide, straight north–south route across the Left Bank, the boulevard Saint-Michel, which took over much of the old right-of-way.

From the earliest times at least fourteen different names for the rue de la Harpe have been recorded, several of them used concurrently. To some, the street was known by a standard or an inn or a school; to others by the people who lived there. It was the street of Reginald the Guitarist or Reginald the Harper, the street of Old Jewry, the street of the Old Buckler, the street of new Saint-Michel, and so on.

A standard of King David playing a harp finally won out and gave the street its present name. The standard is said to have identified the house of Reginald the Harper but may bear some relation to the fact that in the eleventh and twelfth centuries there were Jewish schools on the rue de la Harpe, between Huchette and Saint-Séverin.

The first recorded synagogue in Paris, built in the tenth century, stood on the corner of the rue de la Harpe and rue Monsieur le Prince, approximately four blocks south. Nothing at all is known about it, except that it was just inside the wall of King Philippe Auguste, which encircled and protected Paris. When the Jews were expelled from Paris and their synagogue confiscated in 1182, Philippe Auguste gave their houses to twenty-four drapers and eighteen furriers.

The rue de la Harpe has been the heart of the Latin Quarter for centuries. Roger de Beauvoir in *Paris Chez Soi,* published in 1855, describes it as it was in the early sixteenth century, when Latin, though losing ground to French, was still spoken. To quote his description:

> There was a time when a mass of strange costumes could be seen milling around the greasy, dirty street. There was first of all the mire, the first doctor of early times, who sold his drugs and unguents in the street, escorted by a child with a monkey that was bled by the "practitioner" on request [for

what we can't imagine]. Then followed the hanging sleeves and furs of a professor as grave as Erasmus, the flowing cloaks of the students mixed in with the jackets of the men-at-arms, the pointed hats of the Jews, and later on the wig of Dr. Diafoirus. . . . How many little working girls, the girl-friends of the students, did these black, filthy houses not shelter? Girls singing like canaries in their cages, the fright-ful cages of the seventh floor of the rue de la Harpe. The whole anthill of the schools . . . begins every morning to move its thousand legs from the bottom of the rue de la Harpe—the medical student who goes off, nose to the wind, hand in pocket, looking at his colored anatomical plates; the high school student buying a cake; the law student ogling a shop girl; the tutor taking the rich man's son to his exam for the baccalaureate. The point is that rents were reasonable; even so, no chance that a Chinese, a Turk, an Arab, or even an Englishman would lodge there. It is a special people that enlivens this quarter; a people with ink on its fingers and in its lips; an undisciplined, haughty, noisy people, the people of the schools, the drinking joints, the furnished rooms; the rue de la Harpe with its thousand side streets is the "heart of the students."

Today it is not the "heart of the students" but the heart of the tourists. As you have noticed, the Arabs and the Vietnamese, if not the Chinese, the Greeks, and the Turks, have found their way to this quarter and have changed the business of the street from one of student housing and small food shops and workshops to one of restaurants, cafés, boutiques, jazz clubs, and hotels. The street must be seen at night, and Saturday night is the best night of all.

The "frightful cages of the seventh floor" are now restored as studios (one room and a cubby of a kitchen and bath) renting for large sums, and are snapped up before the rental signs are put up.

No. 33 is a narrow, one-window house called La Petite Bouclerie. Remember, the street was once called the street of the Old Buckler. The name is written inside a sculpted stone frame above the door.

Look up at **nos. 35**, **45**, and **47**. You will see elegant eighteenth-century houses with impressive doorways, rounded stone window-frames, and sculpted façades. The old coach entrances are now filled in, the courtyards occupied by restaurants; but up above, the ceilings are twelve feet high and the rooms are large and bright. The cellars, once filled with mud from Seine floods or used as wine cellars, are fast giving way to restaurants and movie houses.

Look in the courtyard of **no. 35**, past the entry on the right. You'll see a staircase with a classified (historically recognized) iron railing and a wall of beige building stones.

This wide street is a pleasant place to walk, despite some poor-quality clothing stores. In pleasant enough weather musicians and singers vie for the corner of rue de la Harpe and rue de la Huchette, one block north. Enormous crowds gather and often richly fill the empty hat in appreciation of good music or just the pleasure of the spectacle. We once heard a violinist who really was first class, probably on holiday from a symphony orchestra.

Rue de la Parcheminerie

Turn left into the **rue de la Parcheminerie**. In the Middle Ages this street was the "bookshop" of the rue de la Harpe. Before 1530 it was called rue des Escrivains (street of writers); then it was renamed for the parchment the writers wrote upon. The first parchment paper was thick and rough and lent itself poorly to handwriting. It was only in 1380 that the experts developed a grain so tight they were able to write the whole Bible in one small volume. The scribes who worked here were privileged souls, exempt from taxes and held in high esteem, though their morals were infamous. This street has been cleaned up and widened, and so transformed from its former dark-alley appearance to a quiet and pleasant residential street.

The odd luxury of the street is **no. 29**. It was built in 1750 for a gentleman named Claude Dubuisson. One of its beautiful doors was removed when the building served as a wine depot. Each pair of the tall, curved, graceful windows, all three stories of them, opened onto a large room. Today these rooms have been divided into apartments; the previous occupant, who was there during the restoration of the splendid façade, explained to us that the original walls were so thick, architects today could squeeze in the necessary bathrooms.

The second door of no. 29 now opens to **The Abbey Bookshop**, competition for Shakespeare and Company, especially since the former offers free coffee. Opened in 1989, the shop has a large and carefully chosen selection of books in English,

The Abbey Bookshop

especially Canadian books. The shop's owner, Brian Spence—Canadian, intelligent, informed, and charming—claims that in this busy and crowded part of the Latin Quarter, his bookstore is a refuge for the poet, the scholar, or the pilgrim. The piles of books teeter as you squeeze past. Join the Canadian Club of Paris for a small fee and attend book discussions, artists' shows, and wonderful outings, often hiking or biking.

The recently built **Hôtel Parc Saint-Séverin**, at **no. 22**, benefits from a sunny, open site in this neighborhood of crowded, twisted streets. Room number 70 is the hotel's penthouse suite, with a circular terrace that spans views from Notre-Dame to Montmartre.

In 1935 plans were drawn up that called for a complete modernization of the area, a transformation of these winding, narrow streets into neat, airy thoroughfares flanked by modern apartment buildings. But then the campaign to save old Paris took over; the Ministry of Cultural Affairs classified every possible treasure and forbade the destruction of most of the buildings, though they could be restored. Alterations were usually permitted in the interior, hence the opportunity for profitable conversion to new commercial uses and to luxury apartments. And so the restoration goes on, but always far behind the rise in demand.

The medieval name of the rue Boutebrie, on your right, connects the street to the rue de la Parcheminerie. It was known as the street of illuminators, rue des Enlumineurs, when the other was the street of writers. This was the book center of Paris, and Paris was the intellectual center of the world. Follow the continuation of Parcheminerie to the rue Saint-Jacques and turn left.

Rue Saint-Jacques

Cross the rue Saint-Jacques to the store side—the better to see the back of the church of Saint-Séverin, which was smothered by shops until the street was widened a hundred years ago. The stores on this street change with time and style, but many of their names—the Cloister, the Pilgrim, Tentations—still tell the history of past centuries.

To the left of no. 31 rue Saint-Jacques and to the right of no.

27, on the right corner of the wall that juts out, there is a plaque that tells of the death of a soldier, a policeman who was killed at the barricade in 1944. On the adjoining wall, high up, is an etching by Salvador Dalí of a strange sundial. At **no. 21**, **Man'Ouché**, they make *galettes Libanaises,* which are prepared on a large metal dome, called a *tannour.* These crêpes can be covered in a variety of spices and filled with a wide choice of ingredients. After being removed from the *tannour,* the crêpes cool and become crispy. They make an excellent snack or an easy lunch.

A new and charming hotel, the **Hôtel Henri IV**, at **nos. 9–11**, is clean and cozy. In the lobby there are tables for breakfast and newspapers to read while you eat. If you stay in a room in the front of the hotel, you will have a beautiful view of the back of Saint-Séverin; and because it is a new hotel, the rooms are soundproofed and are just as pleasant and quiet on the street side as they are in the back. The hotel even offers umbrellas by the front door for the typically rainy Paris days.

Métamorphoses, at **no. 15** rue du Petit Pont, is true to its name: it changes its wares. It was originally an eccentric 1900s store. Today, Suzanne Sauvanaud (a poet as well) sells strictly jewelry—80 percent is old pieces and the rest is a collection of mainly Art Deco reproductions made by the same companies that made the jewelry in the 1920s and using the original molds. Her stock may be more expensive than others in Paris (still very reasonable), but the quality and selection are superior. The store and front window are crammed with treasures, so take your time.

Polly Magoo, at **no. 5** rue du Petit Pont, is a trendy bar with a fancy mosaic-tile exterior. It was once located at no. 11 and was a place where people gathered to play chess, but the chess disappeared when the bar moved to its larger, swankier location.

Quai Saint-Michel

Cross the street to the corner of place du Petit Pont and the quai de Montebello, and walk right, toward the Pont au Double. You will pass in front of the famous bookstalls of Paris and be across the street from Shakespeare and Company (Walk 1). The book-sellers (*bouquinistes*) represent one of the oldest trades in Paris, and one that has changed very little. The men and women lucky enough to get a spot on the parapet to hang their metal boxes consider themselves a special breed. They love the out-doors and the freedom to open and close at will. When the *quai* is quiet, they sit and read, or sleep, or knit, or smoke, or play chess with their neighbors. Story has it that they are never sick and live to very old age. Most of them have a specialty, but many buy whatever looks salable.

The real fear of the *bouquinistes* is the automobile. The noise is deafening, the air polluted, and the traffic so dense and steady that they see themselves as under siege. Even worse are the huge tourist buses that park themselves directly in front of their stalls. Although plans to transform the *quai* into an expressway have been abandoned, the fear is always there.

Many of the bookstalls offer the usual fare of pages torn from old books, reproductions of Daumier prints, and modern paintings of children with large liquid eyes. But many have a specialty worth a closer look. We found the stalls between the Petit Pont and the Pont au Double more interesting than those near the Pont Saint-Michel. Some stalls down, M. Lanoizelée has a serious stand. He collects first editions, many of which have inscriptions from the author on the flyleaf.

On the west corner of the Petit Pont, stall no. 1, opposite no. 9 quai Saint-Michel, is the stall of Véronique Le Goff, who has followed M. Korb as the president of the *bouquinistes'* union. Participants pay a yearly fee of $50. The union offers an annual literary prize that is celebrated with a fine repast and copies of the speeches in its journal, *Bouquinistes des Quais de Paris*. Union members also help each other out in bad times.

Go back to the corner of the Petit Pont and the quai de Montebello. Diagonally across the street you will see the usual souvenir and poster shops that fill the quai Saint-Michel, but tucked in between are serious galleries and entrances to choice apartments that look out on the Seine and the bustle of the *quai*. A gallery of fine engravings has moved out to make way for a *métro* elevator for the physically handicapped. We once lived in 13 quai Saint-Michel, and the building quaked during the underground drilling.

No. 15 is home to an elegant hotel, **Les Rives de Notre-Dame**. We were impressed by the beauty of its décor. We visited the wonderful sitting room with its glass roof sheltering wooden vaulting, Provençal fabric–covered couches, and caged birds singing. This is a four-star hotel with only ten rooms, so reserve early.

Sartoni-Cerveau, at **no. 15**, begins a row of serious collectors' stores. M. Sartoni-Cerveau's shelves are packed with antique books and etchings. The major topics of his collection are travel, maps, landscapes, and decoration. His motto is "The love of books unites us."

The cupboards on the walls of the **Galeries Michel**, at **no. 17**, are filled with original seventeenth-, eighteenth-, and nineteenth-century prints. M. Michel, whose father ran the gallery before him, is both informative and friendly. Now his daughter works there as well. The labels on his cases cover any subject you might think of—circus, interiors, romantic, mountains—as well as individual artists. M. Michel will be glad to give you a chair and a standing wooden frame to rest a folder on and leave you on your own. Prices range from numbers with one zero to numbers with many. Most of M. Michel's business is done with collectors by mail, despite his location on this very busy street of tourists. Ask to see the back room, which is a small museum of fine etchings.

Gibert Jeune: there are three of these, two on the *quai* and one around the corner, on the place Saint-Michel. They are offshoots, though now separate, of the older firm of Gibert, chief bookseller to generations of students at the Sorbonne and the Lycée Louis-le-Grand, farther up the Boul Mich.

Gibert Jeune, like every other Paris enterprise that can get away with it, sets up displays of merchandise on the pavement outside to catch the fancy of the passersby. These take up a good half of the pavement, and although they create a minor pedestrian traffic jam, it's a lot of fun. Take your time walking through the crush during morning and evening rush hours. At those hours parking is not tolerated on that side of the *quai,* and cars tear along in the outside lane a foot or two from the pavement.

The first Gibert Jeune, at no. 23, offers art books, guidebooks, and books for collectors (about dolls, playing cards, trains, buttons, pipes, anything) at remainder prices.

The second Gibert Jeune, no. 27, has perhaps the largest selection of school books in Paris; these range from beginning readers in the back of the store to Keynes on economics in the front. When secondary school starts, in the fall, lines stretch around the corner, and students wait for hours with their lists of books in hand. The shop closes at five, the line at three.

The third, and the largest, Gibert Jeune is at no. 5 place Saint-Michel. Turn the corner and you will see a book and stationery shop literally in the street. Every morning and evening the stands are carried in and out. The ground floor has all kinds of stationery and office supplies. Enjoy yourself buying new kinds of pads, pencils, and paper clips.

It is certainly time to sit down at the corner café, **Le Départ**, for espresso, fresh lemonade, hot chocolate, or beer. If you like lemonade with bubbles, ask for a *siphon* (seltzer bottle) with your *citron pressé*. Le Départ is a choice spot for people-watching.

You are now back where you started, but there are a few more remarks we would like to make. The *métro,* with its easy map of instructions, will take you anywhere faster than a taxi. This particular entrance is one of the seventeen remaining in Paris that were built around 1900 by Hector Guimard, the architect of the period. Go to see the façade and interior of one of his prize-winning houses, at no. 14 rue La Fontaine, in the sixteenth arrondissement. Sometimes the art of the period, Art Nouveau, is called Style Métro because these subway entrances typify the imaginative floral spiraling that marked the style so clearly. Note the curved squares on the sides of the *métro* entrance. We watched painters one day, as we sat at the café, preparing to put on three layers of paint to get the exact soft green coloring they wanted.

An Art Nouveau show at the Museum of Modern Art in Paris in 1960 appropriately used a *métro* entrance as the passageway

Art Nouveau métro *railings designed by*
Hector Guimard

into the exhibit. The appreciation of 1900s *métro* entrances soared, but the Museum of Modern Art in New York managed to buy one before Paris realized their future worth. The entrance in the place Saint-Michel is missing its curved arch. It has been replaced by a straight pole, typical of the Art Deco of the 1930s, which holds up the rectangular nameplate.

Look across the street at the very high, large fountain that marks this central outdoor lounge and meeting place. On a Saturday, after school had begun, Alison's daughter, Elana, who was spending a semester with her grandparents in order to attend the Ecole Active Bilingue J. M., went with Sonia on the hunt for a special history book. What they found were at least a thousand students staking out territory on the *place* to hawk their secondhand school books. It was a lot of fun pushing through the shouting and the hustling and bustling.

The fountain was built between 1858 and 1860 by Davioud to hide the back wall of an apartment building that ruined the view down the boulevard. This accounts for the unnatural height of the fountain/monument. Four red-marble columns surround a bronze statue of Saint Michel, by Duret. With outspread wings, he stares down at a demon in the water below. At the time of its construction, the work was not appreciated, as evidenced by this rhyme in the press:

In this execrable monument
one sees neither talent nor taste
The devil is worth nothing at all
Saint Michel isn't worth the devil.

If you look down the boulevard, you will see how jammed it is with people and sidewalk vendors. The Musée National du Moyen Age is three blocks south, away from the *quai,* and the Sorbonne, five. The rue Saint-André-des-Arts, to your right, is a busy, funky street that leads to the Saint-Germain-des-Prés area.

Walk · 3

Saint-Germain-des-Prés

In my last letter, I told you that the guillotine is taking care of some dozens of rebels every day, and that about the same number are shot. Now I want to inform you that several hundreds are to be shot every day so that we will soon be rid of those scoundrels who seem to defy the Republic even at the moment of their execution . . .

—From a loyal republican to his section

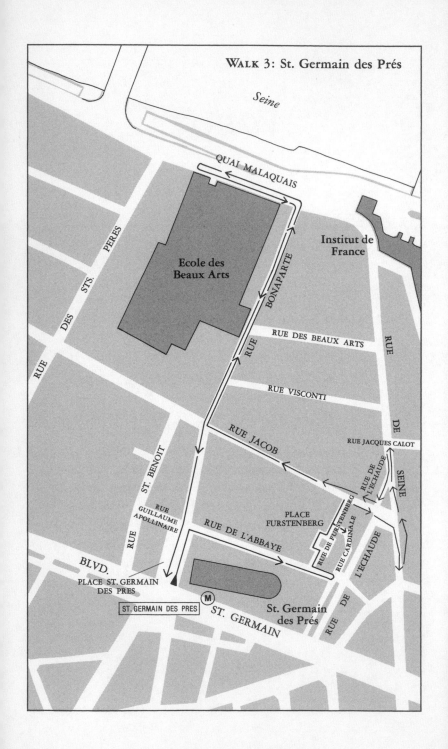

WALK 3: St. Germain des Prés

Seine

QUAI MALAQUAIS

Institut de France

Ecole des Beaux Arts

RUE DES STS. PERES

BONAPARTE

RUE

RUE DES BEAUX ARTS

RUE VISCONTI

RUE

DE

RUE JACOB

RUE JACQUES CALOT

ST. BENOIT

RUE DE L'ECHAUDE

SEINE

RUE DE FURSTENBERG

PLACE FURSTENBERG

RUE GUILLAUME APOLLINAIRE

RUE

RUE DE L'ABBAYE

RUE CARDINALE

RUE DE L'ECHAUDE

BLVD.

PLACE ST. GERMAIN DES PRES

Ⓜ ST. GERMAIN DES PRES

ST. GERMAIN

St. Germain des Prés

Starting Point: Place Saint-Germain-des-Prés, 6th arrondisse-
ment
Métro: Saint-Germain-des-Prés
Buses: 39, 63, 86, 95

As you take in the busy and curious scene of Saint-Germain-
des-Prés, wander over to the hollyhock-filled garden on the side
of the church at the corner of rue de l'Abbaye and the place
Saint-Germain. We suggest you begin this walk by taking a seat
in the garden and reading a bit about the illustrious abbey and
the bloody events of the French Revolution that took place on
and around this spot.

In Roman and Merovingian times, up to the early eighth
century, this area consisted of open fields (*prés*) stretching westward away from Paris, and there was a temple to the Egyptian
goddess Isis on the site where the church of Saint-Germain now
stands. The modern suburb of Issy-les-Moulineaux took its
name from this ancient temple.

In 542, Childebert, son of the first Christian king, Clovis,
went on a crusade in Spain to punish the Visigoths, who,

though Christian, were believed guilty of heresy. The inhabitants did not defend themselves in any way, and Childebert laid siege to their key city, Saragossa. Despairing of their fate, the Visigoths paraded around the walls of the city in hair shirts, carrying sacred gold relics and the alleged tunic of Saint Vincent. The men chanted psalms; the women, with hair unkempt, sobbed hysterically, as if in mourning. Childebert was fascinated by this procession, and when he saw the relics the Visigoths carried, he offered to lift his siege in exchange for these treasures. He returned triumphantly to Paris with the sacred tunic and the objects of gold. There is evidence, however, that the Bishop Germain (later Saint Germain) of Paris, as well as the chronicler of this tale, Gregory of Tours, considered Childebert a fool to have settled for so little. They felt his father, Clovis, would have done better.

In any event, the bishop took the opportunity to get Childebert to build a church to house the sainted relics on the location of the former temple of Isis. There, a magnificent basilica with marble columns and gilded rafters was built in two years. The outside was covered with gilded copper and gold mosaic radiant in the sunshine. The church was called Saint-Germain-le-Doré (Saint Germain the golden).

Three hundred years later, Norsemen, drawn by the glitter of what looked like pure gold, descended on Paris and ransacked the church four times in forty years, between 845 and 885. They were disappointed each time, for the true gold relics that Childebert had brought back from Spain, along with the tunic of Saint Vincent, lay safely somewhere in the countryside. In the meantime, the devastated church was left a ruin for more than a century. Then, in the beginning of the eleventh century, it was rebuilt. The central bell tower dates from this reconstruction and today is the oldest church structure in Paris.

What decided the fate of this area for many centuries was the establishment of an abbey, with rights to the land and its revenue over an enormous area stretching from the Seine all the way to what are now the suburbs of Paris. The abbey also received exclusive jurisdiction in all religious and legal matters within its territory. The fortified walls that enclosed the abbey proper formed a square between the present boulevard Saint-

Germain and rues Jacob, Saint-Benoît, and de l'Echaudé. The size and riches of the abbey of Saint-Germain rivaled those of the city of Paris.

The bishop's abbey was his palace, his clerics were his court, and the peasants who lived outside the walls (bakers, butchers, prison guards) were his servitors. This imitation of courtly life did not go unnoticed by the king, who kept a close watch on the rival power just outside his city walls.

The most interesting tales come to us from the thirteenth century and concern the perennial conflict between the monks and the students of the nearby Latin Quarter. The students used to come to talk and sport on the fields that stretched along the Seine north of the abbey. They made noise, trespassed on areas the clerics would have closed to them, and troubled the peace of the local residents—as students are usually accused of doing. In return, the residents of the abbey harassed the students at every opportunity. From time to time this hostility broke into violent conflict.

The worst of these confrontations took place in 1278, when the Abbé Gerard built some houses along a path that the students customarily used in going from the Latin Quarter to the playing fields. The students saw this as a provocative impediment to their passage and proceeded to dismantle these structures. The abbé rang the tocsin, summoning monks, vassals, and serfs to defend the rights of the abbey. Chroniclers tell us that an armed company fell on the students with swords, pikes, and clubs, shouting, "Kill! Kill!" The students took a terrific beating. Two were killed, one blinded, several badly wounded. Prisoners were paraded bareheaded through the marketplace and thrust into the abbey's dungeons, on the site of the present Hôtel Madison, at no. 143 boulevard Saint-Germain.

However great the provocation offered by students, the abbé was felt to have overreacted. The students appealed to the papal legate and the king and, surprisingly, got a quick and sympathetic response: perhaps this was because both the church and the crown had come to feel that the abbey was too rich, powerful, and arrogant for anyone's good. The leader of the abbey forces was exiled; the chapter was compelled to build and endow two new churches in memory of the slain students;

the parents of the victims were granted substantial indemnities; and the students were confirmed in their legal use of their sporting meadow, the Pré aux Clercs, so called because the term *clerc* denoted all men of instruction, whether or not they were members of the clergy. The students were overjoyed at this victory, and in the following years continued to exercise whatever rights of destruction they felt appropriate.

Three centuries later, Henri II, plagued by student uprisings, decided to dampen their ardor and sent Parliament orders to pursue persons guilty of acts of violence. Parliament's action culminated on October 6, 1557, with the burning at the stake of a student named Croquoison, who received the bleak mercy of being strangled before being burned on the Pré aux Clercs. This seems to have been the last major incident in the student-monk war, although their mutual animosity produced incidents well into the eighteenth century.

In the spring of that same year, 1557, the people of the *quartier,* as well as those who came streaming in from all over Paris, had been treated to a more dramatic execution at the stake. Two Huguenots who had been captured at a secret religious meeting two weeks earlier and had refused under torture to abjure their faith were brought into the square that is now place Saint-Germain, in front of the church, and asked one last time to renounce their heresy in order that they might be strangled before being burned. If not, their lying venomous tongues were to be ripped from their mouths. They refused. After the executioner had done the terrible deed (to the roaring approval of the crowd), the heretics were bound and hoisted onto the stakes, which were placed high above the wood in such a manner that the lower halves of the bodies would be reduced to ashes while the top halves were still intact.

Less gruesome stories are told about the fairgrounds, an area that stretched from the boulevard Saint-Germain to the Luxembourg Gardens and which were a central feature of the abbey's power. Every year for a month after Easter, a great fair was held. This was one of the great medieval fairs, drawing

The bell tower of the church of Saint-Germain-des-Prés

people from Spain, England, Burgundy, Flanders, and the Holy Roman Empire, as well as from all over France. Here were hundreds of stalls selling every kind of product and service available then; troupes of performers, dancing bears, and minstrels; the most impressive swirl of colors, aromas, and noises a commoner would ever find. This fair served as a gathering point for students as well as courtesans and men of state. The rest of the year the area was far from deserted. There was always some activity, and it seems to have been the place to find whomever it was you sought in Paris. In addition to attracting courtiers, merchants, and students, the fairgrounds were frequented by a group of Italian ruffians, called *braves,* ironically, since they always hung out in groups of five or six. The *braves* were available, at the right price, for carrying out whatever vengeance one might seek, as the following story illustrates.

In the court of Henri III there was a nobleman whose mistress dumped him rather rudely. Having given her large sums of money in happier days, he wished to collect his "loans." His former lady, believing that, in love, money loaned is money given, refused to comply and sought vengeance. One night, the nobleman was returning home after a walk through the Saint-Germain fairgrounds. On the *champ crotté* (the dunged field of the cattle market), which was understandably solitary, a band of *braves* jumped him and held him by the nose, which the leader began to cut off with a knife. The victim's screams aborted the full operation, and the nobleman was left watching his assailants flee as his nose dangled by a thread. The nose was sewn back on but, in the testimony of a contemporary, slightly off-center. The story had unpleasant results for some of the actors; one does not lightly cut off a nobleman's nose. One *brave* was hanged, and the lady and her friends had to buy their way out of trouble, no doubt with the hapless victim's money.

Henri III, too, appreciated the promenade, where he would stroll in the company of his *mignons* (literally "cuties," the name given to his favorite young men, with their curly hair, powdered faces, and makeup). The king and his entourage rapidly became the butt of student jokes. Returning one day from Chartres, the king had several students imprisoned for following his suite with long pieces of curled paper and shouting out loud in the middle of the fair, "*A la fraise on connaît le veau*" (You can tell the calf by its birthmark—a French proverb that meant, in this context, "You can tell the gay by his curls").

The monastery reached the end of its twelve-hundred-year history when the forces of the French Revolution moved in and took over, replacing intermittent violence with the organized violence of the Terror. The revolutionaries filled the abbey's jail until it was overflowing with prisoners (aristocrats, clergy, and common people), and then set up tribunals to thin out the crowd. These tribunals made use of "guest houses," which stood on the corner of the rue de l'Abbaye and rue Bonaparte, just outside the entrance to this garden. These houses had extra rooms called *chambres à donner* (rooms that could be given to guests of the abbey). These rooms, which once provided shelter and comfort, were turned into tribunals of condemnation—swift and deadly. The stories about the trials held there are hard to believe.

One concerns Mlle de Sombreuil, a carefully brought up young lady who rarely left her house unaccompanied. One day, however, she left alone, on a terrible mission. Her father, a prisoner, was scheduled for one of the infamous swift trials in which no one was ever found innocent. When she appeared at the tribunal, she begged for her father's life. The guards found the situation amusing and offered to make a deal. If she would drink the still-steaming blood of the latest victim, they would spare her father. She did, and her father lived, for a few days.

During September 2 and 3, 1792, these tribunals carried out the ostensibly judicial massacre of more than two hundred victims. Each defendant was dressed in his best clothes, because he had been told when arrested that he was being sent away. The questioning that followed was strictly pro forma. The defendant was found guilty regardless. After this mock trial, the prisoners were led out of the tribunal into the courtyard of the abbey and were there hacked and stabbed to death by two rows of hired citizens, in many cases local residents.

On September 3 alone, 168 men and women, including several of Louis XVI's ministers, his father confessor, and surely many "irrelevant" people, were executed in this fashion because Judge Maillard (nicknamed "the Slugger") insisted on having them killed at once. The executioners, however, were soon to rue their zealous slaughter when they learned that as a prize for the day's work they could claim the victims' clothes. The clothes were so badly cut up that they were worth little. The massacre continued with the slaughter of the king's personal Swiss guard. Late in the afternoon, another judge came onto the scene and, drinking to the nation, shouted to the executioners (whose arms still dripped with blood): "People, you slaughter your enemies, you do your duty!" On September 4 the slaughter was followed by a long auction of personal effects while the pile of corpses lay in this garden, alongside the church.

In all, the number of citizens killed in Paris during the month of September 1792 is estimated at 1,614. Many victims were burned at the door of the prison, and even at the door of the church, but the largest number were massacred in front of the tribunal, at the corner of the rue Bonaparte and boulevard Saint-Germain.

After the Revolution, Paris was irrevocably changed, including the role of the church. The church of Saint-Germain was reconsecrated, but simply, as the parish church it is today, and the abbey was relegated to serving, as it still does, the social needs of its parishioners. The neighborhood today is an intellectual center of Paris in which the church of Saint-Germain-des-Prés simply happens to be found.

Now it is time to look at the garden itself, the square Laurent-Prache. This quiet spot, in the midst of a confusion of cars and people, is a flowered and shady retreat in summer and a startlingly bare sculpture garden in winter. Many of the pieces are Gothic remains from a medieval chapel. You will find a gargoyle whose spout was in the shape of a dog's head. Unfortunately, it was broken off and stolen by a "lover" of Gothic architecture.

The first piece of sculpture before you as you enter the garden is most unexpected; it is the strange and powerful bronze head of a woman, dedicated to Guillaume Apollinaire, sculpted by his loyal friend Pablo Picasso. The bust sits on a four-foot-high white stone pedestal; it is dated 1959, although Apollinaire died years before, in 1918, at the age of thirty-eight.

Picasso and Apollinaire, the artist and poet, were favorites of the arty café world and were courted by all the would-be artists and hangers-on who spent their days drinking and talking together.

One of these admirers, an employee of the Louvre Museum, wishing to show his appreciation and respect for the two, presented each of them with a statuette. Picasso and Apollinaire thanked him, put the objects away, and thought no more about them. Several months later the guards at the museum, shocked out of their negligence by an important theft, realized that a variety of other objects were missing as well. It wasn't long before suspicion fell on the guard, who led them directly to his friends, pleading that he had simply given Picasso and Apollinaire the statues as gifts. Because he was not a French citizen, Picasso was let off with a few sharp words; but the case was different for Apollinaire. The officials not only entangled him in the ubiquitous French web of paperwork and procedures but also questioned him so harshly that the poet was driven to ask why in the world they didn't accuse him of stealing the *Mona Lisa*. That did it. The *Mona Lisa* had just been stolen, and Guillaume Apollinaire was put in prison.

The situation might have been merely ludicrous, but Apollinaire's patriotism turned it into tragedy. He was born in Rome of Polish parents named Kostrowitzki, but he fell in love with France with an intensity that led him to change his name and nationality and to fight valiantly in the First World War for his new country. To be accused of stealing the nation's treasures and imprisoned was too great a blow. He died soon after his release from prison, a disappointed and unhappy man. It is, therefore, particularly suitable that tribute was finally paid him with the placing of this statue here, among medieval remnants and archways; amid the treasures of the France that was so dear to him.

These treasures are fragments from the thirteenth-century chapel of the Virgin, which stood within the walls of the abbey, diagonally down the street, at the present **no. 6 bis rue de l'Abbaye**. The chapel, begun in 1245, took ten years to build and was the work of Pierre de Montreuil. The remains that you see on the two walls of the garden, pieced together stone by stone, make clear how delicate this masterpiece of thirteenth-century flamboyant Gothic must have been.

The chapel was partly destroyed in 1794, when the refectory and library next to it exploded and burned. It was completely dismantled in 1800, when the street was cut through. Additional remains of the chapel decorate the garden of the Musée National du Moyen Age.

If you have not been in the church yet, you may wish to go now, or you may enter later, when the walk ends back here. Pass through Saint-Germain's modern clear-glass doors, which keep concert music in and street noise out. This is one of the few churches that has kept its original interior painting. The vaulting is sky blue sprinkled with stars. Each gilt pillar is decorated differently. Today we are accustomed to plain stone, but medieval churches were very colorful. For example, originally the entire façade of Notre-Dame and the interior were brightly painted and gilded.

The entrance to the garden Laurent-Prache was actually the site of the Revolutionary tribunal. It was here that the incredibly bloody hacking to death of 168 persons took place. This street was cut through in 1800, and shortly after was given the whitewashing name of rue de la Paix (street of peace), but finally took the name of its earlier history, rue de l'Abbaye. The place de la Concorde, on the Right Bank (see Walk 7), the site of most of the guillotine murders and crowd madness of the French Revolution, has somehow managed to keep its name, despite its violent past.

Rue de l'Abbaye

Until 1997, **no. 18 rue de l'Abbaye** was the site of the well-known bookstore Librairie Le Divan, owned by Gallimard, one of the most distinguished publishing houses in Paris. This corner spot, stuffed with books on tables and shelves, was an introduction to all the publishing houses and bookstores dotting the streets behind: Seuil, Hachette, Gallimard. The city, which owns the property, increased the rent so much that Gallimard made the momentous decision to move—to the far reaches of the fifteenth arrondissement.

Why was the rent suddenly so high? Who could afford it?

Christian Dior. And who moved into the famous American Drugstore? Armani. And who bought half of Arthus Bertrand? Louis Vuitton. What happened was a takeover by the big names from the Right Bank's rue Saint-Honoré. Now nearly every store on the Right Bank has a branch somewhere on the Left, and the concept of chain stores has taken over Paris.

M. Brenner of Galerie La Hune, which you will soon visit, says these big names are bringing the showcases of high luxury here, more for advertising than actual sales. M. Brenner and the group he represents felt that this intrusion would take over and destroy the soul and spirit of Saint-Germain, and that the oldies—Hemingway, Natalie Clifford Barney, Camus, Sartre—would have put up a fight. The group wanted everyone to sign their petitions. They wanted to preserve their bookstores, galleries, and artisans. They wanted to save the neighborhood's soul.

Saint-Germain is the heart of Parisian culture, the soul of learning, and the meeting place of intellectuals. The books sold at Le Divan were the source of debate and discussion that animated the cafés on the boulevard. Concerned members of the neighborhood started the organization SOS Saint-Germain-des-Prés, Save Our Souls, with headquarters at La Hune. Their petition read, "The undersigned ask the public officials and legislators to do everything they can to maintain the cultural affairs that mark Saint-Germain as the genius of the *place*."

A meeting was held April 22, 1997, at the Café de Flore to inaugurate the organization and make their case known. Juliette Greco, a longtime resident and famous actress and singer, with the help of actors Jean-Paul Belmondo and Catherine Deneuve and singer Charles Aznavour, pleaded their case with the minister of culture, Philippe Douste-Blazy. Despite their efforts, today many publishers have moved out and fabric stores have taken over galleries.

Before you enter **La Hune**, take a look at **no. 16**, the spot where the refectory of the abbey once stood. Unfortunately, the door is usually locked, but try it anyway. The refectory was built by Pierre de Montreuil in 1239. Nearly five hundred years later, in 1714, a library was built over the refectory. During the Revolution the refectory served as a magazine for gunpowder, which exploded on the night of August 19, 1794. The refectory collapsed and fire broke out, completely destroying it and the library above. Fortunately, most of the manuscripts were saved, including the original *Pensées* by Blaise Pascal, written on little bits of paper.

It was thought that no trace of the refectory remained. But a few years ago the government was in the midst of putting up moderately priced housing on this spot when the workers uncovered the marvelous former outside wall of the refectory. Its two and a half flamboyant windows, tall and graceful and intact, had been covered by plaster and totally forgotten for almost two hundred years.

The wall is preserved on the right-hand side of the entrance hall to the apartments. Some of the stones below are also part of the old wall. The monks' cells in the cellar are now filled in with brick walls and serve as storage rooms for the tenants. Niches for holy statues dot the walls.

Now visit La Hune (literally, crow's nest), at **no. 14**, a fine and refined gallery whose exhibitions and *vernissages* (openings) are always wonderful. Notice the bronze door handle in the shape of a man's face. When you leave the gallery, look at the back of the man's head on the handle. The artist is Igor Mitoraj.

Past La Hune, enter no. 14 and walk to the back of the courtyard. To the right you will find a neat, small white stucco house. We saw it years ago when the place was in ruins and overgrown with bushes. To see into **no. 12**, look through the door. The building was once a small rectangular cloister, built in the thirteenth century, plainer than the larger one across the street. The bays have been filled in and rebuilt, but the shape remains the same. If you look all around, you will see the perfect symmetry of the four sides.

Inside **no. 13** are the remains of the abbey's larger cloister (built in the thirteenth century, restored in the seventeenth), in which the priests could stroll. Remember that the rue de l'Abbaye did not exist at that time and these cloisters were in fields surrounding the church. Note the three floors built above the arches of the cloister. Curtain-like vines drape the walls—green in summer, red in the fall.

Nos. 11, 9, 7, and **5** have recently been restored. **Rubelli,**

The front and back of the doorknob of La Hune at no. 14 rue de l'Abbaye

at no. 11, shows decorator fabrics in an ultramodern setting. Between nos. 9 and 7 is a parish office whose garden offers a fine view of the church. At no. 7 a hook for a pulley is attached to the gabled top window and there is a side entrance to the church.

Look into the glass door of **no. 8**, a grandstanding apartment house (built in 1963), to see a variously marbled, tiled, and flowered entry. Notice the spectacular wooden sculpture shaped like a series of abstract totem poles. In the courtyard is a carefully tended (and that is unusual) walled garden with a pool.

Nos. 1–5 are the remains of the palace built in 1586 for

Cardinal Charles I of Bourbon, the abbot at Saint-Germain. The unusual style is marked by a sharply slanted slate roof and open pediment and particularly by the use of both brick and stone for the façade. The few remaining examples of this style are the houses on the place des Vosges (see Walk 4) built under Henri IV, and the apartment houses that form the prow of the Ile de la Cité, facing the famous statue of Henri IV. Brick is, in general, rarely used in Paris. When you spot some turn-of-the-century brick apartment houses here and there, you will probably agree that stone suits Paris better.

Until recently these buildings were hidden by a temporary wall that also hid a gallery, a garage, and a social services center. Now the Institut Catholique owns two-thirds, and one-third is still the social services office for this parish. The institute is closed on the weekends, but on weekdays you can enter the door with names and doorbells, at no. 5, to see the restored stone staircase and, through the metal grille, the lovely garden. The main staircase at no. 3 originally served as the grand entrance to the abbey from the rue de Furstenberg, behind you.

No. 8, **Flamant**, is a home interiors and furniture store, which also has an entrance on the place Furstenberg. If you go in the entrance on the rue de l'Abbaye, you can see the remains of an old pillar that once stood in the chapel of the Virgin. The chapel was first damaged when the neighboring refectory exploded in 1792, and the opening of the rue de l'Abbaye, in 1800, completed the destruction, leaving only this pillar. The store sells beautiful décor in a shabby-chic style and has a small restaurant that serves sandwiches and salads. The wares are lovely, but the staff less so.

No. 6 bis is another of the many decorating shops in this area. These wallpaper and fabric specialists often collaborate with their neighbor **Manuel Canovas**, at **no. 6**. Canovas was the first to move here. He also has showrooms at nos. 7 and 5 place Furstenberg. Note the Art Nouveau floral motif of the building.

For a light bite, pack a vegetarian lunch at the very busy **Guenmai**, at **no. 2**. This was once a Greek restaurant, Au Vieux Paris, opened by M. Nico on December 6, 1941, during the German occupation. When meat supplies were limited, M.

A stone pillar from the thirteenth-century chapel of the Virgin

Nico would call his best customers and serve them the meat he had concealed beneath puréed potatoes. The building has been scaffolded and unused for years, which is surprising in this coveted neighborhood.

Rue de Furstenberg

Retrace your steps to the rue de Furstenberg. When Egon de Furstenberg was abbot of Saint-Germain-des-Prés, in the last decades of the seventeenth century, he opened a new entrance to the palace, one that led into the rue du Colombier (street of doves), now the rue Jacob. This entrance descended from the grand staircase of the abbey into the rue de Furstenberg.

The square in the middle of this short street, with its four pawlonia empress trees and old-fashioned light globes, is a picturesque spot. Benches were removed when it became too much of a hangout. Although the trees are named after Anna Pavlova, daughter of Czar Paul I of Russia, they are Chinese (some sources say Japanese) in origin. The trees are admired in the spring for their perfumed mauve blossoms and large leaves.

The three smaller ones are recent replacements. Symmetrical houses were built next to each other on either side of the square; **nos. 6** and **8**, still standing, and recognizable by their low doorways and brick-and-stone painted façades, were stables of the abbey.

This is the spot filmmakers choose in Paris for romance. Remember that Martin Scorsese filmed the final scene in *The Age of Innocence* in this square. In the film, Newland Archer sits on a bench looking at, but never going up to, the apartment of Mme Olenska, to finally join the woman he loves. Edith Wharton did not put Newland in the place Furstenberg, but in the more formal setting of the place des Invalides, which was perhaps more fitting for his controlled rather than romantic response.

Walk through the stable archway of no. 6, across the courtyard to the center door, to the **Musée National Eugène Delacroix**, home of the painter for the last six years of his life, 1857 to 1863. This is an exciting small museum, with changing exhibitions, fine drawings, and small sketches of Eugène Delacroix's completed masterpieces. Through the museum windows, look to see a small cream-colored building with a pebbled garden. This was the infirmary of the abbey, where the invalids were kept, more as protection for the healthy outside than to help the sick within.

After the museum, go outside and downstairs to Delacroix's atelier. It is a beautiful room with a huge skylight, high ceilings, and oak floors. It was here that Delacroix created his last works, which were exhibited at the Salon of 1859.

In the street once more, walking left toward the rue Jacob, you will notice at the point where the street narrows a sculpted stone torch on the pillar of **no. 4**. This is the remains of the decoration of the Court of Honor, a place where ceremonies were performed when the palace on the rue de l'Abbaye was Furstenberg's private domicile. The house was sold to the government in 1797 and taken down. Only this pillar, an entry, remains.

Directly across the street is an ultra-chic Canovas retail store of items made with superb fabrics available at reduced prices.

As you head out to the rue Jacob walk to your right, down the small, picturesque **rue Cardinale**. The street once lay within the boundaries of the Abbaye Saint-Germain and was named for

A stone torch on the pillar of no. 4 place Furstenberg

the abbot, Guillaume de Furstenberg. It was originally the abbey's open-air tennis court but became a street in 1701. The house at the elbow of the street, **no. 3**, has an attractive terrace with wrought-iron grillwork and a sagging roof that evoke a picture of this city's lost past. A few steps to the right of this house, at **no. 5**, is **Cipango**, selling beautiful, creative jewelry made only from natural stones. Half the store is an atelier where the jewelry is made. Open from 11 A.M. to 6 P.M. daily.

There are interesting shops on your way to the rue Jacob: choice seventeenth- and eighteenth-century antiques at **Yveline** and, at **no. 1**, **Aux Armes de Furstenberg**, a fine antiques shop, almost an institution, specializing in scientific instruments, globes, and military objects. One more decorating shop, at no. 1, has replaced a serious bookshop. Spot the exposed stone and beams inside.

We are going to turn right on Jacob; visit the rue de Seine, packed with galleries and sights to see; and then return to visit the rue Jacob.

In front of you and across the street, **no. 6** houses a curious shop, the **Huilerie Artisinale**, the kind that defies the chain stores. The Huilerie resembles a perfume store, with its many bottles of different oils. You can sniff and taste. The young people here are members of a family that has been pressing oils in Burgundy since 1878. They sell to fine restaurants and to you.

At the corner, look to where rue de Seine and rue Jacob meet. This Japanese-type garden, with stones, fountain, and grasses, is lovely amid all the buildings and stores. There is often a bird perched on the highest stone.

Rue de Seine

Turn right onto the **rue de Seine**. The rue de Seine is lined with galleries, some of which are constantly changing. We cannot describe them all in detail, so if you are an art aficionado be sure to allow plenty of time to explore.

The **Hôtel de Seine**, **no. 52**, in this central location, is a good choice to stay. It is up-to-date, with telephones, color TV, individual safes, and reasonable prices.

No. 54 is an important, recently restored building, twelve windows wide. Note the stone pillars on the second floor, the mansard roof, and the tiny balcony.

Così, at no. 54, sells a good, quick, inexpensive lunch of brick oven–baked bread with scads of toppings. This Così is the original one and has spawned the popular chain in the United States. Open every day from lunch to midnight.

At the corner, at **no. 56**, look up at the gable (*pignon*) roof on this 1744 building. Odd, because these pointed roofs facing the street were outlawed in the early 1500s. The rain gathered between the rooflines, instead of falling on the street below, causing serious water damage. There are only about thirty of these left in Paris.

In front of you is the wonderful **Buci food market**, one of the best in Paris. Find the old street name incised in stone at the corner of **75 rue de Seine**, RUE DE SEINE and RUE DE BUSSY 16. The *16* refers to the sectioning of Paris before the city was divided into its twenty arrondissements.

Return to the right side of the rue de Seine. On this street, **nos. 73**, **71**, **65**, and **63** are "old houses." Train your eyes to recognize differences from the other buildings.

The ironwork at no. 73 is classified. The **Galerie de Buci** has exceptional paintings and sculpture.

At **no. 69**, you will find **Fish à la Boissonnerie**, which is owned by an American, who explained that the name of the restaurant is a play on the expression "drink like a fish." You can see that the restaurant was once a seafood store (*poissonnerie*) and that the owner has added tiles to the mosaic above the door to change the name to "boissonnerie." His partner owns Così, directly across the street.

No. 63, once the home of poet Adam Mickiewicz, the national poet of Poland, is beautifully restored with lovely wrought-iron balconies. **No. 57**, with its four *mascarons,* three women on the second floor and a man on the third, is typical of eighteenth-century decoration. The three-windows-wide balconied façade is classified.

Jacqueline Subra, at **no. 51**, collects quality estate jewelry and antiques. If you go through the first courtyard, through a building, and to the second courtyard, you will find a small garden with bushes and flowers set out in a pattern—a rarity in Paris.

At the back of the courtyard of **no. 49** is a charming shop called, appropriately, **Au Fond de la Cour**. Here you will find a tremendous collection of colorful majolica, serving dishes of all kinds (we have never seen so many variations of an asparagus plate), and furniture designed for greenhouses.

Now we come to a watering place with some of the old artistic spirit of the neighborhood. Sit outside a 1900s café at

Fish à la Boissonnerie restaurant

La Palette, **no. 43**, a lively hangout for actors, artists, and cinema people. It is off the beaten track of the boulevard, the café food is good, and the service is informal. Walk past the tables on the **rue Jacques Calot** to find an amazing statue by Arman that is almost symbolic of the café and the neighborhood. The statue of a woman is sliced in vertical layers to show her many talents. Walk all around her and find all the signs of artistic creation: a pile of books, a painter's palette, brushes, a violin, and more.

A remnant of the French Revolution sits directly across the street, at **no. 34.** The building is a *temple d'amitié* (temple of friendship). These temples were built during the Revolution to replace churches. The words *à l'amitié* (to friendship) are inscribed on it. This neighborhood was rich in such Revolutionary clubs, but very few remain. At our last visit, the building was under construction.

At the corner (and officially at **no. 40** rue de l'Echaudé) is an ornate apartment building dating from 1910. It is interesting to compare the curves and lush decorations on this façade with the more sober seventeenth- and eighteenth-century buildings in the neighborhood.

Keep going on the **rue de l'Echaudé**. At **no. 6**, **Pixie & Co.** sells expensive toys, figurines, and other interesting playthings. The store next door specializes in *Le Petit Prince*.

Rue Jacob

From the rue de l'Echaudé, turn right onto the **rue Jacob** to visit this famous street. Streets in Paris are often named after famous people, important places, or interesting signs, but rarely do they get the name of a Biblical patriarch like Jacob. The name was given in memory of a vow taken by Marguerite de Valois, whose colorful life has left its mark on the history of this area and is worth recalling in some detail.

Marguerite, known as "chère Margot," was the daughter of Henri II and Catherine de Médicis. She was the sister of two kings and the wife of Henri de Navarre, later Henri IV. In addition to having this noble background, she was beautiful and learned. Her memoirs are among the best written by nobility, but when the French refer to "chère Margot" with a knowing smile, they are thinking less of what she wrote than what she left out.

As one historian put it, "She knew love at eleven," and thanks to this early start, she was able to collect a long list of lovers in the course of her career. She had, naturally, good teachers: her brother Henri III and his flamboyant *mignons,* as well as her cousin and husband, Henri, who is recorded as having had fifty-six mistresses.

Margot was married in 1572 at the age of nineteen to the Protestant Henri de Navarre (second in line for the throne) very much against her Catholic convictions and the will of the Pope. This mattered little compared with the determination of her brother Charles IX.

It took more than marriage to slow Margot down. She had her establishment; her husband had his. All went well until one day, in 1583, when Margot's brother Henri, now Henri III, denounced his sister's debauchery before the entire court. The actual cause of his anger was that Margot had openly parodied him and his court of homosexuals.

A "sliced lady" representing all the arts

This denunciation made it harder for Henri de Navarre to put up with Margot's scandalous behavior, and finally, in 1587, under social pressure, he put her away in the Château d'Usson, in Auvergne, where she managed to seduce her jailer. She made the best of her exile—eighteen years of being served by a severely restricted court—writing memoirs and adding to her list of conquests. Nevertheless, she missed Paris and swore to raise an altar to Jacob if ever she was allowed to return. Jacob had also suffered exile, had worked and waited fourteen years for Rachel, and had finally been able to go back home, where he had given thanks to God for his safe return by building an altar.

The happy day came in 1605. By this time Henri de Navarre, now Henri IV, had long since divorced Margot and married Marie de Médicis. The king installed Margot in the château of the archbishops (an ironic touch) of Sens, located on the Right Bank of the Seine at the entrance to the Marais quarter. (See Walk 6 for the Hôtel de Sens.)

Margot was then fifty-two, fat, and bald, but as insatiable as ever. Her weight was so great she ordered the doorways widened. Her hair was so thin she snipped locks from the heads of her blond valets to use for her wigs. Jean Duché, in his *Histoire de France Racontée à Juliette,* claims that Margot wore around her ample waist amulets containing pieces of the hearts of her dead lovers.

The Hôtel de Sens became a place of revelry. Margot's lover of the moment was the twenty-year-old Count of Vermond, but finding him perhaps too old, Margot brought in the eighteen-year-old son of a carpenter from Usson. Vermond couldn't stand this. He lay in wait for his rival and shot him in the head right in front of Margot, who was returning from her religious devotion in a nearby church. Margot was enraged. She had Vermond pursued and arrested, and when he was brought before her, she cried out, "Kill the wretch. Here, here are my garters. Strangle him!" They cut off his head instead, while Margot looked on.

But all this blood and gore depressed her, and two days later she decided to leave the Hôtel de Sens and inhabit a house she was then building on the Pré aux Clercs, at what is now nos. 2–10 rue de Seine. She remembered her vow and built the convent of Petits Augustins (now no. 14 rue Bonaparte) in the back of the garden of her château. There she installed fourteen Augustinian friars, who took turns every two hours singing praises to Jacob with words and music written by Margot. Five years later she chased them out, claiming they sang badly. The name of the street is all that remains of Margot's celebrated gesture of thanksgiving.

This street is what we call one of the hidden streets of Paris. The unknowing eye sees shop after shop below five-story apartment buildings that show little decoration and little difference from one to the other. In fact, there are gardens, courtyards, staircases, even ceilings to discover on the rue Jacob.

The building at **no. 5** is the spot where one of the towers of the surrounding walls of the abbey stood. It was twenty feet in diameter and stood next to the dovecote (hence the old name of the street, rue du Colombier) of the abbey.

Enter the courtyard of **no. 12** and go through the archway. At the back you'll find a small garden and a shop selling jewels and pashminas. Note the stone steps of the staircase, the old railing, and the rafters. No. 12 also has an antiques shop that has replaced an old bookshop that was once the meeting place for lovers of Paris. The Huysmans Society met here every Saturday from three to six. Joris-Karl Huysmans was the famous nineteenth-century writer who described Paris in a manner so poetic, so unbelievably full of love that first editions of his books today are collectors' treasures and are sold at auction for very high prices. Huysmans could write about the smells of Paris trash in a way that would make you mourn the passing of the open garbage truck.

No. 7 dates from 1640 and was once called the Hôtel Saint-Paul. Racine lived here with his uncle in 1656, when he was seventeen years old. Pierre Frey, another big decorating name, has moved in, replacing an art gallery.

Richard Wagner lived at **no. 14** for six months, in 1841–1842, in poverty but on the verge of his first operatic success with *The Flying Dutchman*.

A new building for this street, **no. 18**, built in 1928, is a nice example of Art Deco architecture, not often found here. Inside is **Gaggio**, which sells Venetian goods. The store is filled with lush velvet fabrics, hand dyed and printed with wooden stamps. There are elegant jackets, slinky dresses cut on the bias, fabrics for furniture and drapes, and home accessories such as chandeliers made from Murano glass. The shop can custom-make anything for you, including Fortuny silk lamps. The fur-trimmed capes are so fabulous they made the youngest, unmarried member of this team want to plan a winter wedding just so she could have a reason to wear a cape.

In the seventeenth century, **nos. 9**, **11**, and **13**, built next to the old abbey wall, were all one house, belonging to a member of Parliament, M. Chabenat de la Malmaison. Later, the building was the Hôtel de la Gabelle, the main office for the collection of the salt tax. No. 9 is now an expensive art gallery.

The antique dealer who owned part of no. 11 never appraised—or even found—what was certainly the most valuable treasure his store had ever seen. A later owner who renovated the space uncovered fabulous painted beams in the ceiling. There are hundreds of rafters in Paris but none like these remarkably well preserved and painted ones. They date from the end of the fifteenth century; the painting, however, was done later. Various trades of the City of Paris are pictured in the medallions in the center. The entire ceiling had been hidden (and preserved) by plaster. Very skillful restoration has saved most of it. Imagine the beauty of this room when it was two floors high and the fireplace on the side wall was huge enough to reach this high. The last time we were here the building was in transition. If there is a business here, go in and ask to see the first floor (our American second floor).

When you reach the entry to nos. 11 and 13, stand back and take a look. The tall, rounded doorways are topped by the typical eighteenth-century mask decorations called *mascarons*. These two must have been done either at different times or by different people. One of the nicest pieces of iron sculpture, a flamboyant S projecting tridents, to ensure privacy, is attached to the wall above the two doorways.

If you can enter no. 11 (push the release button and the door might unlatch), turn left just before you reach the court-yard, go up a few steps, and you will find an imposing wide stone staircase. What is truly impressive about it is that the

Mascaron at no. 11 rue Jacob

stone banisters and railing were cut by hand—a tremendous task, in comparison with the already difficult one of turning a banister in wood. This Louis XIII style is often used for wooden staircases, as is the case on the upper floors of this building. In summer this wide stairwell is a cool, quiet spot; in winter, when it gets dark early, turn the *minuterie* light on until you have seen it all. Please be discreet and polite if you meet residents.

Hôtel Millisime, **no. 15**, decorated in warm Provençal fabrics and colors, is one of several charming, not overly expensive hotels in this neighborhood. They serve breakfast in their beau-

Mascaron at no. 13 rue Jacob

tifully restored vaulted cellars. These hotels are always popular, and you must book far in advance for the spring and summer.

Much has been said and written about **no. 20**, but today little can be seen. A small temple of friendship, like the one on rue de Seine, is hidden in the courtyard behind an iron door. If you try to look in, the concierge will peer out from behind her curtain and call a huge dog, who will bark loud and long, though he is safely behind a high wall. The garden and the temple were owned by Michel Debré, former right-hand man to de Gaulle and then to Pompidou.

Natalie Clifford Barney, an ardently Francophile expat, lived here. In her youth she was called "the Amazon" or "the Sappho of 1900." She was beautiful, intelligent, and at the forefront of a literary movement that championed women's independence. In her *première étage* apartment she received a procession of the greatest writers and artists of the twentieth century: Hemingway, Joyce, T. S. Eliot, Colette, Rilke, Apollinaire, Anatole France, Max Jacob, Anna de Noailles, and many others. She was a legend to the people, a lesbian in her personal life, and catholic in her hospitality. She once hosted a boat trip around Greece for fifty friends. She did as much for the artistic life of the quarter as did the well-known cafés on the boulevard Saint-Germain.

As you leave the courtyard notice the classified wrought-iron banisters and gate and the consoles of phoenixes in the entry hall.

Nos. 17 and **26** are two bookshops that indicate the range of specialized bookshops in Paris. One is agricultural and horticultural; the other, specializing in maritime books and overseas editions, shows maps and prints in the window. Look also at the old houses above the shops.

Within the crevices of **no. 19**, down hallways, through doors, past the old offices of the publishing house Editions du Seuil, there is a private house and garden with a view of the back of the Delacroix museum. Prudhomme, an active pamphleteer against the *ancien régime*, lived back here. He was an editor of the *Revue de Paris,* a Revolutionary journal, and it was in the quiet of this garden that he wrote the incendiary articles that led to numerous arrests of citizens during the Terror.

No. 21, the **Hôtel des Maronniers**, with its courtyard of chestnut trees that can be seen in winter through glass walls, is one of the many attractive medium-priced hotels on this street.

At **no. 25**, the **Hôtel des Deux Continents** is another favorite of the rue Jacob. For high season reserve two months in advance.

No. 28 is a shop selling rare stones and minerals. **Claude Boullé** specializes in stone slices that look like seascapes or the countryside. The stones, which come from Tuscany, are inexpensive and full of wonder.

Twenty years ago the Editions du Seuil, an important French publishing house, took over the lovely private home and front garden of **no. 27**. Ingres, the champion of classical painting, lived here more than one hundred fifty years ago.

No. 29 replaces a traditional hotel with a whole new look for this Saint-Germain neighborhood. **La Villa** is a trendy, Memphis-decorated hotel. It is rated as a four-star hotel (more luxurious than most in this area), and the furniture and colors have all been carefully chosen to make a high-fashion statement. Try their bar and popular jazz club at night.

Across the street, on the corner to the right (technically, 21 rue Bonaparte), was Mme Castaing. She bought the most curious and interesting colonial empire objects, mainly from the nineteenth century. She was also an eccentric who would, for example, buy a dress at Chanel and improve on it by removing the sleeves. After her death her old shop became an outpost of the restaurant **Ladurée**. Ironically, the décor is Asian colonial, with hand-painted walls and tented ceilings, a style often represented by Mme Castaing. Do not skip stopping in for their famous *macarons,* two meringue cookies sandwiching a rich ganache filling. They come in all different flavors, from the typical *chocolat* and *café* to the seasonal and more whimsical, such as bitter orange or summertime's strawberry-poppy. The atmosphere here is much more pleasant than that at the original Ladurée, near the place de la Madeleine (see Walk 7).

Rue Bonaparte

Despite too many cars in the road and too many people on the sidewalks, the rue Bonaparte is still a favorite of visitors and Parisians. The shops are rich with the art of today and yesterday; nobility of all ranks lived on this street; and although the colorful history of the street is less obvious, it is nevertheless there to see and imagine.

Seven hundred years ago there was no street here at all, simply open fields that belonged to the abbey. You will recall the stories of the university students battling violently with the priests of the abbey over the use of these lands. These conflicts were settled only in 1368, when the monks built a wall and moat around themselves for privacy and safekeeping. At that time they also dug a canal, sixty-five feet wide and twenty-five feet deep, which ran from the Seine down the present rue Bonaparte to the corner where you are now standing, at rue Jacob and rue Bonaparte.

Here is where this arm of the river, la Petite Seine, emptied its waters into the moat of the abbey. Boats sailed up and down, bringing in and taking away goods. But the canal's most important function was to provide a natural division between the field frequented by the students, which was a small piece of land that covered the area between what are now the rues Jacob and Visconti up to the rue Bonaparte (called the Petit Pré aux Clercs), and the larger field on the other side of the canal favored by the priests (called the Grand Pré aux Clercs).

For almost two hundred years the little Seine characterized the *quartier,* and when it was eventually filled in, in 1540, it gave its name to the paved road that took its place, rue de la Petite Seine.

In 1606, when the famous Margot received a gift from her ex-husband, Henri IV, of a piece of land on the rue de Seine, she built the beautiful château whose walled gardens and walks cut through the rue de la Petite Seine, closing it off from the river itself. But Margot was generous with her new domain and allowed her meadows and gardens and shaded walks to go on giving pleasure to the simple folk of the neighborhood.

Marie de Médicis, who was Margot's successor as wife to Henri IV and whose money no doubt paid for Margot's château, was jealous of the latter's reputation for generosity and her popularity with the people. And so Marie tried to outdo Margot by building the Cours de la Reine (the queen's way), a wide and beautiful road on the Right Bank of the Seine, parallel to the present Champs-Elysées. These two ladies, Marie and Margot, spent more time outfoxing each other than Henri spent thinking about either of them; his constant love was Gabrielle d'Estrées.

Margot's gardens and the convent of Petits Augustins, which she had built farther up the street, lasted until 1628, thirteen years after her death. At that time her property was divided among many, and the street was once again opened, this time named the rue des Petits Augustins. Look across the street to see this old name cut in stone on the corner.

The name Bonaparte was not given until the year 1852. Why is there no rue Napoléon in Paris? Was he too formidable a hero? Perhaps the idea of the republican Bonaparte is more acceptable.

And now for the street, to find what is new and what remains of the old. Your route will turn right at the corner of Bonaparte and Jacob, continue up the right side to the top, and then cross to the other side and back down the street to return to the place Saint-Germain.

The door to the courtyard of **no. 21**, on the left, gives you an idea of the grand houses that surrounded the abbey in the sixteenth century. The garden of Queen Margot's palace on the rue de Seine extended all the way to the other side of this street, just a few yards up from here. The grand house before you now was built in 1760, around the courtyard of an earlier one, for Prévost de Saint Cyr, and was lived in during the period of French constitutional history known as the Consulate (1799–1804) by the Princess de Rohan-Rochefort, who was secretly married to the Duke of Enghien. After the Revolution these houses changed their tenants and their appearance, as the neighborhood turned popular. Today it is once again a street of high rents, coveted apartments, and very special shops and galleries. It is also one of the most heavily trafficked streets in Paris.

This large courtyard is picturesque, with its thick ivy, its ornamental ironwork on the balcony windows, and the large iron hook for a pulley on the dormer, or mansard, above to the left.

If you wish to buy a fancy gown, visit **Vicky Tiel** in the courtyard. Elizabeth Taylor has been a customer here and is an old friend. It was through Vicky's husband, who was Richard Burton's makeup artist, that the initial contact was made.

We were told that D'Artagnan's stables were here, but then again we were also told that about the rue Saint-Gilles, on the other side of town.

Continue up the street to the corner of rue Visconti. The façade, the door, and the courtyard of **no. 19** are classified.

You are now at the intersection of the rue Bonaparte and the rue des Beaux-Arts. If you wish to take the time to see a beautifully appointed hotel, called simply **L'Hôtel**, walk a few steps down to the right, to **no. 13 rue des Beaux-Arts**. Wander in under the atrium and walk to the back of the reception rooms, where there are bowers of plants and perhaps still a parrot flying free. Oscar Wilde is memorialized; he had a room here, as did Jorge Luis Borges.

Return to the rue Bonaparte, where art galleries abound and the twentieth century seems to be king. **No. 5** sells Deco and Nouveau *objets* of high quality. Most of these galleries don't open until 11 or 11:30 A.M., and then close at 1 P.M. for an hour, for lunch. No. 5, like no. 21, is typical of the eighteenth century, presenting an impressive wall and entry on the street and apartments that look down on the beautiful courtyard. Note the plaque on the outside wall: HERE, FORMERLY 5, RUE DES PETITS AUGUSTINS, WAS BORN EDOUARD MANET, 1832–1885.

If you have walked to the end of the street, you've reached the quai Malaquais; to the right is the Institut de France, home of the French Academy, where the renowned dictionary writers and protectors of the purity of the French language work. Election to the Académie Française is open to only forty "immortals," who choose their own colleagues. The ceremony of admission calls for an ornate dress uniform complete with sword. These swords are much too expensive for most academicians to buy themselves, so friends usually contribute to the cause. Later you can visit Arthus Bertrand, which makes these swords. Across the *quai* there is a romantic footbridge over the Seine to the Louvre.

The little low house across the street, at **no. 4 rue Bonaparte**, with dormer windows and with a hook and wheel for loading above one of them, was built in 1620. Cross the street to look up at it. This site was originally a hospital run by the Brothers of Charity, until Queen Margot forced them out in order to build her neighborhood estate. There is a huge art supply store named Paris Art, serving the Ecole des Beaux-Arts (school of fine arts), down the street. Look at their painted signs and note the large gap between the words *Paris* and *Art*. In that gap used to be the word *American;* it was painted over in the recent upsurge of anti-American sentiment.

There are two modern art galleries at **no. 6**. Look up at the roof garden on top of the building and at the small corner room that leads into it. This building was redesigned and restored in the eighteenth century.

At **no. 8**, **Félix Marcilhac** has collected some beautiful pieces of Art Deco and Art Nouveau. They are few but extremely fine.

Librairie E. Rossignol, also at no. 8, is an antiques bookshop that has been passed from father to son since 1906. They publish a yearly catalogue and maintain special-interest files in order to notify customers of relevant acquisitions.

At **no. 10**, **La Porte Etroite** has exactly that, a narrow door—also the title of a book by André Gide. This bookshop was probably a hallway at some point in its history.

At **no. 12**, now closed, M. Roux-Devillas once spent his days surrounded by memories of the past. He specialized in old books, old documents (autographs), and old scientific instruments. The collection ranged from sundials and eighteenth-century dental tools to treaties signed by kings and other rare documents. One home inventory of the wife of a French lieutenant general in Martinique in 1791 divided her possessions into three sections: furnishings, silver, and slaves. All the slaves were identified and described in the same way: name, job, age, and price. There was Jurançon who took care of the boats, thirty-two years old, and worth 3,300 francs; Caroline, no duties, five years old, worth 500 francs; and Lucille, who was too old and incapacitated to do or be worth anything at all, but was listed simply to note her existence, "*laissée pour memoire.*" Documents of this kind formed the basis of historical research on slavery today.

The **Ecole des Beaux-Arts** is at **no. 14**. This site is a ministage for the history of Paris. The first record of inhabitants dates from 1603, when Marie de Médicis, Henri IV's Italian wife, brought five priests from Florence and built a charity hospital for them here. These priests were also surgeons and pharmacists. Clearly Marie de Médicis felt she needed more than serving ladies to accompany her to her new country, so she established, in effect, for her use as well as for that of others, an Italian hospital and an Italian pharmacy. The Brothers of Charity Hospital moved three years later to the corner of the rue des Saints-Pères and the rue Jacob, where it became a large and important hospital, lasting until 1937, when it was taken down.

After the removal of the original hospital, the eccentric Margot built her promised altar to Jacob here. The convent remained until the Revolution, at which time it was forced to close down. It was left abandoned, but not for long.

During the French Revolution it was the "sacred" duty of each citizen to remove every symbol of religion and royalty he could find. (See Walk 2 for the altering of street signs.) A young painter and critic, Alexandre Lenoir, was quick to see the threat to all the art treasures and manuscripts in Paris. After eloquent and anguished pleading, he received permission to take or buy all the treasures he could find, to store the books and manuscripts in two other convents, and to store the art treasures in this one. Thus followed frenzied years of snatching books from fire, saving statues of precious metal from the mint, and rescuing kings from their coffins at Saint-Denis. Lenoir survived the Revolution only to be killed when he was pierced by a bayonet as he threw himself upon Richelieu's tomb in the church of the Sorbonne to save it from a mob in 1839.

He was unable to save the row of statues under the first balcony of Notre-Dame (the one that the beggars in *The Hunchback of Notre-Dame* climb to save Esmeralda from the hands of the hunchback). These statues—meant to represent the kings of the Bible but done in the anachronistic style of Merovingian kings—were thought by the mob to be kings of France and were pulled down. They were presumed lost until a few years ago, when they were found buried in the basement of an apartment house in the seventeenth arrondissement. They are now in the Musée National du Moyen Age. But Lenoir got whatever he could, however he could, and gathered it in—until this old convent became an amazing storehouse. When the Terror was over, Lenoir could stand back and look at the most eloquent creations of eighteen centuries of French art. He was inspired to make this cave of Ali Baba into a museum of French monuments. In 1795 that became a reality. Chroniclers describe the display of treasures as the most beautiful and impressive ever gathered in one place. It lasted through various French governments—the Directory, the Consulate, and the Empire. Napoléon, in his zeal to preserve the glory of France, showered gifts and privileges on it. Perhaps that is the real reason for the present name of the street. But Louis XVIII made the regrettable decision (for Paris anyway) to close the museum and disperse its contents. He allowed each locality to reclaim its old art treasures. The monastery here was then turned into the Ecole des Beaux-Arts, familiarly called just Beaux-Arts.

Enter the courtyard, if you can. On the right, high in a niche, should be a statue of Alexandre Lenoir. He was missing on our last visit, but we hope he was gone only for cleaning and restoration. The classified and odd remains of doors and pieces of sculpture that decorate the courtyard have been taken from châteaux. The classical wing at the back, just cleaned, was put up in 1858 and was the original building of the school. Go through the main door to see the neoclassical frescoes, the lecture rooms, and the students' work in progress.

When you are back in the courtyard, facing the street, enter the middle of the wing to your left and go into the delightful Cour du Mûrier (court of the mulberry tree), which was a cloister of the convent. The pedestals in each cloister bay are capped by pieces of Roman sculpture (mostly legless and armless) made by students who won the Grand Prix de Rome. This coveted prize allowed the winner to go to Rome to study the antique and Renaissance masters in the Villa Medici. The prize is still being given today.

The students at Beaux-Arts were among the most disruptive in the student revolt of 1968; they destroyed and damaged a good deal of the school. At that time, the school granted all sorts of student demands, including one to separate the faculties for painting, architecture, sculpture, and so on, in order to improve the level of teaching, which the students felt was too general. The administration, cleverly, has continued this division to such a degree that it has weakened the communal power of the students. Classes are held all over Paris, painters never see sculptors, and even the famous costume ball of the Beaux-Arts has not been held since the uprising.

Once, when we were sitting on a stone ledge in the big courtyard on the quai Malaquais, wondering where the spirit of art students had gone, we were suddenly doused with cold water from a balcony above. Amid gales of laughter, we were told how lucky we were it hadn't been ink or paint.

Return to the rue Bonaparte, to **no. 20**. This building is one that marks this area as Henri IV's. Of all his women, Gabrielle d'Estrées was the one he loved the most. In the back of this courtyard is a house in which their son, César de Vendôme, once abbot of Saint-Germain, lived. He was born illegitimate in 1594, recognized the following year, and would have been king had Louis XIII not been born.

If it is unlocked, go into the courtyard of **no. 28** to look at the elegant open staircase with its fountain and thick, flowering vines.

This next section of rue Bonaparte (between rue Jacob and rue de l'Abbaye) seems to belong to **Nobilis**, an important interior decorating firm. They occupy **nos. 29, 31, 38**, and **40**. At no. 29 they sell finished goods made from their own fabrics, including very nice traveling bags and lap rugs. Very chic and expensive.

At **no. 25**, **Simrane** sells high-quality, very attractive cotton cloths, napkins, and place mats made in India but in French style. Note the rare books at **no. 27**.

The **Hôtel Saint-Germain-des-Prés**, at **no. 36**, has one of the most charming lobbies in Paris. The back wall is a sheet of glass sandwiching a beautiful display of flowers growing in a hothouse against the stone wall of the building. The building is eighteenth-century, and although the décor reflects this, every room provides all the modern amenities at reasonable prices. August Comte lived here between 1818 and 1822.

Fabrice (one of a chain), at **no. 33**, specializes in jewelry and accessories that are always unique and avant-garde.

To the right is the small **rue Guillaume Apollinaire**, named for the artist whose statue sits across the street, in the garden of the church. The restaurant **Le Bonaparte** is a pleasant spot when the cars are not too close.

At the end of the street is the famous restaurant **Le Petit Zinc**, which has moved here from the Buci market. The interior is an authentic Art Nouveau setting. The decorations were brought here from other buildings, but the tiles, wrought-iron railings, bar, and furniture seem to have been made for the room. Moderately priced.

Continue on the rue Bonaparte, on the opposite side of the street from the church of Saint-Germain, to the very proper and dignified **Arthus Bertrand**, which is now cut to one-half its size by the coming of **Louis Vuitton**, the very expensive leather-goods store enthusiastically patronized by Japanese tourists.

Enter Arthus Bertrand, a one-hundred-and-fifty-year-old firm that specializes in museum reproductions of jewelry and honorary medals. (They reproduce the Louvre's artifacts, but in sterling silver or eighteen-carat gold.) This is a serious shop: the merchandise is exhibited in cases, and you must sit at the table and have trays brought to you for inspection as the saleswoman consults a separate price list. The shop engages one hundred and eighty employees to make their jewelry. Arthus Bertrand is especially famous for military medals and decorations. They supply 80 percent of the medals awarded in African nations and the individually designed academician's swords for the Institut de France. The latter range in price from $10,000 to $20,000. Claire Chretien told us how much she personally enjoys designing the swords for the academicians.

Notice the Wallace fountain in front of no. 24 (see Walk 1).

You now come to a wide pavement once used in the summer months for late-night plays, pantomimes, and acts by sword-swallowers, fire-eaters, and chain-breakers. A stage was set up here, and crowds gathered to watch, as in medieval times. The hat was passed for contributions. As another part of the "refinement" of the area, Les Deux Magots has extended the restaurant into this spot, behind a row of hedges. The square is now quiet in the evening.

Take a table at the famous café **Les Deux Magots**, or its rival, the **Café de Flore**. You are now in the heart of what was, and to some extent still is, the artistic and literary center of Paris. Before the First World War, Picasso and Apollinaire were already installed at the Flore, in the back, although they were

Anytime at Les Deux Magots

also habitués of the even more popular cafés of Montparnasse: the Dôme, the Rotonde, and the Closerie des Lilas. How many cafés can one frequent?

The "lost generation" of expatriates after the First World War, some of whom drank themselves into oblivion, frequented both Saint-Germain and Montparnasse. One distinction between the two areas seems to have been that writers favored Saint-Germain-des-Prés; artists, Montparnasse. Reread Hemingway's *A Moveable Feast* and *The Sun Also Rises* for the feel of those days gone by.

Les Deux Magots was the birthplace of surrealism, the Café de Flore the home of the existentialists. Simone de Beauvoir and Jean-Paul Sartre had their regular table at the latter, drawing young intellectuals like a magnet. Albert Camus came, but not often, because Sartre was supposedly jealous of Camus; at any rate the two did not get on.

Today café life is still fascinating. The talk is at once familiar and tantalizing. It is about ex-husbands and weekend houses or business deals concerning art, films, and books. Most of the publishing houses have offices in this quarter, and a constant stream of intellectuals will be around for lunch or a drink. Tourists come to look at everyone else; the French come to be looked at. It is still true that many of these people know one another, and the neighborhood keeps the character of a small town.

These cafés got their odd names the same way so many other places and streets in Paris did. A small statue of Flora (goddess of flowers and mother of spring) used to stand at the door of the Café de Flore. Visit the interesting room on the second floor of the Flore decorated, as the French say, "in the English style."

Les Deux Magots was the name of a novelty shop that planned to move to this spot from the rue de Buci in 1873, but before that could happen, a bar opened, used their name, and has been here ever since. The *deux magots* are the two wooden statues inside the café on the central pillar, of Chinese dignitaries (most often portrayed in porcelain), which were to be the standard of the novelty shop.

In 1984 the Deux Magots was sold at auction. M. Mathivat,

who has operated the café for decades and is still there, bought it. "I bought it for sentimental reasons," he said. "Don't worry. It will always remain what it has been. I don't want to start a fast-food joint." The auction was carried out in the Chambre des Notaires tradition. After the bidding was finished, the auctioneer lit two candles. As they burned, those with a possible change of heart had the opportunity to come in with a higher bid. Under the law M. Mathivat was not the true owner until ten days later. A bid of 10 percent more than his could still have been accepted.

Before his death, our late friend Georges Perec (author of *La Vie: mode d'emploi*) had ceased to come to Saint-Germain, as have others like him. But the small cafés off the beaten path are still frequented. Cafés play an important role in people's lives, so they are often the subject of literature. They are also the places where literature is made.

Behind the Flore, on **rue Saint-Benoît**, are several restaurants that have outside tables in the warm weather. **No. 26**, **Boutique du Café Flore**, offers fun houseware souvenirs imprinted with the Flore logo.

Le Drugstore, which was across the street from the Flore and the Deux Magots at **149 boulevard Saint-Germain**, was an American institution that famously became popular overnight. The French loved the hamburgers, which they ate with a knife and fork, and they hung out there until closing time, at two in the morning. Armani has now moved in.

In an effort to placate the SOS movement and to keep the genius of the area, Armani has paid for the new windows in the church of Saint-Germain-des-Prés. Their clothes prices are still prohibitive, but their café fits into the general ambience of the neighborhood.

Across the boulevard Saint-Germain visit **Arts et Bijoux**, **no. 147**, an old-timer in the neighborhood. In addition to elegant estate jewelry, there are sculptures of rabbits, cats, and other animals by Marc Poncini, a well-known animalier and the son of the owners. These are objects you want to take home with you.

There are two famous restaurants nearby. **Brasserie Lipp**, at **no. 151** boulevard Saint-Germain, is a restaurant that has done what we would have considered the impossible. The French, as you know, consider themselves the arbiters of fine taste, and the cuisine they would be least expected to copy would be German. The namesake of the restaurant, Lippmann, was an Alsatian who was desperately unhappy about the separation of his homeland from France. Alsatian food and drink are, however, typically German—frankfurters and sauerkraut, along with light and dark beer. The amazing fact is that this dish caught on; it appears today on almost every Parisian menu. *Choucroute alsacienne* is sold fresh in every *charcuterie,* in cans in every grocery, and it is now the raison d'être of countless restaurants in Paris, including Bofinger, described in Walk 6.

In the early 1900s, Lipp was the after-theater place to dine, as the Plaza Athenée was fifty years later. The lovely ladies shown in engravings, picking up their long dresses as they step from horse-drawn hacks, were no doubt going to dine at Lipp. By 1924 the area had become so much the quarter of editors (two steps to Grasset, four to Gallimard, and six to Hachette) and their prize-winning writers that Lipp was forced to enlarge, not like the Deux Magots—which could extend its stomach onto the pavement—but by turning and twisting into the recesses behind the restaurant. In the 1960s, Lipp was the eating place for politicians as well as writers. François Mitterrand, then president of France, used to dine here.

Vagenende, no. 142, is a joy to behold. Here is 1900 in all its fantasy and variety. You will see many a floral door on the boulevard Saint-Germain, but they are a product of the 1970s. This restaurant and the even more fantastic restaurant of the Gare de Lyon (which was shown in the films *Travels with My Aunt* and *Murder on the Orient Express*) are the real thing, built when Art Nouveau was at its height.

Although you have walked and talked and looked for a good two hours, these few streets are only a sample of what the neighborhood has to offer. If you have more energy and a need to shop, wend your way through the streets on the south side of boulevard Saint-Germain, in a triangle between the place Saint-Sulpice and the Bon Marché department store, on the rue de Sèvres—you'll find plenty to delight you.

Walk · 4

Place des Vosges

C'est le coup de lance de Montgomery qui a créé la place des Vosges.

It's the blow of Montgomery's lance that created the place des Vosges.

—*Victor Hugo*

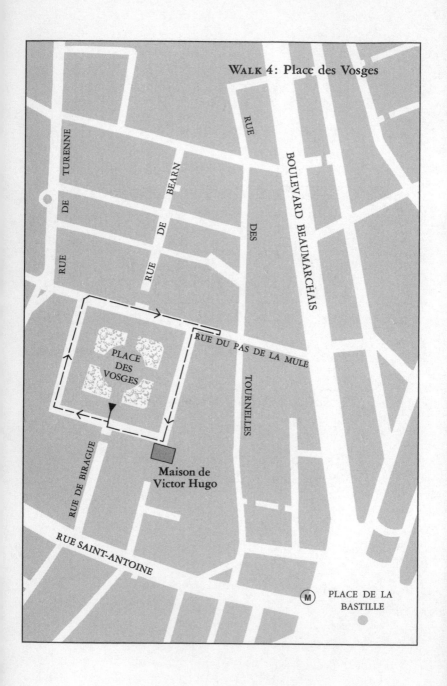

WALK 4: Place des Vosges

RUE DE TURENNE

RUE DE BEARN

RUE

RUE DES

BOULEVARD BEAUMARCHAIS

RUE DU PAS DE LA MULE

PLACE DES VOSGES

TOURNELLES

RUE DE BIRAGUE

Maison de Victor Hugo

RUE SAINT-ANTOINE

Ⓜ PLACE DE LA BASTILLE

Starting Point: Rue de Birague, south entrance of place des Vosges, 4th arrondissement
Métro: Bastille or Saint-Paul
Buses: 29, 69, 76, 96

Walk up the rue de Birague (stop and look at interesting shops) and continue into the place des Vosges (pronounced plass-day-voge) before you. A *place* is a square; this one has a large park in the middle and symmetrical townhouses all around. Sit in the garden near the children's area so that you can watch the children play *à la française* (despite the mix of Hebrew, Yiddish, and Arabic you'll hear). If it is cold, try the café Ma Bourgogne, on the northwest corner of the *place*.

Read the history of this *place* and some of its surroundings. While the Left Bank was inhabited as far back as the sixth century, the Right Bank, or Marais (marsh), was not settled for another five hundred years or more.

In 1407, a *hôtel* (grand private residence) known as Tournelles—for the small towers in its walls—came under the ownership of the crown and replaced the previous royal residence.

It remained the royal residence until 1559 and the joust that cost Henri II his life. The king had fought and won two jousts already that day, but he insisted on a third against the captain of his Scottish Guards, Gabriel de Lorges, sire de Montgomery. At the first pass, both combatants splintered their lances. The king wanted another run; Montgomery was reluctant. Of course, the king, savoring his success, had his way. Once again Montgomery's lance broke, but this time, by a freak accident, the point pushed up the visor of the king's helmet and entered his head above his eye. For ten days Henri suffered. The greatest doctors were called; Ambroise Paré and Andreas Vesalius came all the way from Brussels. Four criminals under sentence of death were decapitated so that the doctors could study their cranial anatomy, but to no avail. Henri died, of infection if nothing else, and his widow, Catherine de Médicis, persuaded her son Charles IX to demolish the palace with its unhappy memories.

Once royalty abandoned the palace, the ground on which it had stood was given over to a succession of improvised roles. The militia used it for its exercises. The city installed stables and used some of the buildings to store powder. For many years the interior courtyard housed an active horse market that attracted many rogues, posing a growing problem for the authorities. The answer was found by Henri IV. The horse market would be replaced by a development project, Paris's first. It would be a spacious, symmetrical public square to be known as the *place Royale*, a *place* of respectable residence and assembly. The parceling of terrain began in 1605, and the first building finished was the large pavilion at the south end of the square. It marked the start of an epoch in domestic architecture and set the example for the remaining construction.

The place Royale was only one of Henri IV's three urbanization projects. Another, a set of large avenues that would radiate out from the *place*, was never built, and the third, the place Dauphine, on the tip of the Ile de la Cité, was only partially completed. (Today at the place Dauphine you will find a splendid statue of the gallant Henri IV on horseback looking out over the Seine.)

The place Royale, however, was the king's pet project, and

he visited the construction site daily to speed the workers along. In his plan for the large square, he reserved the south side for himself and the north for a silk factory *à la façon de Milan*. The east and west sides were to be sold in parcels to private owners.

The Duc de Sully filled 50 percent of the pavilions with his friends. The Duc de Guise did likewise. The result was one that pleased Henri, a convert to Catholicism: a mix of Protestants and Catholics.

The façades were to be all the same, built of brick with *pierre taillé* (cut-stone) trim. The ground floor, planned for shops, was set back to create a covered walkway of four arcades per lot: each building was to have two floors above that, the whole capped with a steep slate roof encompassing another two floors pierced with mansard windows. The style was known as *bleu, blanc, rouge*—for the slate roofs, the white stone trim, and the red bricks. At the center of the south end would be a raised pavilion for the king. Within a year or two, when the silk project failed, the north end was given its own pavilion for the queen and private residences matching those opposite it.

The open space in the center would be promenade, tournament ground, and stage for public events, functions that no street, however wide, could perform. There was no other public square in Paris at this time, and it was Henri's intention that all visiting foreign dignitaries arriving in Paris would enter by the gate just to the east of here, at the Bastille, travel down the rue Saint-Antoine, and then turn into the place Royale from what is now the rue de Birague, where you entered.

In principle, the buildings around the square were to be made of brick with stone trim. In fact, only the first structures, including the Pavillon du Roi, lived up to the plan. It took a long time to lay brick, and Henri was in a hurry. Bricks and mortar were also expensive, especially in a city that had never before (and has never since) considered brick to be fashionable. Nor did the local workers have the skills necessary for this huge undertaking.

In any event, the owners of the later buildings were only too happy to construct them of plaster on wood framing and then paint them to resemble brick, in colors ranging from dusty pink to dark red. Some of this trompe l'oeil is still visible. It is surprising that these masterpieces of French architecture—praised for their concept, size, proportions, and colors—were mostly façade.

The artifice, however, does not seem to have dimmed the square's glory. Although no king ever lived here (the Pavillon du Roi was far too small to accommodate the king and his retinue), the square was inhabited in the seventeenth century by the best society. Before the Faubourg Saint-Germain-des-Prés became the chic neighborhood, the Marais, and especially the place Royale, was the place where anyone who was anyone lived.

Unfortunately, Henri IV was assassinated shortly before the square's completion. The square was therefore inaugurated by the young Louis XIII. This is why the equestrian statue in the center of the square is of Louis XIII, and not of Henri IV.

On April 5, 6, and 7, 1612, a fabulous tournament was held at the resplendent place Royale. Jousting was forbidden, but five equestrian ballets were organized for the cavaliers, each with different exotic costumes—including one group dressed as American Indians. A description of one of the quadrilles will give you some idea of how elaborate these festivities were: the Duc de Longueville and his retainers were dressed in gray violet satin with silver embroidery; the pages and the horses were dressed in red velvet; four winged horses pulled a chariot with two rhinoceroses harnessed to the back; and two giants in blue satin preceded the duke himself, who rode a horse draped with repoussé plaques of silver and gold. There were one hundred and fifty musicians, as well as games, continuous parades, and fireworks at night.

The square was packed with ten thousand people, some crowded onto viewing stands, some at the windows. Members of the royal entourage had been assigned different houses and balconies from which to observe the tournament. In fact, the residents had been required to make their balconies available to the noblemen assigned to them. It was the first time that houses had been built with real balconies; until then Parisians had had only small stone ledges to lean on. Once the place Royale had shown the way, balconies quickly became de rigueur. The common people had to hang from the chimneys or squeeze into the recesses of the arcades.

The place Royale was used frequently in the seventeenth century, for tournaments and spectacles. Visiting ambassadors staged elaborate processions to show off the riches and costumes of their home countries. For many Parisians this was their only contact with a foreign culture, and dress and appearance were carefully scrutinized and criticized. Of one delegation Mme de Motteville wrote, after describing their rich clothes studded with jewels, "In general they are so fat that they give you heartburn, and concerning their bodies, they are dirty."

The place Royale was also the favorite dueling ground for the hotbloods of the French aristocracy. The fashionable ladies of the *place* enjoyed the spectacle, and the swordsmen were encouraged by these ardent admirers. The fights were more than show, however. In 1614, three out of four antagonists were killed in one encounter, and over the years France lost some of its most valiant cavaliers in this square.

In 1626, Richelieu, first minister of Louis XIII, forbade dueling on pain of death. The very prohibition was a challenge to French manhood. Only one year later there occurred a six-man duel (two principals and four seconds, who were expected to do more than hold the combatants' coats) right in front of the Pavillon du Roi. Results: two dead, two fled to England, and two off to Lorraine. The latter two were caught en route, brought back to Paris, and decapitated, over the protests and appeals of the nobility of France. Richelieu was not a man to take insolence lightly. The incident cooled the ardor of the young blades, but only for a time.

In 1643, after Richelieu's death, the last scion of the Protestant Colignys dueled with Henri, Duc de Guise, grandson of the man who had killed Coligny's grandfather, Admiral Coligny, in the aftermath of the Saint Bartholomew's Day Massacre, the slaughter of the Protestants during the religious wars (1572). The duel was supposedly fought to champion two quarreling women, but who is to say that old, unavenged grievances did not enter into it? Anyway, the ladies watched and cheered their men on. Guise was wounded first, but managed to grab Coligny's

Northwest corner of the place des Vosges

épée (sword), hold it, and simply finish him off. This time the king, hoping to end the enmity between Catholics and Protestants, chose not to punish the victor.

Not all the action in the *place* was outdoors. The place Royale was the center of Parisian social life, and such fashionable ladies of the neighborhood as Ninon de Lenclos and Marion Delorme invented a new and durable institution. They met at intimate gatherings called *ruelles,* at which the elegant guests rivaled one another in wit, fine speech, and social finesse. Molière parodied their excesses in his play *Les Précieuses Ridicules.*

The predecessors of the fashionable salons of the eighteenth century, these encounters took place in the hostesses' bedrooms, perhaps because an amazing number of the hostesses were as renowned for their sexual as for their social prowess. Several of the great ladies of the place Royale could hardly keep track of their lovers. We shall meet them later as we visit each house individually.

The fashionable lifestyle of the place Royale spread to the rest of the Marais, and large *hôtels* sprang up everywhere throughout this sparsely settled part of the city. Houses here were larger and more elegant than anything Paris had ever seen. One can imagine the constant visits and receptions of the nobility, the clergy, and the officials who thrived here. The busy streets hummed with ladies carried in their sedan chairs, beribboned soldiers strutting in high boots, and clergy of all levels carrying out their errands.

It was also the era of great changes in interior decoration, brought about mainly by the women. Mirrors replaced paintings above the fireplace for brightness, armchairs were more comfortable than thinly upholstered straight chairs, moveable *torchères* around the fireplace supplied both light and heat. Wallpaper began to replace tapestries, and ceilings, copied from Italy, were painted.

But there was misery outside. The poor lived in the streets as much as possible to avoid their miserable and dingy hovels. People wore big boots that were mud encrusted. The joke was that the favorite color in Paris was brown. When night fell, anyone with honest intentions went home. There was no protection from those who roamed the dark streets. Lanterns were lit on moonless nights only, and one toss of a stone could throw an entire area into total darkness. What guards there were, were generally not interested in losing their lives to some brigand, so they chose to appear only after the battle was done and the bodies lay dead.

Tallement des Réaux, a chronicler of the Marais, reports an incident one night involving the Duchesse de Rohan, a member of the great aristocratic family that lived throughout the quarter. She was returning from a ball when she was stopped by thieves. "Immediately," he recounts, "she put her hands on her pearls. One of these gallant men, to make her let go, grabbed her where women ordinarily defend themselves best; but he was dealing with a tough lady: 'That,' she said, 'you can't carry off, but you can take away my pearls.'" Luckily someone happened along, and the duchess was saved.

Beginning in the eighteenth century, the Marais went into a decline. The center of Paris fashion and social activity moved steadily westward. The aristocracy moved to the Faubourg Saint-Honoré, where the Palais Elysée and the British and American embassies are now located (see Walk 7). The decline continued into the nineteenth and twentieth centuries. The fashionable neighborhoods grew toward the west, in part because the prevailing winds came from the west and carried the unpleasant odors of central and eastern Paris away from the residents of these fine new neighborhoods.

Palaces were abandoned to manufacturing and trade. Heavy machinery was bolted to elegant parquet floors; paneled walls were stripped or covered over; large reception rooms were divided into two-floored workspaces; spacious courtyards were filled with homely utilitarian sheds and shops.

The whole area eventually grew into an industrial center of small enterprise and craft shops, running from the old market, Les Halles, in central Paris, to the Faubourg Saint-Antoine, east of the Bastille. If not for these enterprises, the place des Vosges would have disappeared. They kept the buildings heated, roofed, and occupied.

In the years after World War II, the trend reversed. The newly elegant districts of Passy and Auteuil filled up, and well-to-do Parisians, unwilling to settle in distant suburbs, began to look again at the long-abandoned buildings of the older neighborhoods. The first areas to benefit from the new mode were on the Left Bank. Old residences came to have a new cachet, like old furniture and objets d'art.

Serious renewal of the Marais came later, with a special push from the law of 1962 that required the cleaning (*ravalement*) of the façades of all buildings at least once every decade or so. The law created a massive new industry that transformed the appearance of Paris. Suddenly, black and gray structures took on the colors and details of their youth. Paris became once again a city of light.

The Marais was one of the areas that benefited the most from the new cleanliness; the *hôtels* were spectacular once one could see their lines and details. Some of them were restored by the state; others by developers. There was no lack of customers waiting to pay small fortunes for apartments in renovated buildings. But there was also no lack of residents who were very happy to stay in their old quarters at low rents.

The result was a small, quiet civil war. French tenancy laws made removal hard enough; politics made it even harder. There were abuses on both sides. Tenants organized themselves into defense committees and solicited support. Some of them were eventually scared or bullied into leaving. Later, tenants held up badly needed improvements even when generous provision had been made either for their subsequent return or their relocation into what was often better accommodations. Militant denunciations and calls to resistance covered neighborhood walls. We found one petition in a courtyard and started to copy it down. The concierge came out and asked us what we were doing. She was furious at the "troublemakers" and tried to scratch out the poster as we stood there. She was no doubt on the side of the "improvers." They would bring in better and richer tenants, and that would mean a substantial gain in status and income for her. Can't blame her.

The Marais has become the neighborhood of choice for intellectuals, professionals, and those who want the feel of old Paris. Jacques Lang, the former minister of culture, was an early resident of the restored place des Vosges.

Before you begin a close look at the different houses in the *place,* take a look at the garden and the façades. The railings that you see today, surrounding the garden, are merely a poor imitation of the wrought-iron version with elaborate gold trim that originally stood here. The gate was locked at night, and residents had their own keys.

During the Revolution the railing was almost torn down to be made into spears but was saved because a depot for military equipment already existed in the *place*. The gate was inexplicably torn down, however, during the reign of Louis Philippe, despite the eloquence of Victor Hugo on its behalf. It was replaced in 1839 by the uninteresting grille that you see before you today.

During the Revolution the place Royale was renamed the place de l'Indivisibilité, after the new Republic, one and indivisible. Then, in 1800, the name was changed again. It became

A typical façade on the place des Vosges

the place des Vosges to honor the region that paid its taxes first. Lovers of old Paris argue heatedly for the return of the original, historic name, place Royale. Imagine the confusion between the place Royale and the Palais Royale.

At first glance you might think that all of the houses in the square are identical. But although the architectural plans for the square were strict, the individual owners still managed to put their marks on the buildings in discreet yet effective ways. As we noted earlier, the original plan for each dwelling (*pavillon*) called for four arcades. Each *pavillon* was to have mansard windows, two round *oeil-de-boeuf* windows, and two square windows, all framed by the roofline. Yet every set of windows is slightly different. Look to see how, with time, ownership has changed the original four-arcade plan into any number of variations.

Today, the most noticeable difference between buildings is between those that have been restored and those that have not. When you get inside the courtyards you will see that some with glowing façades are in terrible shape on the inside, and some with marvelous courtyards are in disrepair outside.

The garden before you is the subject of great and ongoing controversy: to keep or not to keep the trees. To preservationists and purists, the large leafy trees are an intrusion. They weren't there originally, and for good reason: they block the view of the *place*. The French have always been devoted to vistas, which is one reason why Paris is such a beautiful city. Here in the place des Vosges, the original garden was minimal—lawns with paths cut on the diagonal—in order to leave an unobstructed view of the whole square.

The trees that are here today are the second set of trees to be planted in the garden. The circle of trees that had surrounded the statue were stricken with dutch elm disease and were replaced. The new trees obstruct more of the view of the entire *place*. When you visit the Musée Victor Hugo, look out of the windows from the second story onto the *place*. You will be astounded to see how magnificent the whole square looks when it is uninterrupted by the trees. You too may be tempted to side with the historical preservationists.

Children move about freely here, in a relaxed atmosphere

that is unusual in a Parisian park. Older people sit on the benches in the leafy shade and converse, knit, and play checkers and chess while their children and grandchildren play happily. The park really fills with children between noon and 2 P.M., when those attending the three schools tucked away in these imposing houses—plus two more schools backing onto the *place*—come out to play. On sunny weekends the grass is packed with hordes of young adults sunbathing and sharing picnics. This park, once the social center of the seventeenth-century upper class, has now become a playground for the highly diverse neighborhood population.

Begin walking at the Pavillon du Roi, at **no. 1 place des Vosges**, the center of the south wing. As you face the pavilion, odd numbers are on your right, even numbers are on your left.

Saturdays and Sundays, from noon to 6 P.M., the Minor String Quartet plays to more than a hundred admirers in front of no. 1. The quartet sells CDs on the spot.

The *pavillon* was never occupied by the king but rather by his *concierge* (gatekeeper), who was the first resident of the building. Since 1666 it has been rented to different tenants, and today it is divided into apartments that are served by the unattractive stairs and elevator built into the right-hand side of the entrance arcade. This blocking of the arcade, done in the eighteenth century, still rankles. Even more important, the stairwell blocks part of the vista from the rue de Birague into the *place*—and, as we have already noted, vistas are serious matters for the French. The building is a classified historical monument and therefore should be returned to its original condition. But how would the residents enter their building?

As early as 1752, the writer Germain Brice said that these three arcades themselves should be torn down to leave the view of Louis XIII's statue unobstructed from the rue Saint-Antoine. This is perhaps too much to ask, but he also wrote:

> It has to hurt to see one of the three arcades under the pavilion blocked to make a nasty stairway which defaces entirely the entrance from the side of the rue Royale [rue de Birague today]. But we have such little care for public embellishments in Paris that we do not hesitate to spoil a vista or an

entire square for the minor interests of some private person who has influence with the officials who are supposed to look after the decorations of the city.

Looking up at the façade of no. 1 you will see that the balcony here is stone rather than wrought iron and that the building is adorned with a bust of Henri IV, which was added at some unknown time. Walk through the arcade and look at the other side of the building from the rue de Birague.

On this side the *pavillon* is decorated with the arms and initials of Henri IV just above the arches; these date from the original construction. In the spring and summer many of the residents fill window boxes on their balconies with flowers, and the building looks more as if it should be part of a narrow Mediterranean street, not a king's pavilion in Paris.

Reenter the *place* and turn to the left, at **no. 1 bis**. This four-arched residence, the Hôtel de Coulanges, was the last to remain in the hands of a single owner, Mme Cotin. More than thirty years ago she undertook the gigantic task of restoring the entire structure. She changed architects and contractors every few years, working first on the façade, then on the interior, then back again. It has been a source of wonder to the neighbors, who watched with great interest. One contractor, M. Sachet, of Sachet and Brulet, said in 1989, with some pride, that this was a prestige job and therefore he had decided to face the building with real brick even though false brick was stated in his contract. He planned to make up the difference in cost himself. He has long since departed and work has ceased.

We haven't seen any progress here for years, let alone someone to ask about the situation. The building is in terrible condition and shows no sign of restoration. Of the six arcades, the last two are in false brick, because each pavilion of four arcades must match, and the first proprietor to restore sets the style of brick for the rest. The next two arcades had already been realistically restored in false brick.

The building has one of the oldest wrought-iron balconies in Paris, built in 1655. Its straight, plain support poles are the sign of its authenticity. There are more of these early balconies in the *place,* but most are more modern, with elaborately decorated supports. The rooms of this *hôtel* are reputed to have kept their seventeenth-century size as well as the painted walls and beamed ceilings that were so fashionable in the early days of the place Royale. The last windows on the right-hand side of the second floor have seventeenth-century interior shutters (*pan clos*).

This grand house, the Hôtel de Coulanges, is famous as the birthplace, in 1626, of the Marquise de Sévigné, née Marie de Rabutin-Chantal. Note the plaque on the wall. This was the home of her maternal grandfather, Philippe de Coulanges. Marie, orphaned at two, lived here for ten years. At seventeen she was married off to the Marquis de Sévigné. She had two children, one of them a daughter, with whom she remained very close. After the death of her husband, who was killed in a duel in 1651, when she was still a very young woman, Mme de Sévigné lived in many different homes, always in the Marais. She was often courted and proposed to, but she chose instead to remain a widow, turning her aspiring lovers into friends.

Meanwhile, her daughter married the Comte de Grignan, who took his new wife to live in Provence, far from Paris and her mother. The separation was painful for Mme de Sévigné, who often disagreed violently with her daughter when they were together but missed her desperately when she was away. Their separation prompted one of the most famous collections of letters in French literature and a picture of high life during Louis XIV's reign. In her last years, Mme de Sévigné lived in the Hôtel Carnavalet, now the Musée Carnavalet (Walk 5). Much of her furnishings, personal belongings, and portraits can be seen there.

In 1627 the Comte de Montmorency-Bouteville hid here in the Hôtel de Coulanges after the duel, described earlier, that so piqued Cardinal Richelieu. As soon as things quieted down, he took off for Lorraine, but he would have done better to have run immediately. He was caught and put to death. Montmorency was well known in the place Royale; he had been the lover of many of the women who lived here.

Fashion has been coming to the Marais in the form of avant-garde designers. The first major designer, at **no. 3**, **Issey Miyake**, combines inventive and practical ideas with high but wearable fashion. He often designs in pleated washable polyester that looks like a piece of sculpture. Most of his customers are between thirty and thirty-five, but one well-known customer is ninety-five. The door to his shop is locked. Ring to be admitted—or you can just look in the windows.

The entrance to the courtyard at **no. 3** place des Vosges can be unlocked by pressing the button marked *porte*. Push the door open and walk into a charming courtyard. This was one of the first buildings in the *place* to have been restored, and the owners are justly proud of their work. The door is open on principle: people should be able to see the interior courtyards as well as the façades. This is also the only building in the *place* with "brick" walls in the courtyard. If you look closely at the front façade of this courtyard you will see that the "brick" is painted, even down to the pipes in the corners. The pipes are painted pink when they are in front of "brick" and ivory in front of the stone trim. The color is bright, but it has a pleasing effect, especially with the small garden and the elegant glassed-in terrace on the second floor of the back section of the building. If you come and cannot get in the courtyard, it can be viewed through the windows of Issey Miyake.

Note the windowed arches on the ground floor below the terrace. They were originally the entrance to a stable; this house was built in 1613, on the remains of the stables of the Hôtel des Tournelles. Two huge bronze urns stand against the back wall.

The front staircase, on your right as you leave, is lovely, with wide stone steps and a wrought-iron railing. During the nineteenth century the banister was remodeled with wooden inlays, which are handsome but, as a resident informed us, not authentic.

As you go past **no. 5**, look at the pavement to see rails installed that used to facilitate the delivery of heavy loads to the factory inside. If you want to see what the factory-filled place des Vosges was like, open the door here and look inside.

Next door—always open—leads you to the back garden of the Hôtel de Sully (described in Walk 6).

Just around the corner, an attractive shop called **Alix** carries inexpensive costume jewelry.

At **no. 9** is the **Hôtel de Chaulnes**, where there is much to see and read about. Press the bell for Galerie N. D. Marquadt to enter the courtyard; the door is always open because of the art gallery inside. This is one of the larger, more elegant *hôtels,* and it is part of a guided tour given by the Monuments Historiques (once a month only), which will take you inside this building and inside the Hôtel de Sully. The tour, given in French, is announced in *Pariscope* and *L'Officiel des Spectacles.* If you understand even a little French, it is well worth going.

The history first, then the present-day offerings. The Hôtel de Chaulnes, built in 1607, was one of the most luxurious houses in the place Royale. Louis XIII stayed here when the tournament inaugurated the *place.* The *hôtel* was also the site of the royal reviewing stand during all the public events that were held here. In 1644 the building was bought by Honoré d'Albret, *maréchal* (marshal) de France, Duc de Chaulnes, and peer of France. The Chaulneses were a wealthy family, and much of the decoration was done by them. When the duke died, his widow remodeled the house to include a new dining room and an oratory in the left wing. In 1655 her third son, a man who was accustomed to living well, inherited the residence. He hired Mansart, the famous architect, to extend the right wing of the house back to the rue de Turenne. Mansart designed a façade with a large triangular *fronton* (pediment) in the roofline.

Today this wing is partially obscured by a gallery that cuts into its center. Mansart also built a monumental staircase to serve this newly expanded wing, but the wrought-iron stair rail was sold to someone in England in the nineteenth century. In the expanded courtyard, the new duke had a huge formal garden planted; it had a fountain and a trompe l'oeil perspective painted on the back wall. One of the few touches remaining today from the Chaulnes era is a room with a painted-beam ceiling, in the left wing. This was the duchess's oratory, but it was later converted into a kitchen and plastered over. It was the thick covering of plaster that happily has preserved the wooden beams for us.

In 1695 the building was sold to the Nicolaï family. They restored it in a neoclassical style, with stucco ceiling decorations, which were recently uncovered when layers of paint were stripped off. Legend has it that during the Revolution, Aymard Charles de Nicolaï hid in his wife's boudoir when the *sans-culottes* (working-class revolutionaries) came looking for him. He was discovered and led straight to the guillotine. The *hôtel* itself was seized and not returned until 1795, after the Terror had run its course. By that time only one of the four Nicolaï brothers still had his head.

Elisa Félix (1820–1858), better known as Mlle Rachel and one of France's most famous actresses, lived here in the mid-nineteenth century. She was renowned especially for her performance in the role of *Phèdre*, which she played for the first time in 1838. Rachel died in Egypt, but her body was returned to Paris, and a great funeral service was held in the synagogue at no. 14, on the other side of the place des Vosges.

Today the entire *première étage* of no. 9 is owned by the Architecture Society, an élite group of one hundred members who use this center for conferences and reflection. They are responsible for the restoration of the building and the cleaning of the façade. They also did some marvelous work in the interior, which you should try to see.

The courtyard of this *hôtel* is very large. One of the first things you notice is a statue of a satyr. Viewed from the side, it has an amusing symmetry of profile. The right wing of the building still reflects the work of Mansart, despite the gallery at the back. Note the arched doorways with the *mascarons* (mask decorations) above them. The large *fronton* gives a pale idea of how grand the newly designed wing must have been in the seventeenth century.

Look in the doorway of the right wing to get a feeling of the volume of the stairway Mansart designed, even though the railing is now gone. In the left wing, through the last second-floor window—if the lighting is right and the curtains are open—you can see the painted pink and green beams of Mme de Chaulnes's oratory. The beams, decorated with a *C* and a *D* for "Chaulnes" and "Dailly" (the duchess's maiden name), were painted in 1654, among the last in Paris to be thus decorated, for that fashion ended around 1650.

There is a second courtyard behind and to the left of the

one we are in now. It is marked private, so be respectful of the owners and just trust our description. The courtyard is a charming, hidden corner of Paris, one that most visitors to the place des Vosges never see. The houses here are privately owned and may have been the stables or servants' quarters of the original estate. In a tiny garden a statue of a girl holding a bunch of roses is surrounded by real roses.

Today, a huge warehouse-like gallery, **Nikki Diana Marquadt**, has moved into the courtyard after the retirement of the owner of a lighting fixtures factory that had been a resident of the *place* since the beginning of the century. While the factory was busy and noisy and full of people, and friendly too, this huge gallery contained only two twelve-foot-high, trophy-shaped sculptures. On the right wall was a ten-foot-square tile mural, decorated with black-and-white photographs of people. The last time we visited, a fashion house rented it for a fashion show. You will surely see something odd when you visit.

In the courtyard, look to your right and through the windows to the restaurant next door. The chandeliers will give you an idea of the luxury of the restaurant.

L'Ambroisie, also at **no. 9**, is one of the points of pride in the revitalized *place*. A Michelin three-star restaurant, it is the only world-class restaurant in the Marais. Sonia and spouse David went there for lunch (dinner reservations were unavailable for at least a month) as an anniversary present from the children. Fifteen years ago lunch cost $250 for two of us. Today dinner for two is about €700.

Chef Bernard Pacaud's food is extraordinarily fine, in nuance and taste. The flavors are subtle, and yet the essence of each ingredient remains clear and distinct on the palate. The menu changes, but there are three standard and supplementary offerings that accompany each meal. The *trou normand* (cleansing the palate between courses) consists of a fruit sorbet set in a sabayon sauce. (The *trou normand* was originally a glass containing a shot of alcohol—calvados, no doubt. Maupassant writes [free translation] in his *Contes de la Bécasse,* "Between each serving, the cleansing of the palate was done with a glass of eau-de-vie that lit a fire in the belly and madness in the head.") Custom continues, but in a much weakened form. The other additions to the meal are a feathery light warm chocolate mousse and a mix of citrus fruits in syrup to help cut the sweet but light desserts.

The décor here is sober and refined. The tables are far apart and the seating is luxurious. Service is, as to be expected, absolutely perfect. Closed Sundays and Mondays, and in August.

Popy Moreni, at **no. 11**, is an ultramodern women's shop, and was the first clothing shop in the *place*. Their collection is avant-garde. No. 11 also houses part of Virgin Records, although they are not visible from the street.

No. 13, **Hôtel d'Antoine de Rochebaron**, once the property of the Marquis de Villequier, was originally one of the most elegant houses of the square, and it is now restored to its grand state. According to a description of the house as it once was, it was a gem, with decorations by all the best artists of the time. Stucco ornaments by Van Obstal were painted by Vouet; an alcove was decorated by Buirette, the foremost wood sculptor of the time, who had *"epuisé tout son savoir"* (exhausted all his skill) in making it. There was a *salon à l'italienne* with a huge fireplace decorated with silver and gold. The salon itself calls for elaboration. It was two stories high, with a ceiling in the shape of a lantern, and was lined with mirrors, a rare commodity in the seventeenth century. A chronicler writes:

> When reclining in this salon, if we look to the right, we see, through the two glass doors, opening on to the place, carriages, people on foot or on horseback, and all that is happening in the place Royale. If we turn to the left, the same thing reflected in the mirrors is presented to our sight, so that, without getting out of bed, in summer as in winter, in sickness or health, we can enjoy the diversion.

After the Marquis de Villequier, the house was owned by the ambassador to Venice, M. des Hameaux, who added to its luxurious appointments, installing precious paintings, furniture, and even more mirrors, brought from Italy. The stables were large enough to hold three carriages and seven horses.

No. 13 place des Vosges

Today we have new wonders of restoration to see here instead. The property was bought by the Société Française de Promotion et de Gestion Immobilière (SFPGI), which administers apartment houses, and the work was financed by the Banque de Indo-Suez. Elegant as the building looks now, the Société's first set of plans was rejected by the Monuments Historiques as being too pompous for a popular neighborhood.

To see the splendid courtyard of no. 13, look through the windows of **Antiquités Philippe Magloire**, specializing in Middle Eastern antiquities. The back wings in the courtyard were re-extended all the way to the rue de Turenne, which was how the building stood in the seventeenth and eighteenth centuries. The wings had been demolished by the twentieth century. The entire back section of the building is therefore new, though built in the style of the eighteenth century, while the front half has been redone in the seventeenth-century brick style.

The garden in the center is a copy of a classical French design, but here, too, old and new merge; it is automatically watered every evening at eight o'clock by sunken sprinklers. Under the garden is a garage for the residents. This is the first underground garage in the place des Vosges. A parking space in Paris is like gold. The entrance to the garage is just past the back grille, on the rue de Turenne, and looks like the entrance to an apartment building of grand standing rather than a garage door.

The apartments are fabulous: parquet floors in the Versailles pattern, restored or rebuilt; huge fireplaces of red marble in the living rooms; ceilings almost sixteen feet high. Many of the rooms have interior lofts accessible by spiral staircases. Elevators have been recessed into the thick walls because the stairs are classified as historical monuments and may not be touched.

No. 15 was one of the last *pavillons* to be restored, but on our last visit restoration was complete. The building looks beautiful, and the exterior has been finished in real brick.

At **no. 17**, the **Galerie de la Place** replaces a previous one, which replaced a previous one. Since the galleries unfortunately change almost yearly, we will let you find what interests you as you walk. You can enter the courtyard. While the exterior of the building looks very plain, there is a beautiful garden within. Be aware that there is often a concierge just inside the door to the courtyard; just smile and take a quick look around.

At **Musatamo**, also at **no. 17**, the Japanese designer can sometimes be seen sitting at a small table, designing men's clothes. The store is spare. Each item stands by itself. Many of the clothes are in black leather.

Next door, at **no. 19**, is the very popular café **Ma Bourgogne**. Stop here for a cup of coffee with steamed milk (*café crème*) no matter what the time of day, and if it is lunchtime, have one of their *charcuterie* platters from Auvergne. Ma Bourgogne specializes in these and in wine from Burgundy and Bordeaux, but the café also serves meals whose prices can add up quickly. The waiters here are characters and enjoy teasing; they offer advice whether asked or not. The café also has a good WC. There has been a café here since 1920. *Note:* Beware of sitting on the curbside. The pigeons may drop gifts from above. Open daily.

In the seventeenth century this building was owned by the Conseiller d'Etat Robert Aubrey, who lived here with his wife, Claude de Pretevel. Tallement des Réaux, the contemporary chronicler of life in the Marais, wrote astonishingly of this couple: "*Elle le méprisait beaucoup, de sorte qu'elle a pissé plus d'une fois dans les bouillons qu'elle lui faisait prendre*" (She hated him so much that more than once she pissed into the soup that she gave him). Hardly an appetizing legacy for a building that houses a café. Fortunately those manners are far behind us.

No. 21 is another one of the larger and more elegant buildings in the *place*, with eight arcades. It was given to Cardinal Richelieu by Henri IV, but no one knows for sure if he ever lived here. Possibly he stayed here briefly while waiting for the Palais Royale to be completed. He bequeathed the building to his grand-nephew, who then passed it on to his son. The son never lived here either, but he is rumored to have made good use of his pied-à-terre to get to know almost every woman in the *place*.

This *hôtel* was restored in the summer of 1978. Residents here have put a lot of money and care into the work. These arcades had originally been done in real brick, and the residents wanted to return them to their original condition. The Monuments Historiques was not eager to do it, but the owners insisted. They went to the brickworks in Versailles, which had made the original bricks in the seventeenth century, and they matched the missing parts as closely as possible. Compare this arcade with the fake paint and etched plaster of the others. The beauty of these arcades has now inspired other residents in the *place* to restore their buildings with real brick.

From out in the street, look at the façade of no. 21, above the fifth pillar from the left, at some stones cut in little squiggles, like vermicelli, the same kind used to decorate the Seine side of the Louvre. Some of these, the sharply cut ones, are new; the worn ones—the sixth to ninth squiggles on the left column—are the originals. M. Balmès, the owner of the antiques shop here, says that the Monuments Historiques helped pay for the restoration of the façade and for the part of the roof that shows from the square and will also pay a small amount for any classified stairways or railings. Other renovations must be paid for by the owners of the building, which is one reason why the work goes so slowly and erratically.

Look closely at the sides of the arcade pillars right above the pediments and you will find little square stone patches. These patches date from the Revolution, when this section of the arcade was used as a forge for making arms. The patches cover the points from which metal curtains were hung to close off the forge. As you walk you will notice many more of these patches in the sides of the pillars. Until around 1930 the arcades were filled with shops of all kinds—butchers, shoemakers, and so on—and each shop walled itself in by setting beams into cuts in the stone. There were so many little shops it was hard to make one's way through the arcade. The last survivor of this era was a shoemaker, who is said to have worked in the arcades as recently as the 1950s.

The courtyard is large and sunny, well maintained and charming. It is usually locked, but you can look through the keyhole. Inside the second floor the original *pans clos* (interior wooden shutters) that were used in the seventeenth century still remain.

On the right is a small private garden (you may see a cat stalking the birds) and the entrance to a large staircase. The stair railing here was unfortunately sold to the United States in the nineteenth century. M. Balmès explains that Englishmen and Americans would come and ask the building owners to sell stair railings, offering them enough money to restore a whole building. The owners were thrilled then, but the current owners are sorry now.

In the back there is a kind of *orangerie* (greenhouse for raising oranges), dating from the latter half of the eighteenth century. No one knows what it was built for, but now it is a small factory with a small, carefully tended garden. On the left were the stables of the *hôtel;* today they make a sunny apartment with a terrace on top. The buildings in this courtyard all seem to vary slightly, which is partly explained by the fact that they were built at different times. But the layout has been the same since about 1750, as shown by Turgot's famous map of that time.

Also at no. 21, **Richelieu** specializes in scientific instruments from earliest times to the twentieth century: clocks, optical devices, navigational aids. M. Balmès has a number of "masterpieces," the graduation projects that guild apprentices have made as a test of their skills and proof of readiness to work on their own. The guilds were all abolished in 1791, so these masterpieces are usually more than two hundred years old. (Today, artisans learn their trade at the Compagnons du Devoir described in Walk 6.) We saw a small wrought-iron balcony and miniature staircases of exquisite detail here. We also learned how lace was made by examining a *carreau*, a box with a square cushion overlaid with a paper pattern stuck with pins to weave the threads around. The threads were drawn from small bobbins, which in this case were still attached to the half-finished piece. M. Balmès is as much a collector as a dealer, and his shop often looks empty. But do try the door. He is usually upstairs, but his wife will wait on you. If you are interested in something special, he will come down to help you. He also knows the place des Vosges very well.

Also at no. 21 the owners of **Les Deux Orphelines** collect eighteenth- and nineteenth-century *art populaire* (country handicrafts) mainly in wood: marvelous ox yokes, wooden shoes, religious statues, and metal objects such as candlesticks, sconces, and planters. The prices are reasonable, and the merchandise is amusing.

Next door is **Max Spira**, a jumble of old and new twenties-style bric-a-brac and furniture. They are open at night.

At **no. 23**, notice the heavy wooden door decorated with thick wooden plaques attached with metal bolts. There are several doors of this kind in the *place,* and each one has its own pattern. Inside the courtyard is a small garden and a vaulted brick entry. This was the Hôtel de Marie-Charlotte de Balzac d'Entragues. Not only her name was impressive; her career was as well. She lived here with her mother, who had been the mistress of Charles IX. Her sister, Henriette d'Entragues, had been the mistress of Henri IV. (Decidedly, these ladies did not bring good luck to their lovers.) Marie-Charlotte was the mistress of the *maréchal* de Bassompierre and gave birth to his son, Louis, in 1610. Their relationship was very stormy, and Marie-Charlotte kept pressing the *maréchal* to marry her. He refused, reneging on his written promise. So Marie-Charlotte consoled herself with a series of lovers of equal distinction or equal means, among them the archbishop of Paris, Jean-François de Gondi, and the financier Le Plessis-Guénégaud. We are told that there is a room in the house that still has painted beams dating from her residency, but we have never been inside.

At **no. 25** is the charming **Guirlande de Julie**. The restaurant's lofty goal is to "make dining an intermission from the absurd, an instant stolen from daily drudgery." The reality is that the interior is decorated in a soothing bower of green and pink and the food is excellent, beautifully presented and served, bounteous, refined, and, with all that, not too expensive. The restaurant's name is from the history of the place. The Guirlande de Julie was a small book of madrigals, each surrounded by a different flower, that the Duc de Montausier offered to his wife on May 22, 1641. The restaurant, like Coconnas, also in the *place,* is owned by the colorful Claude Terrail, impresario of the famous Tour d'Argent restaurant. Closed Mondays.

The courtyard and house on the right side of no. 25 are lovely. The ground-floor window just past the doorway is a large hemisphere of glass usually associated with a shop-front window. This building, however, is occupied as a private home. Formerly there was a trellis with plants rather than curtains, which permitted a glimpse of the living room. Under the frescoed ceiling, a huge stone fireplace on the right wall could hold three men standing upright.

Press the button marked *porte* and enter the courtyard. This is a private home, so please be quiet and look only. Pause for a moment to look around and note the nicely done modern glass door in the rear to the right; the *mascaron* has been lost, but the stairs and their fine railing are still there. This whole right wing is owned by one family, and in the past we have seen their pets—free-flying birds and assorted animals (including chinchillas)—and their very large plants. The left side of the building is much more conventional. In the back of the courtyard, there is a little house redone and filled with bookshelves;

perhaps used as someone's study. The entrance at the back is modern, but the old *mascaron* is still intact above the door.

You have now gone halfway around the square and are standing in front of the Pavillon de la Reine, which is opposite Henri's pavilion, where we started. This one is exactly the same except for the sun emblem of the Médicis on the façade and the very long iron balcony. The small street here, the rue de Béarn, was the exit route for all the parades that passed through the place Royale.

The **Hôtel Pavillon de la Reine, no. 28**, would please a queen more than the Pavillon de la Reine, the central north pavilion of the *place*. The hotel is set back from the street, behind a classical French garden. It looks as if it has always been there, although this spot was once an extremely unattractive garage. The hotel has all the comforts and luxuries of new hotels, and is close to all the new goings-on in the Marais, yet is quiet and private. A simple double room costs €335, a duplex double or a suite, €600. The clientele is largely European.

No. 26 was the *hôtel* of the first *précieuse* (a high-society woman with a *ruelle,* or salon, attended by her admirers and lovers) of the place des Vosges, Charlotte de Vieux-Pont. Today the building itself is not very interesting, but the many galleries that occupy the ground floor are.

No. 24 has a fine wooden door, but the courtyard beyond is undistinguished. This *hôtel,* Hôtel du Maréchal de Geran, does not have as illustrious a history as some of the others, but it did have one famous, or notorious, resident, the wife of the *maréchal* of France, Duc de Boufflers. She was fourteen years old when she was married and she quickly became known for her beauty, caustic wit, and number of lovers. This verse was written about her:

> *Quant Boufflers parut à cour,*
> *On crut voir le mère d'amour,*
> *Chacun s'empressait à lui plaire*
> *Et chacun l'avait à son tour.*

When Boufflers appeared at court,
You would have thought you were looking at Venus;

Everyone tried to please her
And everyone had her in turn.

We are now at the end of one side of the *place,* at the corner where the rue du Pas de la Mule joins the square. Originally there was a house here, and the street joined the square
through the arcades of the house. The marks of the house
are reportedly visible on the side of the wall of no. 22, but
we have never found them. The house was torn down in 1823,
making the northern side of the place des Vosges a too-well-
traveled route for cars headed toward the Bastille and the new
Opéra.

Walk east out of the *place,* to **no. 6 rue du Pas de la Mule**.
This is one of the most fascinating shops in Paris. It was called
the Boucherie (butcher's shop), but it now sells musical instruments. Note above the doorway the metal hooks from which
meat was once hung. The tiled walls are original.

M. Bissonet comes from a long line of butchers, and this
shop was his until his passion for musical instruments gradually
won out. He began by hanging violins and trumpets alongside
his sausages, but eventually the meat vanished, and now the
shop is crammed from floor to ceiling with instruments. His
cold-storage room has become a library of books on the topic,
and his workrooms are now his office and a workshop to restore
the instruments to their original playing condition. He showed
us a silver-etched guitar, a porcelain trumpet, and a tuba made
of Venetian glass. He also played for us a Breton bombardon, a
flutelike instrument that is only twelve inches long and less
than one inch wide but makes an enormous sound. He drew
quite a crowd. The store also had a player piano that made the
sounds of twenty-nine flutes, a mandolin, and violins in addition to the piano; it was built for a merry-go-round in 1920. M.
Bissonet is so agreeable that he might just play an instrument in
the shop for you.

Return now to the place des Vosges to continue the walk.
On the corner, at **no. 22**, is **Café Hugo**. Along with typical café
fare, the café offers free wireless Internet. We had some trouble
using their slow connection, but it is a nice place to sit and

An arcade in the place des Vosges

watch the crowds. In winter, eat in the restored seventeenth-century building; in summer, sit outdoors under the arcades.

The enlargement and renovation of the restaurant about fifteen years ago cost the owner 3 million francs (approximately $500,000). The rule is that the city pays a little more than 24 percent of renovations and the state pays 36 percent. The rest is paid by the owner. In this case, the owner got tired of waiting and did the work on his own. He is very proud of his restaurant, and justifiably so. He was wise to finish his renovations when he did, because the *mairie* (city hall) officials of the fourth arrondissement have just decided not to pay for the cleaning of three of the last pavilions in the *place*.

Press the button above the keypad at **no. 20** to enter the courtyard, and face the front wall (facing the *place*). The wall is in the midst of repairs that were halted twenty-five years ago. An architect known for prefabricated constructions lived here and wanted to restore the façade. He had wanted to finish a nineteenth-century addition: a glassed-in hall on the first floor and a covered passageway on the second floor. Originally the apartments in these buildings had been built without halls; each room opened on to the following. Halls were added later, by taking space from the original rooms, which were usually large enough for the purpose. In this building, though, these halls were built on to the outside of the building.

The architect's plan here was to build a new façade in the original seventeenth-century style that would encompass the hallways and incorporate them into the building. He began construction with hollow bricks, but when the authorities found out, they objected, saying that the original did not have bricks at all but rather plaster painted to resemble bricks. The decision? The building must remain in status quo, that is, the ugly glass balcony and the partially completed work would have to remain as they were.

Years ago, residents assured us that the work would be done within a year, once the architect had died, but construction is still not finished. Of course, the Monuments Historiques assures the authenticity and quality of the work it endorses, so perhaps it's better that unauthorized restorations are stopped. But is a building better in indefinite limbo?

The walls here do serve a purpose, however, in their present condition: they give us a good opportunity to see how these buildings were constructed. Look at the window frames on the right and left of this wall as well as at the corners. You can see how the large stones were used as a frame, which was then filled in with small stones and rubble and covered with plaster. This is essentially the same *colombage* technique used in the sixteenth century, except that here stone replaces the timber framing.

L'Occitane, now a well-known chain, at **no. 20**, sells fine natural bath products. The mural, the brick floor, and the decorations are reminiscent of Provence. Each year the shop sells the new lavender harvest like a fine vintage.

No. 18 was the Hôtel de Marguerite de Béthune, the Duchesse de Rohan and the daughter of Sully, Henri IV's first minister. Married at the age of nine, in 1604, she later had innumerable lovers, many of them residents of the place Royale. Of her nine children, only one daughter survived her. Today the building has little to offer from the seventeenth century other than a frieze in the Greek key pattern on its façade, which can be seen from the street. A glance at the windows of the apartment on the second floor, with their *pans clos,* hints at what riches may lie inside. The courtyard, which is now locked, has been restored only in the entryway. The walls have been lined with wooden cupboards on the right and with pillars on the left. It is all new and somewhat attractive. The rest of the courtyard has not been touched, but take a look at the bronze statue of the gypsy, in the stairwell on the left. She has lost the lantern from her left hand and one earring. The concierge proudly told us that Victor Hugo put the statue there, but we have not found mention of that anywhere else. We do know for a fact, though, that the gypsy was stolen some years ago. A woman resident called the police and got immediate results. The statue was found minutes later at the traffic light on a nearby corner. Her head was sticking out of the back of a pickup truck. She is now firmly attached to her red marble base, which is firmly attached to the floor.

No. 16 was owned in the seventeenth century by a royal counselor named François le Roux, who had the dubious distinction of marrying *"une petit garce qui se donnait pour un quart d'écu"* (a little bitch who gave herself for a quarter of an *écu*). That was slightly less than a *livre,* but in those days a *livre* was a day's wages for a manual worker, so Mme le Roux was not so cheap after all. Anyway, she had a lot of amateur competition in this area, as we have seen. Today the courtyard needs restoration, but take a look at its wrought-iron railing, on the left, and the *mascarons* over the portal and entry.

A most pleasant place for lunch or afternoon tea is **Nectarine**. Lunch is mainly salads and vegetable pies, while a changing array of luscious cakes and tarts will tempt you either for dessert or as an afternoon re-energizer with a cup of tea. A dense chocolate cake is always appropriate; in the summer try their ice creams.

Short-lived art galleries have now been taken over by an appraisal office that will tell you the worth of your own valuables for free in the hope that you will sell to them. By appointment only.

The Hôtel de l'Abbé de la Rivière, **no. 14**, is now one of the best restored in the *place*. The six arcades have been redone in real brick and the wrought-iron balconies have been cleaned of rust. Notice the balcony and the campanile on the roof, which was added at a later date. Step back from the building to look at the roofline and see the arched back of the façade of the building's entrance on the rue des Tournelles. Today this is a synagogue, and the half of the building that faces the place des Vosges is used by the Ashkenazic community (the eastern European Jews who are mostly Yiddish-speaking); the half on the rue des Tournelles belongs to the Sephardic community (Jews who settled in Spain and Portugal; now most are from North Africa). The doors on the *place* are sometimes locked, but you can always enter on Friday evenings and Saturday mornings, when services are being held.

The walls are wood-paneled; the stairs are carpeted with Oriental rugs; plants sit in the entry. The interior resembles a Victorian home. Indeed, this half once was. The chief rabbi of France lived here with his wife and five children. There is an art gallery on the third floor, exhibiting Jewish artists. Visitors are welcome.

The Sephardic synagogue on the other side of the building, entry on rue des Tournelles, serves the growing Oriental Jewish community. It has a large Moorish sanctuary; the stucco pillars are painted with words and designs; and the ceiling, high above the sanctuary, is rounded in a long arch.

No. 14 takes its name from one of its seventeenth-century owners, the Abbé de la Rivière, favorite of the Duc d'Orléans, tutor of the duke's children, and himself promoted to duke and bishop of Langres. This son of a tailor, a veritable model of social advancement through the church, never did realize his dearest ambition, however—to be made a cardinal. The best painters of the era, Le Brun and Mignard, created a fabulous interior for la Rivière's *hôtel*. The decorated ceilings have been preserved in the Musée Carnavalet.

When la Rivière died, a poet composed the following verse:

Ci-gît un très grand personnage
Qui fut un illustre lignage
Qui posséda mille vertus
Qui ne trompa jamais, fut toujours très sage.
Je n'en dirai pas plus,
C'est trop mentir pour cent écus.

Here lies a very great person
Who had an illustrious lineage
Who possessed a thousand virtues
Who never deceived, was always well behaved.
I won't say more,
That's too much lying for a hundred écus.

The *hôtel* was later used as a neighborhood city hall. That role is commemorated by a plaque that is barely legible. Later the building was used as a school.

Next door to the synagogue, there is a public nursery school for children aged two to six.

No. 8, as the plaque tells us, was the home of the poet Théophile Gautier, who lent his name to the technical high school next door.

The **Musée Victor Hugo**, at **no. 6**, was Hugo's residence from 1832 to 1848. Before Hugo's time it was the *hôtel* of the Princesse de Guéménée, Anne de Montbazon. She was the most famous *précieuse* of the *place*. She was married at twelve to her cousin, the prince, and like other premature wives of the day, she never settled into monogamy. Anne was mistress of the coadjutor of Retz; of the financier d'Emery; of the Comte de Montmorency-Bouteville, beheaded in 1627 for his famous duel; of the duke Henri II of Montmorency, beheaded in 1632; of the Comte de Soissons, who died tragically in 1641; and of the counselor of Parliament Auguste de Thou, beheaded in

1642. She did not bring luck to her lovers, but she herself lived to be eighty-one.

The princess is representative of Molière's liberated *précieuses*. These women established a literary style and a new standard for excellence of the French language. They were also sexually liberated, conducting their many affairs with the grudging consent of their husbands. They seem to have thrived on this, marrying at puberty and living to a ripe old age.

Marion Delorme may also have lived here, in a small pavilion at the back, but most historians feel that it was unlikely that the two famous women could peaceably have shared the same house, if only because of the traffic jam that would have resulted. Marion was a match for Anne in every way, in number of lovers and in the brilliance of her salon. She began her career as courtesan to Jacques Vallée, sieur Desbarreaux, a notorious "epicurean" (read: hedonist) and, unforgivable at the time, an avowed atheist. Next came the Marquis de Cinq-Mars, a handsome, stylish courtier who made the mistake of plotting intrigue against Richelieu and lost his head. (The marquis may have died young, but his place in history and literature is assured as the protagonist of Alfred de Vigny's novel *Cinq-Mars*.)

After the execution of Cinq-Mars, Marion is said to have gone on to a long series of lovers, including George Villiers, the first Duke of Buckingham. (You may remember him from *The Three Musketeers*.) Also Louis II de Bourbon, Prince de Condé (called "the great Condé"), prince of the blood and the last of the great feudal barons. He was eight years younger than she and a great success with the ladies. Yet this great wencher had his own wife confined for her alleged unfaithfulness (which even the malicious gossips of the day refused to credit) and wrote his last letter to the king to ask that she never be released. Nice fellow. Last but not least, Marion is said to have gotten Cardinal Richelieu himself into her bed. Ironically, it was Richelieu's niece who was Condé's unfortunate wife, so everything was neatly kept in the family.

Unlike the other great courtesans of her day, Marion died early, in 1650, but as with other legendary figures, there were those who refused to believe she was gone. Some said she lived on to 1706, when she would have been ninety-three, or even 1741, when she would have been one hundred and twenty-eight. In a sense, she does live on. Victor Hugo wrote a drama called *Marion Delorme*, and G. Bottesini wrote an opera of the same name.

The property at no. 6 was large, stretching back to no. 17 rue des Tournelles, with a discreet rear alley for quick exits, a feature that Hugo often used when visiting his mistresses.

Hugo lived here in a rented apartment one floor up, until his disagreements with Louis Napoléon required him to flee into political exile on the isle of Guernsey. Today the museum is on the first, second, and third floors of the building. Start at the top with the history of Hugo's life, move down to his drawings and mementos on the second, and then visit a re-creation of his apartment on the first. Each room is dedicated to a period in his life. The museum has restored Hugo's bedroom with his Louis XIII deathbed and his death mask. Don't miss the romantic and striking Chinese-style dining room that he built himself in his second home in Guernsey. The wall with its bright red chimney and lavish plate collection reveals in how many ways Hugo was remarkable.

Be sure to look out on to the *place* before you leave to get a good view of the whole square above the trees. The museum is open from 10 A.M. to 6 P.M. daily, except Mondays and holidays. Since the museum is free of charge, it is very easy to go inside and take a quick tour of the house.

On this last side of the square there are several galleries, which change often. Stop in those that appeal to you.

Restaurant **Coconnas** is at **no. 2** place des Vosges, although its front door opens on to the rue de Birague, around the corner. This restaurant is owned by Claude Terrail, who also owns the Tour d'Argent, and it is no accident that both places provided locales for the movie *Who Is Killing the Great Chefs of Europe?* This restaurant is casual and moderately priced. The specialty is *poule-au-pot*. The menu no doubt commemorates Henri IV's promise of a "chicken in every pot." The restaurant is open daily.

You have now completely circled the place des Vosges. The area is so rich, now the richest in history and monuments in all Paris, that we have ended this walk here. But if you still have the strength, the walk continues in Walk 5, right outside the *place*. Exit the *place* from the northwest corner, by Ma Bourgogne, and turn left onto the rue des Francs-Bourgeois.

Walk · 5

Rue des Francs-
Bourgeois

*Now the backbone of the Marais, it prides it-
self on the sumptuous homes endowed by
prestigious institutions.*
> —Jacques Chirac, in his dedication to
> the rue des Francs-Bourgeois

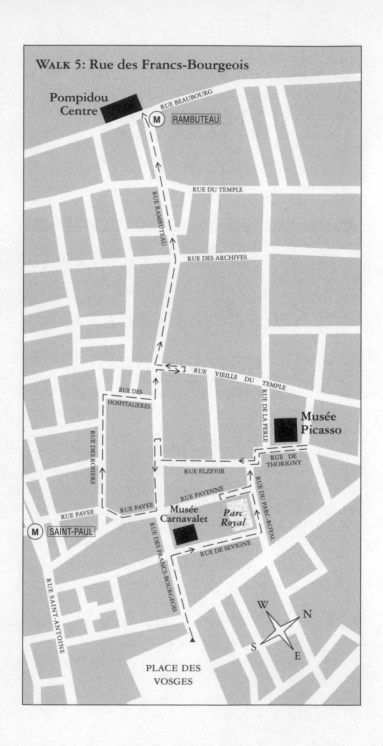

Starting Point: No. 5 rue des Francs-Bourgeois, 3rd and 4th
    arrondissements
Métro: Saint-Paul
Bus: 29

The rue des Francs-Bourgeois with its sumptuous homes that
Chirac is praising today stand on a street named for its poverty.
In the fourteenth century an almshouse was built here. The
poor, too destitute to pay taxes, were called "free citizens,"
hence, francs-bourgeois.

The rue des Francs-Bourgeois marks the different periods in
the city's long history. Now a central Paris street, it once stood
just outside the limits of the city, against Philippe Auguste's
huge and heavy walls that encircled Paris. The street entered the
city limits under the later and wider wall Charles V built around
Paris in the fourteenth century.

In the renaissance of the sixteenth and seventeenth centuries, the aristocracy installed itself along the length of this
east–west axis, parallel to the Seine, between the place Royale,

now the place des Vosges (see Walk 4), and the Palais de Soubise, at the end of the street.

This new heart of the city drew the great lords and powerful financiers to what had been free swampy lands. The neatly bound parcels suited the time's architectural fashion of placing the *hôtel* behind grand double coach doors (*porte cochères*) and between the courtyard and the garden. Chic houses in Paris are identified as *entre cours et jardins* (between the courtyard and the garden). This arrangement allowed for a grand, easy entrance for the horse and carriage, view of the house, and privacy in the garden behind.

The rich competed in luxury and creativity in the construction of these great houses. Among the products of the pomp and circumstance of the society that flourished between the fourteenth and seventeenth centuries, you will see the sumptuous *hôtels* of Soubise, Carnavalet, Lamoignon, Albret, and others. Many are now important museums. Similar residences, less well known, have now recently come into their own, thanks to intelligent restoration.

The street was first called the rue des Poulies, named after a pulley, or wheel, on a loom—for the street was a street of weavers. A generation ago it was still a street of fabrics.

When we first researched this walk, the street had potential but was still dark and, for the most part, seemed uninteresting. Today it is historically restored and booming. The very narrow sidewalks are crowded with shoppers and museum-goers, still mostly French. We are going to give you a description of the great houses and museums, and a limited rundown of the shops because there are so many and they change so often. You will be going back and forth across the street. Be careful crossing.

This shopping street is jam-packed on Sundays. It claimed the right to keep open on Sundays because the rue des Rosiers is open on Sundays, but closed on Saturdays, the Jewish Sabbath. The argument was that if Rosiers could be open Sundays, why not Francs-Bourgeois? Legally, a store can be open on Sundays if the owner is working but not the employees. This ruling was hardly taken seriously, and eventually the shop owners received legal permission to be open. Because much of Paris is still closed on Sundays, this neighborhood is teeming.

In the last edition of this book, the trend was American Western, followed by shoe stores, which are now losing ground to ready-to-wear. Who knows what the trend will be when you walk here today? Styles change often in Paris, though there are a few old standbys.

Hier et Demain, at **no. 4**, has been here for twenty-four years, specializing in thirties Art Deco furniture, objects, and materials, and recently in American jewelry from the fifties, Bakelite, and renovated chandeliers. A find for a collector. It is considered the dinosaur of this ever-changing street. Opens at 1 P.M., Tuesdays through Fridays.

Et Vous, next door, sells elegant and expensive dresses and suits.

No. 5, **Bijoux à Monic**, the other oldie on the street, is an Ali Baba's cave of costume jewelry. They have drawers and drawers of it. If you lose an earring, you can always get a replacement. They say Americans particularly buy the garnet jewelry from Czechoslovakia.

No. 7 is an interesting French restaurant, **Un Piano sur le Trottoir** (a piano on the sidewalk). The name has a double meaning: the word *piano* is slang for the stove in a restaurant. Piano music, vocal performances, and group singing are offered every Thursday through Sunday night. Check the hours.

Origins, also at **no. 7**, allows you to buy the American brand of cosmetics at twice the price. **L'Objet**, at **no. 9**, sells bibelots and estate jewelry.

Enter the ivy-covered courtyard of **no. 8** to visit two wonderful shops that share a single space. The right side, which houses **Imex**, was originally the factory for the coats and jackets they specialize in. The left side of the store is **L'Entrée des Fournisseurs**, an exquisite ribbon and button, tassels and thread store—now a rarity in Paris. On the street, the final store in this building, **Autour du Monde**, sells home furnishings. One of the few remaining American-style stores, it gives off an overwhelming odor of potpourri.

Enter the courtyard of **no. 13**, **2 Mille et 1 Nuits**, to find a collection of decorating exotica. The place glitters.

Archetype, at **no. 17**, specializes in architectural drawings.

Across the street, **Anne Fontaine**'s collection of white blouses, at **no. 12**, is part of the white blouse craze that has hit Paris. Also at no. 12, look at **Cécile et Jeanne**'s creative jewelry. The work has been chosen by the National Museum stores for sale at museums and the Opéra.

La Charrue et les Etoiles, at **no. 19**, is full of miniature figures, especially animals and Viennese bronzes. Bring home a souvenir, perhaps one of the small diorama scenes of Paris peopled with lead figures.

Up at the corner is the French version of Banana Republic, called **Autour du Monde**.

Rue de Sévigné

And now we come to one of the great houses of Paris, the **Musée Carnavalet**. Turn right onto the **rue de Sévigné**. The entrance is on the left, at **23 rue de Sévigné**.

As a result of the elaborate celebrations of the bicentennial of the Revolution, in 1989, the museum was changed from a storehouse for the cognoscenti to an educational institution for the general public. Twenty million dollars were spent on this successful renovation, much of it from American philanthropy.

Mme de Sévigné lived here for twenty years, at the end of the seventeenth century. She is most famous for the letters she wrote to her beloved daughter, who had married and moved to Provence. The letters preserve a way of life full of gossip and stories. Mme de Sévigné's life was the epitome of luxury. It is said that for one of her parties, doors had to be knocked down to allow her servants to carry pyramids of food twenty platters high into her dining room. Guests had to pass notes to one another because they couldn't see around the food.

In the courtyard, look at the bas-reliefs of the four seasons. Compare the central sculpture, *Winter,* by Jean Goujon in 1550, with *Diane* on the right, sculpted by Van Obstal one hundred years later. Compare them to similar sculptures in the courtyard of the Hôtel de Sully (Walk 6). Note the devilish *mascarons* (mask decorations) above the side windows. The statue of Louis XIV was sculpted by Antoine Coysevox, who created the magnificent horses at the place de la Concorde (Walk 7). In time-honored and foolish custom, Louis chose Roman garb and then crowned it with his curly French wig.

Enter the museum through the bookstore. The first room holds a collection of amusing and historical rebus and shop signs. When your customer can't read, you have to show what you're selling. One of the rebuses for an exterminator shows three rats, which is the symbol for the phrase *mort aux rats* (death to rats). Talks about these rebuses are given for children.

The exhibition continues throughout the museum, showing interesting aspects of French daily life. Enter first the original building of the museum, Mme de Sévigné's immense and beloved home. The collection exhibits prehistoric, Merovingian, Carolingian, and medieval pieces that have been in storage for years, as well as the entire collection from the years preceding the Revolution.

The museum doubled in size by incorporating the *hôtel* behind it, Le Peletier de Saint-Fargeau. Le Peletier houses the history of Paris from the Revolution to the twentieth century.

To enter these rooms, dedicated to the Revolution and the Belle Epoque, take the staircase in front of you and follow the long hallway to Le Peletier.

The Revolution is displayed in eleven rooms decorated in the style of the day. The exhibits combine paintings and documents with politically relevant porcelain, a model guillotine, and even a model of the Bastille made from the stones of the original.

After the passion and seriousness of the Revolution and the Paris Commune, the Belle Epoque period is like a glass of champagne. With as much of the original furnishings as possible, the Carnavalet has reproduced several rooms from that period.

Proust's cork-lined bedroom, very dreary (unlike his social life), is here, as well as a private dining room from the Café de Paris, decorated in mauve with Art Nouveau furniture by the master Louis Majorelle. The jewels that adorned the *grandes horizontales,* as the *demi-mondaines* of that time were called (see Maxim's in Walk 7), were purchased by their wealthy, ardent admirers at the famous jewelry store Fouquet, in all its Alphonse Mucha, Art Nouveau glory.

The final room from the twentieth century was a great discovery to us. We entered and immediately realized we had been in this room before. We were in M. and Mme Maurice de Wendel's Art Deco salon, with its sumptuous and theatrical decor. It was originally in their splendid *hôtel* on the quai de New York. The designer was José Maria Sert, the preeminent interior decorator of the period, who completed the salon in 1924. Panels of metal (the Wendel fortune came from iron and steel) painted in crimson and white gold depict the Queen of Sheba's journey across the desert to visit King Solomon. The queen is accompanied by an enormous retinue. Her accoutrements include fireworks, a menagerie, and even palm trees to be planted every evening to provide her with an oasis wherever she might be.

Open 10–6 daily, except Mondays. Entry is free for the permanent exhibitions so you have no excuse for not visiting this fascinating museum. Free entry attracted 600,000 visitors in 2003, however, a lack of funding means that there are not enough guards to keep all the sections of the museum open at all times.

Continue down the rue de Sévigné. You may see a group of high school students fill the street from the Lycée Charlemagne. Push through the crowd of students all dressed in black and smoking, or cross the street.

The owner of the funny American-style store **Lyons Co.**, at **no. 38**, scours the United States for collectibles from the fifties, sixties, and seventies. You can be sure the cookie jar or poster you buy is not a reproduction.

Note the open courtyards of **nos. 46** and **52**. The mother-and-children fountain sculpture at **no. 48** was part of a larger display with water coming from a fountain flanked by two poplars.

The street ahead is **Parc-Royal**, a street of elegant houses and courtyards. **No. 4**, in front of you, dates from 1620 and flaunts the famous fake pink brick of the place des Vosges (Walk 4).

Take a seat in one of the loveliest small parks, the **square Léopold Achille**, and watch society in action on weekends or after school. Here you'll find a mix of Parisian-dressed kids and their chic parents with families from all over the world. The young boys play at kung fu, turning and kicking and yelling, while the girls go up and down the slides. Nothing new. Seen scrawled on the slide: MORT AUX BOURGEOIS and UNE SEULE SOLUTION—LA RÉVOLUTION. Nothing new.

Bust of the Patron of Commerce in the square Léopold Achille, taken from the old city hall

A little farther down, adults sit and sun themselves and read facing a statue of a woman standing among greenery. The statue was originally at the Hôtel de Ville, Paris's city hall, which was burned to the ground in 1870, during the Commune.

Look out through the park's gate at the rue du Parc-Royal. **No. 8** (the German Historical Institute) also imitates red brick. **Nos. 10** and **12** house an inventory and archives of historic Paris. In 1960, no. 10, the Hôtel de Vigny, was saved from destruction by sheer luck. An old gentleman who lived there told his guest, who was an engineer, that his father had said there were painted rafters hidden under the plaster. The following weekend, the engineer returned and uncovered the décor we admire today (if you can get in). Not only did the old gentleman alert André Malraux, then minister of culture, to this find, but he, a puppeteer, put on marionette shows in the courtyard to gather support to save the building. The *hôtel* was saved, and this inspired Malraux to create the Association pour la Sauvegarde et la Mise en Valeur du Paris Historique (the organization to protect and value historic Paris; see Walk 6), one of seventy-seven restoration organizations now active in France. Malraux is also responsible for the crucial decision to have every Paris building cleaned every eleven years. That is how Paris became, once again, the city of light.

Leave the park at the far end and turn up the **rue Payenne** to the **square Georges-Cain**, where it is more shady and quiet. There is a circular parterre of grass, also with a statue of a woman. The graceful seventeenth-century figure, *Flore et Son Char,* by Maillol, poses in the center, holding a scarf.

The wall in the rear is the back of the Hôtel Le Peletier.

The building between the parks was the original *orangerie* (greenhouse for raising oranges) of the Musée Carnavalet and is now the stone museum of the City of Paris. Notice the collection of impressive remains of sculpture on the side wall opposite and the rocks on the ground near the gate. The tree with the biggest leaves, a fig tree, stands in the northeast corner.

Enter the courtyard of the Swedish Cultural Center, **no. 11**, in the perfectly restored **Hôtel de Marle**, across the street on the rue Payenne. Free exhibits and an interesting gift shop. Open Tuesdays through Fridays, 10–1 and 2–5.

Turn left onto the rue du Parc-Royal and walk to the **place de Thorigny**, on your right. There is a friendly circle of benches here, in front of a café.

To your left, find the small, splendid seventeenth-century home of Libéral Bruant. It was until recently a superb museum of the most intricate and fascinating keys and locks. The collection belongs to a private person and at the moment is not being shown.

The façade of the building is classical. Note the four circular bays with Roman personages between them, and the triangular pediment with two fat-winged angels surrounded by horns of plenty. The wall to the left is fake, built for symmetry. This is a common practice. Look for this technique as you visit other *hôtels*.

Directly across the street, the rue de Thorigny leads to the **Musée National Picasso**, which was the Hôtel Aubert de Fontenay. Pierre Aubert de Fontenay built this grand house in 1656. He was collector of the tax on salt, a tax mightily resented by the populace, who derisively called his *hôtel* the *Hôtel Salé* (salt house). Fontenay's joy in the mansion, however, was short-lived. He was allied with the disgraced Fouquet of Vaux-le-Vicomte, and both were relieved of their property and their freedom by Louis XIV. (Visit Vaux-le-Vicomte, a perfect day trip just outside of Paris, for the whole story.)

Two monumental sphinxes flank the entry of this pleasing semicircular courtyard. Note the two pediments, one heavily sculpted with allegorical figures, under the mansard roof. The house has gone through many changes and uses. As a result, none of the original interior remains except for the main staircase, with its sculpture of Roman emperors and its intricate wrought-iron banister. With its bare elegance, the seventeenth-century wrought-iron chandelier could have been designed today. Take in the whole splendid scene. Note the modern touches of open spaces in the walls to allow visitors to peer into different parts of the museum. The house has now been completely renovated. There is a small room of photos that show what the *hôtel* was like before restoration.

The museum houses a collection of works given by Picasso's heirs as a means of paying off their inheritance taxes.

Also in the museum are more than two hundred paintings, sculptures, collages, and Picasso's own collection of Braque, Rousseau, Miró, and Renoir. The works are displayed chronologically, beginning with the Blue and Rose Periods, followed by cubism, a classical period, an eclectic period, much sculpture, and some ceramics. The collection completes a circle with a self-portrait done in 1901 and another painted in 1971. Closed Tuesdays; open 9:30–5:30 from October through March, and 9:30–6 from April through September; €5.50; free on Sundays.

Return to the place de Thorigny and walk down the **rue Elzévir** on the way back to Franc-Bourgeois. On the left, at **no. 10**, find the peaceful back garden of the Hôtel de Marle, on the rue Payenne. This is a favorite spot for fashion photos and television scenes. The trees are often festooned.

Eighteenth-century decorative art is the mark of the **Musée Cognacq-Jay**, at **no. 8**. Cognacq and Jay, serious collectors, made their fortune as founders of the department store La Samaritaine. Here are works by Boucher, Chardin, and Fragonard; pastels by de la Tour; and porcelain of Saxe. Cognacq-Jay was visited mainly by cognoscenti of the eighteenth century. Today it is bustling with elementary school children who come to hear some of their favorite fairy tales—"Beauty and the Beast" and "The Bluebird," by Mme Delaunay and Mme de Beaumont. The storyteller enriches the imagination of the children and leads them to discover and relate to the museum's artworks. They observe the daily life of the eighteenth-century child, the games, the clothes, the activities. Drawing classes imitate the art of the century. The museum has become the place to go for families. Open Tuesdays through Sundays, 10–5:40.

The **Compagnie du Sénégal Afrique de l'Ouest**, at **no. 3**, represents artisan and artistic work from Senegal. They offer a variety of objects and materials. An artist in residence often gives courses to children. Look across the street at **no. 4**, **Lutherie Ancienne–Moderne**, to see craftsmen at work making and repairing violins.

Continue down the street, to Franc-Bourgeois. **Camille**, on the corner, is a busy and happy neighborhood café that serves typical French food.

Look to the right, across the street, at **no. 35–37**, the **Maison de l'Europe**, now a center for international meetings. This was the Hôtel de Coulanges, built in the mid-seventeenth century. It was nearly torn down in the 1960s, but a media campaign saved it. Enter the courtyard to see the arcaded façade, the *mascarons*—each one different—and the wrought-iron staircase on the right.

Directly across the street is the **Hôtel de Sandreville**, at **no. 26**. It has a seventeenth-century Louis XVI façade with wide fluted Doric pillars and a frieze of garlands. The heavily sculpted door is in disrepair. A wrought-iron key plate has been stolen from this door, but the courtyard has recently been magnificently restored. The white stone walls now gleam.

Two doors to the left is **no. 30**, the **Hôtel d'Alméras**. Pierre Alméras was a counselor and secretary to Henri IV. For his *hôtel* he copied the brick-and-stone combination of the place des Vosges. Push the door button and stand at the grille to see a beautiful courtyard, recently restored. The stones glow. Henry IV's bust looks down from the third story, and if the light is right, you will see the beams in the ceilings of the apartments. The superb door and pediment are characteristic of the seventeenth century. The pediment is decorated with garlands of flowers. Two rams' heads rest on wide pillars flanking the door. Another missing key plate. Happens often. If the door isn't open, look through the windows of the gallery to your right.

Turn back to Camille and walk right, to **no. 31**, the **Hôtel d'Albret**, which has recently been restored by the city as offices for the organization, the Center for Cultural Affairs of the City of Paris. Originally built at the end of the fifteenth century for the *connétable* (supreme commander of the royal army) de Montmorency, it has been reworked repeatedly over the centuries. Today it is a striking combination of preservation of the past and twentieth-century design. Examine the façade, with its open-mouthed lions on top of pillars and a man wearing a lion cap. Enter the courtyard. On the right side were the stables; today there is a Louis XIII staircase that ends in stone on the top floor. The cellars have been restored for receptions. The left wing is called "the boat" because of the freestanding staircase

that looks as if it came from an ocean liner. Space was lost in this wing because the building started tipping and needed support when a staircase was removed from the entry.

No. 29 bis still has industries in the courtyard.

The **Paris Musée**, at **no. 29**, reproduces objects from the national museums. **Jean Châtel** sells good men's clothes in an Art Nouveau setting, the historical remains of a bakery. Note the walls and the ceilings.

At **no. 20** is **La Chaise Longue**, selling reproductions of kitchen things used in the 1930s through the 1950s. Find more Art Nouveau panels on what was once a bakery, on the corner of rue Pavée. Bakers and fishmongers were famous for Art Nouveau ceilings and walls. They saw its beauty in its time. These painted tiles are always classified as historical decorations.

The **Hôtel de Lamoignon** is on the corner of the **rue Pavée**, one of the first paved streets of Paris. Before reaching the corner, look at the lovely garden that is part of the Hôtel de Lamoignon. The *hôtel* was originally built in 1555 by Robert de Beauvais, counselor to the king and comptroller-general of the city of Paris. He died in 1568, and the property was purchased by Diane de France, Duchesse d'Angoulême. She was the natural daughter of Henri II. It seems her mother, who was Italian, had refused the king's advances. Not deterred, he had her house burned down in order to kidnap her. Diane was legitimized and became one of the important women of her time, "wise in counsel, beautiful, and the finest woman on horseback."

Notice the square-windowed turret at the corner. A few other such turrets can still be found, one at the Hôtel de Sens (Walk 6). They are the last survivors of what was once a popular design that allowed householders to see what was happening in every direction. The initials *S. C.* carved into the stone on the base of the turret supports mark the limits of the property owned by the Culture of Saint Catherine, then the largest religious settlement on the Right Bank.

In the circular pediment of the entrance wall are statues of two children. One, Truth, holds a mirror; the other, Prudence, a

Entrance to the Hôtel d'Albret, now the
Center for Cultural Affairs of the City of Paris

serpent. Today, the *hôtel* has been completely restored and enlarged. The right wing, built as recently as 1968, and in perfect harmony with the original section, houses the library of the City of Paris. Go into the courtyard, turn right, and go up a few steps and then left into the reading room. Sit down, rest, and admire this beautiful room—its proportions, windows, and view, and the painted beams, with Diane in the middle of a back beam. There is always an interesting exhibition here. When you have finished browsing, take a look at the mausoleum in the courtyard to your left.

Continue down the rue Pavée, to the bookstore of the library. It displays historical exhibitions and carries a fine selection of books on Paris and its history.

At **7 bis** rue Pavée, find a curious bookstore, a long alley that was once a hostelry. Toward the back, the original large paving stones have not been covered over. This is the most eclectic bookstore you can find. Worth a browse.

At the corner of the **rue des Rosiers**, at **no. 3**, turn left to the tea shop called **Le Loir dans la Théière** (the dormouse in the teapot). The first owner named it, and the mural to the right is the French version of Alice and her friends. This is a popular place for tea and cake or Sunday brunch in tatty armchairs.

Return to Pavée and turn left to **no. 10**. This is the **synagogue** built in 1913 by the famous Art Nouveau architect of the *métro*, Hector Guimard. The building is concave, which makes it look taller. The design recalls the shape of the tablets of the Ten Commandments.

Return to the rue des Rosiers and turn left.

The rue des Rosiers was the historic home and first stop for Jewish immigrants and refugees. When Philippe Auguste banned Jews in the thirteenth century, they left the area around Notre-Dame and planted themselves just outside the city walls, on the rue des Rosiers. The area was covered with wild roses, giving the street its name.

The neighborhood continued to play the same role for French Jews as the Lower East Side once did for Jews in New York. When they were forced to leave Eastern Europe because of pogroms at the end of the nineteenth century, the Ashkenazic Jews came here. When Jews fled the Nazis, they again came here. This is also the street the Nazis and the Vichy French invaded and from which they dragged seventy-five thousand Jews away to concentration camps, to Drancy and, worse, to Auschwitz. A later wave of immigrants, Sephardic Jews this time, arrived as a result of the French exodus from Algeria. You will see signs of this history as you walk the streets.

The neighborhood presently suffers additional stress because of the frequently ignored anti-Semitic acts and violence by Muslims against Jews in France. In light of recent anti-Semitic events, increasing numbers of French Jews are immigrating to Israel. They still remember what happened in the 1940s.

In addition, there is a constant drama here that unfolds between the cars that cram and jam and inch forward through a flood of pedestrians who pointedly ignore the automobiles. There is also a fierce battle between the City of Paris and the storekeepers. The city wants to widen the street. The Jewish storekeepers say it will take at least a year, and that people will change their shopping habits and never return.

As it is, the Jewish aspect of the street is threatened by the influx of high fashion. The coming of high fashion on the rue des Rosiers was a kind of public announcement that the Marais and its beautifully renovated buildings had arrived. Twenty years ago, the real estate here was some of the least valuable in Paris. Today, it is some of the most valuable.

Across the street, at **no. 4**, there was a *hammam* (Turkish bath). The most chic, slimmest ladies came from all over Paris to keep fit and beautiful, the better to buy the clothes sold across the street. The bath was first bought by the owners of the Chevignon stores, who dismantled the exquisite tiled walls and pool. The entire neighborhood mourned the loss of this establishment. Since then three failed stores have opened here; the latest attempt is a furniture store.

Note the plaque on the wall: IN MEMORY OF PERSONNEL AND THE STUDENTS OF THIS SCHOOL WHO WERE ARRESTED IN '43 AND '44 BY THE POLICE OF VICHY AND THE GESTAPO AND DEPORTED AND EXTERMINATED IN AUSCHWITZ BECAUSE THEY WERE JEWS.

The owner of a tiny kosher grocery a few doors down was not willing to sell out to fashion when we spoke to him years ago. Today, he's ready.

L'Eclaireur, at **no. 3 ter**, is one of the high-fashion stores that sell ultramodern clothes and *objets*.

The corner of rue des Rosiers and rue Ferdinand-Duval, the center of the Jewish quarter, is marked by the restaurant **Goldenberg**, which serves all the typical Eastern European Jewish dishes. This was the scene of a terrorist attack by Palestinian sympathizers in which four people, including the Arab cook, were killed in the summer of 1982. A sign on your left as you enter reads in part: ON NE CÈDE PAS AU TERRORISME (We don't give in to terrorism). The food at the take-out counter will give you an idea of the quality and variety of Polish Jewish food. Try the blintzes and a cup of tea for a light bite if it's lunchtime.

This corner is a meeting place of the neighborhood. Sundays, when everyone is out socializing, there is no walking up and down the street, as in a *passeo* (pedestrian walkway). People just stand and talk. Pity the poor unknowing soul who starts down this street in a car. To add to the confusion, the street is lined with barricades to ward off terrorists. These barricades exist all over Paris, wherever there is a school or a possible site for a terrorist attack. This much of the ghetto is here to stay.

From Goldenberg's on down, the street is still Jewish. It is dotted with butchers and bakers and Sephardic fast-food *schwarma* and falafel places—especially **L'As du Fellafel**, generally considered the best source for an inexpensive meal in Paris.

At **no. 26**, **Bibliophane** carries a large and wide selection of Judaica.

Two Finkelsztajn shops, the bakery in particular, are worth a visit. **Finkelsztajn**, at **no. 27**, sells only dairy food, the finest breads, cakes, and appetizers. The delicious dark rye bread slices easily and stays fresh indefinitely; not so with a baguette. The specialty of the house is a unique eggplant dip that is smooth and silky, topped with sesame seeds. High quality but very high prices. Try something anyway. The other shop is at no. 19.

Korcarz, up the street at **no. 29**, is an excellent kosher bak-

Excellent traditional Jewish food at no. 27 rue des Rosiers

ery and restaurant. Stop in for a meal or for tea and cake. The busy bakery offers a rich selection of cakes and breads and bagels. Return and turn to the right, up the **rue des Hospitaliers**, to the school on the right. This spot holds many stories. Originally a meat market stood here—hence the heads of bulls on the walls (originally the decorations on two fountains, no

A plaque commemorating the deportation of Jewish children during World War II

longer here). Then it was a Jewish public school—boys on the right, girls on the left. Read the startling plaques on the walls to relive the horror of the Nazi occupation:

ONE HUNDRED AND SIXTY-FIVE JEWISH CHILDREN OF THIS SCHOOL WERE DEPORTED TO GERMANY DURING WORLD WAR II AND WERE EXTERMINATED IN THE NAZI CAMPS. LEST WE FORGET.

The second plaque is an acknowledgment from former students:

TO JEAN MIGNARET, TEACHER AND DIRECTOR OF THIS SCHOOL FROM 1920 TO 1944, WHO BY HIS COURAGE AND AT PERIL OF HIS LIFE SAVED TENS OF JEWISH CHILDREN FROM DEPORTATION.

Recently, similar plaques have been put up on all the public schools in this area to remind us of all the children who were taken by the Nazis with the help of the Vichy government.

Today the right side of the building is a school for special-needs students and the left is a regular (co-ed) public school. Continue up the street to the rue des Francs-Bourgeois.

Rue des Francs-Bourgeois

Directly in front of you is the Swedish Cultural Center, at **no. 38**. The seventeenth-century houses lean toward each other and almost meet at the top. The old-fashioned pharmacy next door, at **no. 36**, is worth entering. Note the back wall of blue medicine bottles, the etched lady in the mirror, the clock in the wall, and the old-style scale.

A l'Image du Grenier sur l'Eau (picture of the hayloft on the water—a street name near the Seine), at **no. 45**, across the street, is a one-of-a-kind postcard store. Here two brothers have assembled postcards from the last quarter of the nineteenth century to 1945 in hundreds of drawers classified by every possible subject. The cards range in price from $1 to $100. If you can bear to mail them, they make a great change from the typical tourist cards you have already sent home.

Cross again, heading left, to an excellent knitting store, **Anny Blatt**, at **no. 40**, famous for its wools. The **Villa Marais**, next door, is a mixture of modern and antique gifts and furniture. They have opened a small *crêperie* on the top floor with dining on a charming rooftop terrace in good weather. Continue up the street, to the corner of Francs-Bourgeois and **Vieille-du-Temple**. You will immediately notice the flamboyant Gothic tower at **no. 54**. This is a reconstruction from the manor house of Hérouét, Louis XII's treasurer, which was destroyed by the last German bombing of Paris, in August 1944, the only building hit in Paris during the war. For years the crumbling building was supported by heavy railroad-type buttresses extending out into the street. Restoring this house became a serious issue. Oddly enough, many said that it had no historic value, was extremely ugly, and was a disturbance to the city and its aesthetic sense. Fortunately, someone found a statute that led the city to classify the building as a historic monument—and this lovely round tower with its flamboyant tracery is still here.

If you are walking on a Saturday or Sunday between 2 and 5:30, do continue up the rue Vieille du Temple (visit a tea place and new galleries on the way), to **no. 87**, **L'Hôtel de Rohan**. Enter the courtyard and turn right into the next courtyard. The

The collector's postcard shop at no. 45 rue des Franc-Bourgeois

Rohans were one of the most important noble families, whose members lived all over the Marais. On the wall to your right you will see the famous and fabulous horses of Apollo, riding out of the stone they were sculpted from. The more you look at these horses, the more detail you see. They were done in 1738 by Robert Le Lorrain.

Return to the rue Vieille du Temple, retrace your steps, and cross rue des Francs-Bourgeois. On the left, see if there is an exhibition of food or books or art or antiques in the flag-bedecked former covered food market.

Across the street, at **no. 53**, is **Ordning & Reda**, a Swedish stationery store. They have wonderful notebooks, pens, and pencils—all arranged by color. To your right try the very pleasant and reasonable restaurant **Au Gamin de Paris**, at **no. 51**. Come here on the early side (before 8 P.M. and before the lines—people wait in the street) for an excellent bistro-style dinner. They have two superb desserts—a chocolate cake (a passion for some members of our family) and a tarte Tatin—sitting in the front window.

Continue down the street to a grand house, **no. 47**, the Hôtel Amelot-de-Bisseuil. It is also known as the **Hôtel des Ambassadeurs de Hollande**. Its remarkably ugly door is reproduced everywhere. Two large and evil Medusa heads stick their tongues out at you. Peace and War are figured in the pediment. The door to the first courtyard is always open. Note the four sundials on the left wall.

The house has a long history, six centuries, but one that is particularly interesting to Americans. It was here that Beaumarchais wrote the comedy on which the libretto for Mozart's *The Marriage of Figaro* was based. Beaumarchais also created a business here called Rodriguez-Hortalez et Cie, which was a front for the exportation of arms to the American colonies in their fight against the English. Beginning with the Revolution, the *hôtel* was left abandoned. Paneling and gold decorations were removed and a dome was covered up. Industry moved in, continuing the destruction. The *hôtel* was divided into stores and small factories; false floors and ceilings were put in place; woodwork disappeared, as well as paintings on ceilings and friezes; buildings, porches, and barracks in the courtyard hid all the wall decorations. Much has been restored, beginning only as recently as 1926. Painted ceilings and the dome have been recuperated.

Farther up on the left of this interesting street is a popular café, **Le Petit Fer à Cheval** (small horseshoe). The street is full of surprises—many interesting shops and cafés, most of which overflow nightly with an international gay clientele. But we are heading back to Francs-Bourgeois to finish up near the Centre Pompidou.

Walk left down Francs-Bourgeois to one of the most architecturally interesting restaurants in Paris, at **no. 53 bis**, on the left. **Le Dôme du Marais** was originally the chapel for the religious order of the Blancs-Manteaux and then was used as the auction room of the municipal pawnshop. The combination restaurant and music room is behind a very small courtyard with tables. It is a large, round spectacular room encircled by a high carved balcony. The ceiling is a colored glass dome (hence the name). The young and hard-working chef offers a superb meal at a moderate price. If you are cigarette-smoked out of small, cozy restaurants, this high-ceilinged place is the answer. Be sure to visit the clever and pretty WC at the balcony level. The restaurant now has musical evenings with varied offerings.

Enter **no. 55**, the courtyard of the **Crédit Municipal**, the government-run pawnshop, known as *mont-de-piété,* or colloquially known as *ma tante* (my aunt). The wall surrounding Paris, begun by Philippe Auguste in about 1190 (see the plaque on the wall), cut across this yard and occupied the space traced on the ground. If you are on the entry side, you would have been outside the boundaries of twelfth-century Paris.

Walk through the far door on the left to see if there is a showing or auction going on. They specialize in jewelry and silver, as well as paintings, rugs, and *objets*. It's fun to watch, and if you can count fast enough in French, you might bid. Add a 15 percent fee.

Walk right through the second courtyard or look into it to see a large tower at the corner of the building. The base is a section of Philippe Auguste's wall, and the building opposite is decorated with *mascarons* of women, lions, and a satyr. Today the building is Munigarde, a storage and security facility for works of art. Turn right toward the street to see a doorway, the remains of a house that once stood there, and an antique column. If you cannot enter this second courtyard, return to the street, walk left, and stand across the street, facing the end of the Crédit Municipal building. There, behind the iron door, you can see the tower of the wall. Many, including us, think it is unjust to close off these historic sites, especially since taxes pay for part of their upkeep, but security is the excuse offered and accepted.

You are now standing next to the largest and most elegant palace in Paris of the old regime, the **Palais de Soubise**, connected to the **Palais de Rohan**, both visitable. Until recently, Soubise was the home of the National Archives of Paris.

The Prince de Soubise, who once lived at 13 place des Vosges, found much wider scope here, as can be seen from this most grand colonnaded courtyard and the large gardens behind and to the side. In order to keep the colonnade level while rising on a hill, the architect cleverly increased each of the pediments under the fifty-six double columns, just enough to compensate for the incline. Imagine the pageantry of the horses delivering nobility to the palace. Four pillars hold up the pediment, and sculptures decorate the windows.

The beautiful rooms, by designer-architect Boffrand in the rococo style, give onto the interior garden. The sun fills these rooms, painted in gold and pale pastels with white sculpted ceilings and panels covered with scenes such as *Venus at Her Toilette* and *The Education of Love*. The palace is closed Tuesdays. Hours are 1:45–5:45 P.M.

The oldest construction in the complex is the medieval gate with its two round towers and escutcheons on the walls on the **rue des Archives**, about a hundred yards to your right around the corner. This is all that the Prince de Soubise left from the fourteenth-century fortress that was originally built by Olivier de Clisson. But this remnant is a great boon, especially for the residents who have the pleasure of seeing a piece of the Middle Ages illuminated at night.

The strongly Catholic Guise family bought the palace in 1553, and enlarged it considerably. It was here that the St. Bartholomew's Massacre, the slaughter of the Protestants during the religious wars (1572), was planned.

The national archives themselves have now moved to an electronically up-to-date building on the rue des Quatre Fils, around the corner. Among the archives are a letter from Jeanne d'Arc and Napoléon's will. The palace is now used for receptions—a kind of republican return to royalist elegance.

The shop on the corner sells mementos of French history—medals, seals, facsimiles, and the like. They make wonderful gifts.

Rue Rambuteau

At the corner of the rue des Archives, the rue des Francs-Bourgeois changes its name to the **rue Rambuteau**. This is a typical market street, with its competing bakeries and *charcuteries,* some now Asian. After one block, turn right onto the **rue du Temple**, and go a few doors down to the new **Musée d'Art et Histoire du Judaisme**. It is housed in one of the grandest palaces in the Marais, the Hôtel de Saint-Aignan, at **no. 71**. Inside, in contrast to this grandeur, is a typical wooden Jewish house from a ghetto (*shtetl*). There are elaborately illustrated wedding contracts, silver artifacts, and art by Modigliani and Chagall.

A historically and artistically significant statue has finally found a home in the courtyard of the museum. The statue of Captain Dreyfus by Tim, a serious cartoonist, tells the captain's story metaphorically. Dreyfus's large uniformed body is covered in some sort of mud encrustation, and he holds a broken sword, a symbol of his fraudulent disgrace. In 1894, Captain Alfred Dreyfus of the French army was accused of spying for Germany, and thus of being a traitor. France was divided between anti-Semites (the army, in particular) and Dreyfus's republican supporters. Zola was one of the important champions who successfully defended the Jewish Dreyfus. The French recognize the Dreyfus Affair as a blot on their escutcheon.

Look around this splendid courtyard and spot another of those false walls on the left.

Return to Rambuteau, turn right, and cross the rue Beaubourg. Enter the pedestrian zone that comprises the **Centre Pompidou**, commonly known as Beaubourg, and the Fontaine Igor Stravinsky.

A huge "hardware" store, **Leroy Merlin**, is at **no. 52** rue Rambuteau. Like paper goods in France, hardware has its own style and is a lot of fun. If this is your thing, be sure to visit the basement of the BHV mentioned in Walk 6.

Directly across the street is the entrance to the Centre Pompidou. Six hundred and eighty-one designs were submitted for the Centre Pompidou, and much to their surprise, two young architects, Renzo Piano and Richard Rogers, from Genoa and London, respectively, were chosen. The fact that their French was limited made it easier for them to disregard the heated and constant criticism surrounding the building's construction. When the center finally went up, with all its color-coded entrails of ducts and pipes (water, gas, air, and electricity) on the outside, most Parisians were horrified. The architects defended these radical innovations, claiming to have saved interior space, now free of metallic structures, pipes, heat, and water ducts.

Twenty years later, the center required drastic restoration, and reaction to it is still sharply divided. It is, however, the most visited attraction in the city, surpassing the Eiffel Tower, which was also once maligned. When you consider the metal Lego effect of the Eiffel Tower, the ultramodern glass pyramid planted in the classical Louvre courtyard, the glass walls of the New Grand Library that let the sun shine on the books and the readers researching belowground, the huge stone hulk of the Bastille-Opéra that fills an entire street, and the towering Arch of the Defense, you must credit the French with courage.

The museum houses many free exhibit areas, the largest open-stack library in the city (a separate and long line forms on the Beaubourg side for users), special exhibitions, a bookstore, and the rich Museum of Modern Art with works from 1914 to the present.

There is a fee to climb up the caterpillar escalator to see Paris spread out all around you. This will also give you a bird's-eye view of the musicians, magicians, and fire-eaters (*cracheurs de feu*) in the plaza below.

Free entry to most of the museum was inspired by the idea of making it a people's museum. It succeeded. But there are drawbacks. The museum is a hangout for the down-and-out and for the avant-garde of pop culture. The inhabitants are not happy with the noise, crowds, and late hours, but the *place* is always lively and fascinating.

Walk up the hill of the plaza to the street. **La Librairie Galerie** has an immense collection of posters and postcards. Continue straight to the left, to the **rue Saint-Martin**. Enjoy a crêpe from the vendor at the intersection. The goodies on the street are a jewelry shop, a pen and paper store, a Quimper pottery shop, and a working bakery making croissants and more. Eat them fresh and hot, just out of the oven. If you don't indulge when in Paris, you're making a mistake.

To find the **Fontaine Igor Stravinsky**, turn left off Saint-Martin before the church of Saint-Médard. Kids love this spot. The brightly colored sculptures are by Nikki Saint-Phalle, and the intricate and mechanical metal automatons by Jean Tinguely were inspired by Stravinsky's music and are an expression of the New Realist movement. They bob happily in the large rectangular fountain. Find the different elements in the fountain: the key to the sun, the nightingale, the serpent, the firebird, the spiral, the heart, life, the elephant, death, ragtime, and love. A conductor starts the players on their water dance. Playing children surround the fountain in the daytime; the restaurants are filled at night. Try the outdoor tables at the red-painted **Brisemiche** for a two-course, reasonably priced menu.

For reasons of space we have not detailed all the streets in this area, but that does not mean that you should skip them. They are laced with historic buildings, interesting shops, and restaurants. If you continue on the rue Saint-Martin, you will pass several good restaurants, in particular, the one-star **Benoît**, at **no. 20**. This first-rate restaurant dates from 1912, and has passed from grandfather to grandson. The grandfather, like his friend the famous chef Ferdinand Point, weighed well over three hundred pounds. The bistro used to serve the workers at Les Halles, the old Paris market. Now the bistro borders on becoming a restaurant with twenty-two employees instead of the usual ten to twelve. They still serve typical bistro food—cassoulet and soups (more elegant)—but keeping the old spirit.

You could keep wandering and make your own discoveries here or head back to the rue Beaubourg to the *métro* Rambuteau or walk straight south on rue Beaubourg, which changes its name to rue du Renard, passes in front of the Hôtel de Ville, and crosses the Seine onto the Ile de la Cité and to Notre-Dame.

27 28 29
JUILLET 1830

Walk · 6

Bastille to Eglise Saint-Gervais

Today, nothing happened.
—Louis XVI in his diary,
July 14, 1789

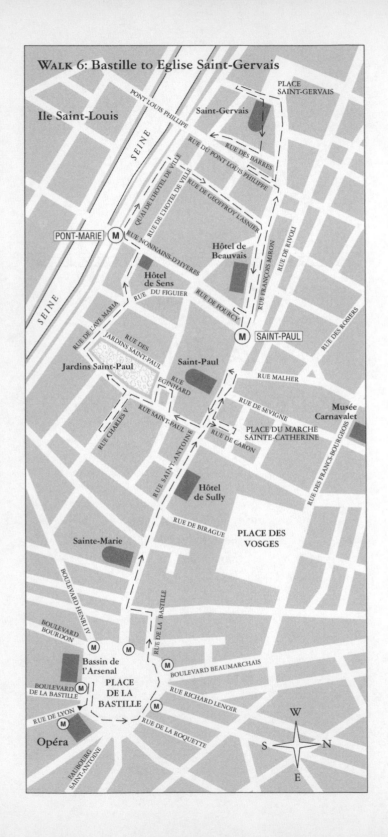

WALK 6: Bastille to Eglise Saint-Gervais

PLACE
SAINT-GERVAIS

Saint-Gervais

Ile Saint-Louis

SEINE

PONT LOUIS PHILLIPE

RUE DES BARRES

RUE DU PONT LOUIS PHILLIPE

QUAI DE L'HOTEL DE VILLE

RUE DE L'HOTEL DE VILLE

RUE DE GEOFFROY L'ASNIER

RUE DE RIVOLI

PONT-MARIE Ⓜ

RUE NONNAINS D'HYERES

Hôtel de
Beauvais

RUE FRANÇOIS MIRON

Hôtel
de Sens

RUE DU FIGUIER

RUE DE FOURCY

SEINE

RUE DE L'AVE MARIA

Ⓜ SAINT-PAUL

RUE DES ROSIERS

RUE DES
JARDINS SAINT-PAUL

Jardins Saint-Paul

Saint-Paul

RUE
EGINHARD

RUE MALHER

RUE DE SEVIGNE

Musée
Carnavalet

RUE CHARLES V

RUE SAINT-PAUL

RUE DE CARON

PLACE DU MARCHE
SAINTE-CATHERINE

RUE DES FRANCS-BOURGEOIS

RUE SAINT-ANTOINE

Hôtel
de Sully

RUE DE BIRAGUE

PLACE DES
VOSGES

Sainte-Marie

BOULEVARD HENRI IV

RUE DE LA BASTILLE

BOULEVARD
BOURDON

Ⓜ

Ⓜ

Ⓜ

BOULEVARD BEAUMARCHAIS

Bassin de
l'Arsenal

BOULEVARD
DE LA BASTILLE

Ⓜ

PLACE
DE LA
BASTILLE

RUE RICHARD LENOIR

RUE DE LYON

Ⓜ

Ⓜ

RUE DE LA ROQUETTE

Opéra

FAUBOURG SAINT-ANTOINE

W

S   N

E

Starting Point: Place de la Bastille, 4th arrondissement
Métro: Bastille*
Buses: 20, 29, 65, 69, 76, 86, 87, 91

The **place de la Bastille** stands today on what was the site of the fortified door known as the Porte Saint-Antoine in the protective wall of the city. In 1356, Etienne Marcel, the provost of the merchants of the City of Paris, had this fortification built as quickly as possible as part of his campaign to take control when France was in turmoil. The king, Jean le Bon, was imprisoned by the English, and the dauphin, Charles V, was the nominal head of France. Charles, however, was only twenty years old, and Marcel assumed that the young ruler could easily be overwhelmed and that this was the opportunity for Marcel to shift power to the bourgeoisie.

*Historical artifacts inside this *métro* station relate to the history of the Bastille. To fully understand their significance you should read the history here before visiting them. However, if you leave the station to follow the walk while you read the history, you will be required to pay again to get back into the tunnels where the artifacts are located. The decision is yours—the description of the interior of the station is on pages 188–89.

This new portion of the wall was attached to the older wall of Philippe Auguste (see Walk 5), enlarging the enclosed, and thereby protected, area of the city. The entry at the Porte Saint-Antoine had a drawbridge and two huge towers called a *bastille,* which was the term for a detached fortification.

Etienne Marcel's treachery against the French dauphin included attempting to obtain the keys to the gate in order to deliver them to the king of Navarre and the English on July 31, 1358. However, the men guarding the gate refused to turn over the keys, and instead hacked the provost to death with axes and threw his naked body in the Seine. Subsequently, Charles V regained control of Paris and had the wall completed. The Porte Saint-Antoine was enlarged, first by the addition of two more towers to create a fort, and then with two more; together, these established the structure that would become known as the prison of the Bastille.

The fort was a huge, oblong structure with thick, high, crenellated walls, eight round towers, a drawbridge, and a moat. In the seventeenth century, Richelieu turned it into a prison. Members of the aristocracy were often committed by a family member or a rival politician. A secret letter (*lettre de cachet*) sent to the king for his signature could put someone away.

The reasons for imprisonment were often peculiar. Voltaire was in the Bastille twice, once for writing malicious verse, another time for challenging the Duc de Rohan to a duel. The prison was not for brutal criminals, and being locked up in it was not considered a disgrace. Quite the contrary. Prisoners could keep a servant, bring their own silver and porcelain, and make arrangements for receiving lovers. The Marquis de Sade draped his walls with fabric; Cardinal de Rohan had a dinner party for twenty. The prison was criticized as an expense to the state and unnecessary.

And it became, of course, the symbol of the French Revolution. Near the end of the eighteenth century, the price of bread had risen sharply, and on July 14, 1789, a mob gathered at the Palais Royale and prepared to make trouble. The revolutionaries were short of powder for their guns, and rumor had it that there were one hundred and twenty-five barrels of gunpowder in the Bastille, so off they went to storm the Bastille to get the gunpowder to start, in effect, the French Revolution. There were some intermittent shots during the day, but at about four o'clock an assault on the main gate began where no. 5 rue Saint-Antoine is now located. Six hundred thirty-three revolutionaries attacked thirty-two Swiss guards and fifty-two pensioners. Eighty revolutionaries and only one Swiss guard were killed.

The revolutionaries forced the governor of the Bastille, the Marquis de Launay, to give up the gunpowder and release the prisoners. He gave up the keys and was rewarded by being cut to pieces along with six Swiss guards.

Who were the prisoners? Four forgers, one accomplice to an attempted murder, a count accused of incest sent there by his family, and a madman. Hardly the makings of revolutionary symbolism, but that didn't matter to the angry mob. This was the start of the Revolution. On that day, Louis XVI wrote in his diary, "Today, nothing happened."

General Lafayette eventually gave the key to the Bastille to U.S. President George Washington. The eighteen-inch key is now on view at Mount Vernon.

Today, the location of the ancient walls of the Bastille is marked in the pavement of the *place* in brown bricks. There are many of these bricks in the traffic circle, but they can be hard to see because of the constant traffic. Those at the entrance to the rue Saint-Antoine are usually easy to find.

July 14 became a national holiday in 1880. Bastille Day is celebrated July 13 with a grand ball at the Bastille from 8 P.M. on, with fireworks at the Eiffel Tower, and with a military parade on the Champs-Elysées on the fourteenth at 10 A.M.

Five years after the Bastille was torn down, in June 1794, the revolutionaries, ever vigilant in their campaign against the enemy, brought the guillotine from the place de la Révolution, better known today as the place de la Concorde, to the place de la Bastille for three days. It was far from idle—seventy-three victims were beheaded in that time.

The *place,* however, was more frequently used as a location for large, symbolic public monuments. In 1793 the first fountain was erected, a colossal plaster figure of the goddess Isis spouting water from her breasts. In 1808, Napoléon's minister of the interior placed the first stone for a new statue of an elephant that would commemorate the arrival of water through the subterranean canal from the Ourcq River into the city. Napoléon wanted the statue to be so monumental that one could enter through a leg and climb an interior spiral staircase to a viewing platform in a tower on the beast's back. The bronze was to come from cannons liberated from Spain, and the pachyderm's trunk would spray water.

The wood-and-plaster model was over sixty feet high and nearly fifty feet long. The project was abandoned, though the model stood for thirty-five years, serving as a nesting place for millions of rats. Victor Hugo used it as a hiding/living place for Gavroche in *Les Misérables*. You can see what the elephant looked like in a fascinating copy of an engraving on a wall of the Bastille *métro* station.

In 1830, a law was passed to create a monument to commemorate those who died in Les Trois Glorieuses, July 27, 28, and 29, 1830—the three days of fighting that marked the end of the reign of Charles X, ultraroyalist brother of Louis XVI. A column was designed to stand on the foundation that had been built for the elephant, with the bones of the honored dead laid to rest inside. The Colonne de Juillet is divided into three portions to represent the three days, with the names of the dead inscribed in gold in each section. It is topped with a statue of the golden spirit of Liberty breaking his irons and scattering light. The monument is dedicated: A LA GLOIRE DES CITOYENS FRANÇAIS QUI S'ARMÈRENT ET COMBATTENT POUR LA DÉFENSE DES LIBERTÉS PUBLIQUES DANS LES MEMORABLES JOURNÉES DES 27, 28, 29 JUILLET, 1830" (To the glory of the French citizens who armed themselves and fought to defend the public liberty on those memorable days of July 27, 28, and 29, 1830). The column was completed in 1840 and soon became a favored site for suicides. As a result, the interior was closed.

There are several things to see in and around this hectic traffic circle, and we advise that you walk around only in the crosswalks and with the light. If you arrived on the *métro* there are a number of things to see in the corridors before you leave the station. If you came by bus you should invest in a *métro* ticket to enter the station. Use the entrance on the rue de Lyon, on the right of the Opéra if you are facing that building. Go down the stairs, pay, and take the hallway to the right, marked with the sign SORTIE RUE DE LYON—OPÉRA BASTILLE, BLVD. DE LA BASTILLE, JARDIN DU BASSIN L'ARSENAL. This leads you to a hallway with copies of historic engravings of the place de la Bastille. Among the panels is the famous Fragonard drawing of the interior of the Bastille prison, with the elegantly dressed women arriving to visit their wealthy imprisoned relatives; the elephant statue; and the demolition of the Bastille. These panels will help you understand the history of this area by providing images of what is no longer here.

The *quai* for *ligne 1, direction Château de Vincennes*, is an elevated *quai* with glass windows offering a view of the canal below and the houseboats docked in the marina. On *ligne 5, direction Bobigny,* is the remains of a piece of the protective wall (*contrescarpe*) that once surrounded the Bastille.

Back outside in the *place*, go down to the banks of the canal if the weather is nice. Known as the **Bassin de l'Arsenal**, this marina was built to connect the Canal Saint-Martin with the Seine. In the summer it is charming, with flowers and fantasies of life on the river in a neat little houseboat.

Back in the *place,* the most notable building is the Opéra, which is built on the site of a small Jewish ghetto known centuries ago as the Cour de la Juiverie. The Opéra de Paris-Bastille opened in 1989 to celebrate the bicentennial of the French Revolution. It could not be more different from the Opéra-Garnier, built in 1875. This, however, is not a surprise, because in the past forty years Paris has been choosing a bold approach to modern architecture.

The Opéra de Paris-Bastille is almost four blocks long, a huge hulking building, sectioned alternately in glass, metal, and stone, and free of any decoration. The building itself has been declared by many critics to be a complete failure. In the rush to complete it, materials were slapped on, and the large stone slabs that make up the façade have been falling off, requiring netting to be strung across the front to catch them. But the building takes on a different aspect each night as the lighting magically changes its appearance. The Opéra-Garnier, in contrast, sits on a small island of land, and it is sculpted, pillared, arched, and decorated to the very top of its famous copper, gold, and stone dome.

The wide high steps of the Opéra de Paris-Bastille, called *les grandes marches*, take you inside, where there is another staircase, geometrical, unadorned, curving high as it reaches the top. The Garnier's doubled, marbled staircase, illuminated with chandeliers sitting on caryatids, was made for a different time— a time for beautiful people in their grand clothes to descend and be admired. The Paris-Bastille, however, has a different function. Like the Centre Pompidou, it seeks a wider, more popular audience.

The main auditorium, narrow and high with few side balconies, is centered directly on the stage. The seats are made for comfort, with individual heaters underneath. Other auditoriums are used for smaller musical performances.

New technology makes it possible to perform several operas in one week. A series of elevators allows an assembled stage set to be brought up from below with the push of a button. We saw this remarkable feat with our own eyes by taking a tour (in French) of the building. For rehearsals, there is a second stage that is an exact duplicate of the main stage. Eight opera sets are made each year for both the old and new opera houses by teams of painters, tapestry workers, carpenters, sculptors, seamstresses, milliners, and designers in a work area of seventy-five thousand square feet in the bottom of the Bastille.

Unfortunately, buying tickets is complicated. The automatic telephone service never connects to a real person, and the voice is French. The best method is to try to navigate the Internet. Tickets range from €5 to €180. Good luck.

Next door to the Opéra is the brasserie **Les Grandes Marches**, named for the uninspiring steps. Until 1990 the restaurant was known as the Tour d'Argent, in recognition of one of the eight towers in the Bastille known as the Tour du Trésor, where Henri IV kept his savings. (According to his minister, Sully, Henri IV had nearly 16 million *livres*, quite a treasure.) The restaurant used to be graced with a large, highly visible red neon sign proclaiming the name of the restaurant. Apparently this less-than-sophisticated display of the name was more than the world-famous Left Bank restaurant of the same name could stand. Claude Terrail, owner of that Tour d'Argent, sued for exclusive rights to the name and won.

Four years ago, Elizabeth and Chris de Portzamparc completely redid the interior of Les Grandes Marches, making it very modern, with a touch of Art Deco. Especially notable are the chairs, which look amusing but are very comfortable to sit in. The restaurant is known for its shellfish. It also has a special arrangement whereby, during the *entr'acte* (intermission) at the Paris-Bastille, operagoers can make a reservation and eat immediately following the end of the performance. Many stars of the opera stage have dined here and signed the guest book.

Continue around the *place* to your right. The **rue Richard-Lenoir** is known for its food market, **Marché Bastille**, on Thursday and Sunday mornings. This is one of the less expensive food markets, and people come from far away to shop here. Even though prices may be lower than at other markets, the quality remains high. A short walk down the street takes you to another Wallace fountain (see Walk 1). Notice the complete Art Nouveau *métro* entrance on the **boulevard Beaumarchais**.

Between the rue de la Bastille and the rue Saint-Antoine is the **Café des Phares**, a neighborhood hangout. The café hosts a philosophy debate every Sunday morning at eleven, drawing people from all over Paris. This was the first of about twenty *cafés philos* in Paris, many of which are near the university on the Left Bank, and many more all over France.

At the corner of the rue Saint-Antoine is a plaque commemorating Charles de Gaulle's famous World War II motivational speech: LA FRANCE A PERDU UNE BATAILLE! MAIS LA FRANCE N'A PAS PERDU LA GUERRE! (France has lost a battle! But France has not lost the war!) France, he insisted, had to continue to fight in order to be present when the German enemy was crushed and, thereby, recover its liberty and grandeur. NOTRE PATRIE EST EN PÉRIL DE MORT. LUTTONS TOUS POUR LA SAUVER! (Our fatherland is in danger of death. We must all struggle to save it!)

Beaumarchais, writer of The Marriage of Figaro *and* The Barber of Seville

Rue de la Bastille

Leave the *place* on the **rue de la Bastille**. This small street came into being when the Bastille turned the rue Saint-Antoine into a dead end, and Parisians needed a way around the fortress and out of the city. Today the street's attraction is its good restaurants. The chief example is the brasserie **Bofinger**, at **no. 3**. Outside, the *huîtrier* (oyster shucker) arranges and opens his fresh oysters in brimming bins; inside, patrons dine in luxury in magnificent Art Nouveau rooms. A colored-glass skylight dates from the restaurant's restoration, in 1919. For reservations in this nonsmoking room, ask for the *coupole* (dome). The restaurant's specialties are the *fruits de mer* (seafood) and *choucroute* (an Alsatian mélange of sauerkraut and sausage cooked in beer). Bofinger is very popular for late-night meals after the opera. Reserve in advance and have a quintessential French experience. Across the street, at **no. 6**, is its little sister restaurant, **Bistrot de Bofinger**, with a simpler menu and lower prices—a less elegant but still comfortable setting with similar food.

At the corner, at **no. 2**, is **Le Bistrot du Dôme**. Under the same ownership as the famous café Le Dôme in Montparnasse, this location specializes in very fresh fish. We began our lunch with a plate of tiny gray *crevettes* (shrimp) that had been lightly fried, which we ate whole like gourmet popcorn. Our meal was delicious, the prices were moderate, and the staff was friendly.

Turn left onto the rue des Tournelles into a tiny island at the junction of the rue Saint-Antoine and Tournelles. This triangular intersection boasts a statue of Pierre-Augustin Caron de Beaumarchais, watchmaker and author of the comedies that inspired Mozart's *The Marriage of Figaro* and Rossini's *The Barber of Seville*, and who lived in this neighborhood in the eighteenth century. Behind his statue is **Fauchon**, a fine foods store. This shop fills a social need created by a custom that is still de rigueur in France—you do not go to dinner at someone's house empty-handed. Fauchon sells expensive food gifts and ready-made food entrées. They also have gorgeous pastries, which, of course, are not cheap either. See Walk 7 for information on their original shop.

Art Nouveau at Bofinger, no. 3 rue de la Bastille

Rue Saint-Antoine

Across from the statue you will find the **rue Saint-Antoine**, which you are now ready to explore. At first glance it appears to be a busy and uninteresting commercial street. While the Left Bank was inhabited as far back as the sixth century, the Right

Bank, or Marais (marsh), was not settled for another five hundred years or more because the area was too wet to be habitable. Even at the height of the Middle Ages, in about the thirteenth century, this land was still largely field and meadow, much of it church lands. The major buildings were churches, chapels, convents, and monasteries, with smaller dependent structures nearby. The only built-up street was the rue Saint-Antoine, which was the major road into Paris from the east.

One hundred years later, the Marais was to become the center of fashionable Paris. The rue Saint-Antoine, because of its width from what is now the rue de Sévigné to the place de la Bastille, offered the best site in the city for the jousts and games that were the delight of the court and for the solemn processions, arrivals, and cortèges that were the public pageants of the day. When the center of Paris—that is, the Ile de la Cité—became dangerous for Charles V in the fourteenth century (a very troubled time, complicated by war with England, civil conflict, and urban uprisings), he moved to the Palais Saint-Pol (Saint Paul), near the Bastille, where he could take care of business and pleasure and yet still be able to get out of town in a hurry. The king's presence in the neighborhood drew wealthy courtiers, who built large residences that, with their fields and gardens, towers and walls, seemed like so many châteaux in an urban setting. One of these, called the Hôtel des Tournelles because of the small towers that marked its walls, came under the ownership of the crown in 1407 and replaced the Palais Saint-Pol as the royal residence. Tournelles was on the north side of the rue Saint-Antoine and included the area that is today the place des Vosges. (See Walk 4 for information on the Hôtel des Tournelles.)

The custom of games, processions, and spectacles in the rue Saint-Antoine continued throughout the sixteenth century with the addition of autos-da-fé at which heretics (that is, Protestants) were burned for the salvation of their souls and the edification of the populace. It was here that Henri II, in June 1559, engaged in the joust that cost him his life and ended the role of Tournelles as royal residence, a story recounted in Walk 4.

No. 5 rue Saint-Antoine was the entry courtyard to the Bastille prison stormed by the revolutionaries on July 14, 1789. **No. 7**, La Bastoche, is a small pre-Revolutionary house remarkably like the Petit Châtelet in Walk 1.

The large church at **no. 17** is the reformed **church of Sainte-Marie**, open only during Sunday service, at 10:30 A.M. Originally this was a mansion owned by several illustrious people in the fifteenth century, including Charles VI and his brother Louis d'Orléans. In 1554 the *hôtel* was bought by Diane de Poitiers, Henry II's favorite mistress; in 1566 it went to the renowned architect Philibert Delorme.

The mansion's destiny as a church stems from Jeanne Frémiot, a woman born in 1572 in Dijon. She married the Baron de Chantal and gave birth to a son, who married Marie de Coulanges and fathered the future Marquise de Sévigné. Jeanne, who was widowed at a young age, devoted her life to the religious order of the Visitation Sainte-Marie (also known as les Visitandines). She became the mother superior of this order devoted to the education of young girls and care for the sick. A century after her death, Jeanne became the only married woman to be canonized by the Catholic Church.

In 1618 the religious order came to Paris, and in about twenty years the convent owned a vast property just inside this eastern edge of the city, including the mansion where the church now stands. The famed architect François Mansart built the chapel in the form of a huge rotunda inspired by the Santa Maria rotonda in Rome. Many of Mme de Sévigné's relatives and other aristocrats were laid to rest in its chapel.

In 1637 Mme de La Fayette sought shelter in the convent to escape the attentions of Louis XIII. He continued to visit her, but she succeeded in keeping the relationship platonic. On the other hand, Cardinal Mazarin's niece Hortense Mancini was locked up in the convent to terminate her less than virtuous behavior. She took her revenge by putting black ink in the stoup (the receptacle for holy water in the church), and watched as the nuns smeared their foreheads with ink.

During the Revolution, the convent was demolished, leaving only the chapel, which became a revolutionary club. In 1803, Napoléon, in an effort to equalize all religions, gave the chapel to the Protestants. Today the exterior is not very attractive and needs cleaning.

One door down from the church stands one of the more impressive *hôtels* of the Marais. The **Hôtel de Mayenne**, at **no. 21–23**, has been partially refurbished, and it demonstrates the vast difference between restored and unrestored buildings. The school in the center is dark and depressing. The office buildings on either side are glorious. Eventually the school will be demolished. The *hôtel* was built in the classic seventeenth-century style of the Marais—combined brick and stone capped with a steep slate roof, just like the Hôtel de Sully farther down the street.

The school was added above the rounded pediment in the center portion over what was once the grand entry to the *hôtel,* built in the style known as *entre cour et jardin* (between courtyard and garden). This architectural plan called for a wide entry flanked by two taller façades that formed the wings of the main building, which was centered between the courtyard and garden. The wings were used for the horses and servants, while the center of the house held the reception rooms and living quarters of the noble residents. The restored Hôtel de Sully at no. 62 rue Saint-Antoine, farther on in this walk, is built on the same architectural plan.

Originally the Hôtel de Mayenne was the Hôtel du Petit Musc, bought by Charles VI in 1378 and given to his brother Louis d'Orléans. In 1562, it became the Hôtel de Boissy, under the ownership of the Marquis de Boissy. Henri III's *mignon* (homosexual friend) Quélus was brought here after he suffered nineteen stab wounds in a vicious duel, along with two other of Henri's *mignons*, against three supporters of the Duc de Guise. At 5 A.M. on April 27, 1578, the six men met in the place des Vosges. After the dust settled, two were dead on the spot, one died the next day, two survived their wounds, and Quélus lingered for thirty-three days in the Hôtel de Boissy before expiring. In an effort to save him, Henri ordered straw be strewn on the rue Saint-Antoine to muffle the noise of the traffic and then ordered the street closed to all.

Ironically, in 1613 the property came under the ownership of the nephew of the Duc de Guise who had incited the fatal duel thirty-five years earlier. Henri de Lorraine, son of the Duc de Mayenne, asked architect Jean Androuet to design his new *hôtel*. Androuet was only twenty-three years old at the time; eleven years later he was also the architect for the magnificent Hôtel de Sully, farther down the street. After passing through many aristocratic hands, the *hôtel* was leased to the Christian School of the rue des Francs-Bourgeois—hence the name on the present façade.

Today, the rue Saint-Antoine is primarily a commercial street, as this section attests. Stores selling inexpensive kitchenware are popular. **No. 32** has an amusing façade based on *Alice's Adventures in Wonderland*. Tiles portray characters from the children's book, including Alice, the Dodo, and the White Rabbit, along with a bottle labeled BOIS-MOI (drink me). Originally this was a children's dress shop called La Petite Alice, but today the shop is an unrelated tanning salon. The next street on your right is the rue de Birague, which leads into the place des Vosges, the subject of Walk 4.

Across Saint-Antoine, on the next block, **no. 53** is nicely restored with different styles of iron balconies. Back on the right side of the street, at **no. 52**, in the front of the natural foods store Naturalia, is an example of the building beams that were used to make seventeenth-century houses. The employees here have no information on the history of the building, but go inside anyway and see how massive these support beams were, and while you are there, note the coffered tin ceiling.

The **Hôtel de Sully**, at **no. 62**, is one of the finest *hôtels* of the Marais. Built between 1624 and 1630 by the architect Androuet, it was not actually owned by the Duc de Sully until 1634, when Sully was already seventy-four years old and married to a much younger and faithless wife. She was so blatant in her affairs that when he gave her housekeeping money he supposedly said, "Here is so much for the house, so much for you, and so much for your lovers."

For a good view of the façade, cross the street to get some perspective. In typical early-seventeenth-century style, the street façade was built to impress, something it does admirably,

Spring and Summer at the Hôtel de Sully

especially when compared with its tasteless neighbors. Two two-story pavilions are divided into three windows each and are crowned with stately pyramid-shaped roofs with an ornate semicircular window. Between the pavilions is the spacious courtyard's entry for horse-drawn carriages. During the Revolution, this center section was filled in the same way as the Hôtel de Mayenne is today. The splendid interior was crowded with workrooms, and the gardens were covered over with sheds and lean-tos. In 1951 the building was restored.

Enter the courtyard. The two wings leading to the main body of the house (the section straight ahead of you) were used for stables, a garage for carriages, the kitchens (noise and cooking odors were kept far from the reception areas, guaranteeing cold meals in drafty rooms), and housing for the vast staff required to maintain a home of this magnitude.

Look up at the sculptured bas-reliefs above the doorways. On the body of the *hôtel* are male figures representing two of the four seasons. Fall holds a bunch of grapes and has a hunting dog frolicking at his feet, and Winter is a balding old man with a serpent wrapped around a staff. Spring and Summer are in the back, on the garden side of the principal building. The wings of the building are decorated with four female figures representing the elements. On your right are Water with a rainbow behind her and a dolphin at her feet, and Earth with a lion; on the left are Air, in wind-swept draperies with a chameleon (reputed to live on air), and Fire, with electrified hair and a salamander (a mythical animal said to be able to withstand the heat of fire). The fashion for these symbolic sculptures dates from the end of the sixteenth century. You can see more of them in the courtyard of the Musée Carnavalet in Walk 5. We have always admired the allegorical sculptures in the Carnavalet but, in comparison, these are carved with more depth and in greater detail.

Pass between the two sphinxes with broken noses and enter the building. A little off center, to the right, is a staircase that was already dated by the time it was built. It consists of two straight runs of stairs parallel to each other and covered by a vaulted ceiling. An apocryphal story has the Duc de Sully reprimanding his wife for letting her lovers use the main staircase. She could have her lovers, he said, but they were to stay off the staircase he used. Inventories show, however, that her rooms, contrary to tradition, were on the ground floor and he was on the *étage noble* (our second floor).

On the left is the portion of the *hôtel* that is open to the public. The large room with painted beams is a bookstore. It stocks an excellent collection of books on Paris, including books in English. The other rooms are open only once a year, in September, as part of *le jour du patrimoine* (heritage day). Passing back into the gardens, remember to look up at Spring and Summer over the doorway. Spring holds a bird in one hand and a cornucopia in the other; a vase of flowers stands next to her. Summer also holds a cornucopia—hers is filled with wheat— and her scythe.

At the back of the garden is the *orangerie*—a large, formal greenhouse that all self-respecting noblemen had in order to grow their own supply of fresh fruit in the winter. This is one of the two remaining *orangeries* left intact in Paris. In the back right corner of the garden is an entrance to the place des Vosges (see Walk 4). Sully enjoyed entering the square and promenading under the arcades. Today, if you enter the *hôtel* from the *place,* it is like stepping through a magic doorway and being transported back in history to a private seventeenth-century home.

Return to the rue Saint-Antoine. A little farther down, on the left side of the street, are several food stores. At **no. 75** note the three gold horse heads, the required standard for a horse butcher. Horse butchers have become rare in Paris and are generally located only in working-class neighborhoods. **No. 77** houses a cheese shop that will mail vacuum-packed cheeses to the United States. When we stopped in, they had a wheel of Comté cheese in the front display case that was nearly two and one-half feet wide.

Across the street, at the level of **no. 84**, is the entrance to the rue Caron, which leads to the **place du Marché-Sainte-Catherine**, one of the most charming squares in Paris. In the thirteenth century this area was the priory of Sainte-Catherine. In 1767, when the Jesuits were driven out of their property at

101 rue Saint-Antoine (and out of France), the religious order of Sainte Catherine took over the Jesuits' property and demolished their own to make room for a market.

Today the *place* is a picturesque spot to sit quietly on the benches or to have a meal in any one of the several restaurants that line the square. These include **Le Marché de la Place**; **Ariang**, a Korean barbecue restaurant; and **Pitchi Poï**, a Polish-Jewish establishment that specializes in smoked fish and blinis. We enjoyed a meal at the **Bistrot de la Place**, which, at the time, was festooned with chandeliers waiting to be shipped down to the owner's newest venture—an inn in the south of France. Those chandeliers may be gone, but will they have been replaced by others? The interior is very eclectic, and the chandeliers add an extra element of fun. If you are lucky enough to have good weather, take a table outside and relax.

Return to the rue Saint-Antoine. **Nos. 101** and **99** rue Saint-Antoine are the addresses for the **Lycée Charlemagne** and the **church of Saint-Paul-Saint-Louis**. This was the location of the first Porte Saint-Antoine in the Philippe Auguste wall in the twelfth century. We will see traces of the wall behind the school later in the walk. The door was one of the four principal entrances to the city and stood here until 1382, when it was replaced by the door at the Bastille.

In the mid-sixteenth century, two *hôtels* were built here. In 1580, the Cardinal Charles de Bourbon, the uncle of the future Henri IV, gave one of these *hôtels,* no. 101, to the Jesuits. The Jesuits made it a retirement home for the superiors of their order. In 1594, however, a graduate of a Jesuit college made a failed assassination attempt against Henri IV, and Henri, in a rage, expelled the Jesuits and gave the property to the Hiéronymites (a Spanish order of priests who took Saint Jerome as their patron saint). They stayed only three years, to be replaced by artists favored by the king. In 1603 the Jesuits regained control of the *hôtel,* and this time they firmly entrenched themselves by buying the neighboring properties.

The Jesuits built the church of Saint-Louis between 1627 and 1641. It was the preeminent church of the Marais and provided the confessors for Louis XIII and Louis XIV. Mme de Sévigné was baptized here. During the Revolution, the *hôtel* became a repository for more than a million books taken from convents that were suppressed by the regime. Many of the volumes were stolen or sold by weight—three *sous* a pound. The *lycée* (high school) that now occupies the site was begun in 1804, and the buildings of the school look as though they have hardly changed since that day. Although closed to the public, the school is said to have some very fine wrought-iron stair rails and an important frescoed ceiling painted by Gherardini in 1690 in what was then the Jesuits' library.

The church, Saint-Paul-Saint-Louis (commonly called the Eglise Saint-Paul—its official double name was given to commemorate the original Eglise Saint-Louis, which was destroyed in the Revolution), was originally built during the reign of Louis XIII. Today, Saint-Paul lacks the delicacy of earlier Gothic churches that inspire a feeling of spirituality. Information provided by the church states that "this façade, inspired by Saint-Gervais, was little appreciated in its time and was found too heavy. Today, it seduces you with its nobility." To most, its baroque façade still appears heavy, dark, and over-ornamented. Divided into three sections, the statues are modern (the originals were broken during the Revolution), while the clock dates from 1627 and was rescued from the original church of Saint-Paul.

The interior is also oppressive with sculpture, although most of its treasures were lost in the Revolution. During the Revolution, the church's religious relics were also sold. The hearts of Louis XIII and Louis XIV were sold to the painter Saint-Martin. He wanted to use them to make a paint pigment called "mummy," which required mixing ground organic material with oil to achieve a brown glaze unavailable from any vegetable or mineral. This pigment was rare and highly sought after. Saint-Martin used part of Louis XIV's heart because it was the larger of the two. At the Restoration he returned the hearts and received a gold snuffbox from Louis XVIII in thanks.

In the seventeenth century this church was the site of awe-inspiring ceremonies for which no excess was spared. In his *Guide de Paris,* written in 1685, Germain Brice described the interior: "There is no altar in the kingdom that is more richly decorated and where there are more reliquaries, vessels, candelabras, chandeliers, lamps, and other similar things unknown to our ancestors, who liked simplicity in the house of God, and that the new orders have invented to warm the cooling devotion of the last few centuries." The church is still heavily decorated with an elaborate altar surrounded by paintings, arches, Corinthian pillars, chandeliers, and balconies and is capped with a heavily sculpted rotunda. One of the more charming decorations is the two huge shells for holy water given by Victor Hugo on the occasion of his daughter's marriage. Contrast this interior with the simplicity of the interior of Saint-Gervais later in the walk.

Rue Saint-Paul

Backtrack to the **rue Saint-Paul**, known for its Village Saint-Paul, an antiques center. Turn right into this street, which was named for a seventh-century church that disappeared with the invasion of the Norsemen in the ninth century. The street led to a busy harbor on the Seine that was also a swimming and washing area. Henri IV swam here accompanied by his subjects, while the ladies of the court were tucked away in a nearby tent where they could spy on the naked and cavorting men. The scene inspired this verse:

> *On y accourt pour voir l'homme en son naturel*
> *Et tel qu'il est sorti des mains de l'Eternel.*

> We came running to see man in his natural state
> And as he came from the hands of the Eternal.

No. 44 is an old one-window-wide building with an exposed beam over the door. **No. 47**, the **Cygne Rose**, is owned by an Englishwoman who serves as an unofficial helper to English-speaking tourists in the neighborhood. Her shop specializes in antiques and unusual gifts. **No. 31** is actually the arched entrance to the tiny pedestrian **rue Eginhard**. This street makes a ninety-degree turn in the middle and ends up on the rue Charlemagne. A few steps in on the right is a small gated and locked garden. In the center is a memorial that was recently placed here to commemorate a Jewish family that once lived on this spot. The inscription states:

ICI ONT VECU MONSIEUR ELIAS ZAJDNER
MORT POUR LA FRANCE À L'AGE DE 41 ANS
ANCIEN RESISTANT DÉPORTÉ À AUSCHWITZ PAR LES NAZIS
EN MAI 1944 AVEC SES TROIS FILS. ALBERT, ÂGÉ DE 21 ANS
SALOMON ET BERNARD ÂGÉ DE 15 ANS
MORTS DANS LE BLOC DES EXPÉRIENCES.
NOUS N'OUBLIERONS JAMAIS.

Here lived Mr. Elias Zajdner
died for France at 41 years old
resistance fighter who was deported to Auschwitz by
    the Nazis
in May 1944 with his three sons. Albert 21 years old,
Salomon and Bernard 15 years old
who died in the medical experiments.
We will never forget.

We got the whole story from the daughter, Mme Sarah Yalibez, a Holocaust survivor. She was one of nine children living here with her parents when they heard rumors that Vichy officials were gathering Jews and taking them away. Where, they did not know. Mme Yalibez's mother left Paris, and some of the younger children had been sent to live with Catholics in the country. On the day the rest of the family was to follow them into hiding, the twins opened the door to Vichy officials. One brother jumped out the back window and survived the war in hiding. Albert considered jumping too, but he stayed because he said he was needed to carry his grandmother's suitcases on the journey. Mme Yalibez, who was fifteen and a half when she was taken, survived Birkenau, but the others did not survive at Auschwitz. The twins were killed in Mengele's medical experiments on twins.

Mme Yalibez was very pleased that the French government finally let her put up a memorial fifty years after the war. Her requests had been rejected since after the war, but she was determined. When she applied yet again in 1995, the government had a new policy and had begun making public gestures to atone for the crimes of the Vichy government. The neighbors were not happy when the memorial was placed and immediately planted a row of trees to block the view. Mme Yalibez pulled up the trees and asked the city to plant grass. It did, and locked the gate.

Return to the rue Saint-Paul. On the left side of the street note **nos. 28**, **26**, and **20**. They are all old and attractively restored.

On the right side of the rue Saint-Paul is a treasure trove of antiques and collectibles. **No. 27** to **no. 1** is known as the **Village Saint-Paul**, an enclave of antiques shops selling everything including postcards, paintings, furniture, Art Nouveau glassware, keys and locks, and rustic farm tools. Some of the shops have a folder with a list of the participating stores and a map of the interconnecting courtyards that will help you uncover all of this charming complex.

In the twelfth century the basements under these buildings were used as dormitories by the religious orders and as a hospice for travelers. The property was just outside the city walls and served those who arrived when the gates at Saint-Antoine were closed. We have been told that the vaulted cellars under nos. 21 and 9 have been restored.

The Village Saint-Paul sells more affordable, less elegant antiques than those sold at the Antiquaires du Louvre or the Village Suisse. Here the stores are generally open from 11 A.M. to 7 P.M. from Thursday through Monday. Take time to wander through the stores. Meet Annie at **Le Puceron Chineur** (the flea market prowler), which sells solid silver and silver-plated items. She is very friendly and will help to orient you to which shops are open and what to see. Wander down the rue Saint-Paul and through the courtyards of the Village to appreciate antique dolls, Art Nouveau and Art Deco objects, kitchenware, keys, lamps, paintings, and knickknacks of all kinds and prices.

In the courtyards pause to enjoy the old buildings that have been renovated for reduced-price housing. In 1996 the media revealed that some of these apartments, coveted for their prime location and low rents, were occupied by relatives of high city officials, though the scandal has not changed the neighborhood in any visible way. At the far side of the first courtyard, exit to the **rue des Jardins Saint-Paul.** In the sports terrain across the street is the largest surviving piece of the Philippe Auguste wall and two stone towers. To your right, at the end of the street, is the back of the Lycée Charlemagne and the church of Saint-Paul. To the right of the Village's exit from the center courtyard is a lovely trompe l'oeil door painted to look like the flower-draped entry to a private garden. It is the back door of the atelier **Un Autre Regard**, a painting gallery on the rue Charlemagne. (If you have not been wandering in the courtyards, go in the entrance from the rue Saint-Paul marked 15–17–19.)

After you have taken the time to wander through the courtyards and found a few treasures to carry back home, you may find yourself tired. If you wish, you can stop walking here and return to see more, including the beautiful Hôtels de Sens and Beauvais, another time. You are near two different *métro* stops: walk back up rue Saint-Paul and, making a left onto the rue Saint-Antoine, go past the church and the *lycée,* and you will find yourself at the *métro* Saint-Paul. Or continue down the rue Saint-Paul, toward the Seine, make a right at the river, and walk two blocks to the *métro* Pont Marie.

If you are ready to continue, then return to the rue Saint-Paul. At **no. 20** is the **Thanksgiving** restaurant and its associated food shop around the corner, on rue Charles V. The two are owned by an American woman, who does the cooking, and her French husband, who does the buying. Thanksgiving's menu is mostly Cajun cooking, but its small store supplies Americans, and the French who admit to liking American products, with foods from all regions of the United States. Their weekend brunch is mostly American and is especially popular, serving pancakes, lox and bagels, and other American breakfast foods. Reservations for brunch are required.

No. 22 is a bookstore, **The Red Wheelbarrow**, which sells books in English. Unlike the Abbey Bookstore and Shakespeare and Company, their books are all brand new, organized, and neatly shelved. The store is bright, with light and friendly English-speaking employees, and the owners, Penelope and Abigail, are often there as well. Penelope opened her first bookstore in Canada at the age of nineteen and later moved to Paris, where she opened The Red Wheelbarrow in 2001. She told us that the neighborhood has a huge Anglophone community, drawn by the English department of Paris VII (a section of l'Université de Paris) nearby, and that the bookstore has become a community center for English speakers in Paris. She and Abigail also own a children's bookstore around the corner, at no. 13 rue Charles V.

On the corner of Saint-Paul and Charles V, at **no. 25** rue Charles V, is another good restaurant, **L'Enoteca**, an Italian wine bar. The restaurant offers delicious Italian food paired with a choice of about 360 Italian wines chosen by three sommeliers. Make reservations for dinner.

Detour down the **rue Charles V** with its nicely restored buildings (no. 23, for example). At **no. 14** is **L'Excuse**, which serves French nouvelle cuisine and is quite expensive. Then stop at **no. 12**, the **Hôtel de la Marquise de Brinvilliers**, also known as the Hôtel d'Aubray. Today only the doorway capped with a *mascaron* (mask decoration) of a man has been restored. But it is the story of one of its residents that is most remarkable. The Marquis de Brinvilliers, Antoine Gobelin of the famous tapestry family, married Marie-Madeleine-Marguérite de Dreux d'Aubray in 1651. The marquise turned out to be astonishingly immoral, even in an era when the nobility were allowed considerable latitude.

By her own account, she "deviated from virtue" at seven and was a regular partner of her younger brothers. (Contemporary historians would probably reexamine her history for indications of sexual abuse.) Her father gave her an extremely generous dowry of 200,000 pounds when she married at twenty-one. She had three children, although their parentage was uncertain because she did not restrict her attentions to her husband. She became the mistress of the knight Godin de Sainte-Croix, a man introduced to her by her husband. Her husband said nothing, but her father objected, and he had Sainte-Croix arrested as he rode in her carriage on the Pont Neuf. Sainte-Croix was imprisoned in the Bastille, where he made use of his time by learning about poisons from an Italian named Exili.

When Sainte-Croix was released, he and the marquise established Exili in a laboratory to make poison for them. His concoction included venom of toad, arsenic, and vitriol. The marquise had, by now, spent her considerable dowry, and she set her sights on her inheritance. As a result of her charity work, she had access to patients in the city hospital, the Hôtel Dieu. She used this opportunity to experiment with proper poison dosages, and when she thought she had it right, she poisoned her father. He was evidently stronger than the sick hospital patients because it took ten tries to do him in. Four years later, in 1670, the marquise killed the older of her two brothers and attempted to poison his wife. Her younger brother was next, although she failed with her younger sister, a Carmelite nun. Next she set her sights on her husband, but Sainte-Croix thwarted her because he was afraid that if her husband died, he would be obliged to marry this dangerous woman.

Not content with just her family, the marquise persuaded Sainte-Croix to assassinate the tutor of the two illegitimate children she had conceived with Sainte-Croix. She had had affairs with the tutor and two of his cousins, one of whom fathered her sixth child. The assassination attempt failed because the lucky tutor, on the balcony across the courtyard, had seen the marquise hide Sainte-Croix behind the fireplace.

In 1672, Sainte-Croix died suddenly of natural (!) causes. As soon as the marquise heard the news she rushed to his house to retrieve the box that contained her letters. She made such a scene that the authorities became suspicious and confiscated the box. In it they found thirty-four letters detailing their crimes and twenty-seven recipes entitled "curious secrets." She fled, taking asylum in a convent in Belgium. She was lured out of the convent, however, by an agent of the head of the Paris police and was arrested.

She wrote a confession that admitted to having set fires, to losing her virginity at seven, to having poisoned her father and brothers, to having attempted to poison her sister, to incest, to adultery, and to attempted abortions. On July 15, 1676, she was condemned to make a confession at Notre-Dame and to be beheaded and then burned in the place de Grève, her ashes scattered to the wind. She was exempted from having her hand cut off for her patricide.

Mme de Sévigné witnessed the execution and wrote up the events in a letter to her daughter. The executioner spent a quarter hour preparing the woman for her death, but "finally, it's done. Brinvilliers is in the air: after the execution, her poor little body was thrown in a very big fire, and her ashes are in the wind. . . ."

Return to the rue Saint-Paul, pausing to peer in the nameless shop at **no. 25** rue Charles V to see if the gentleman within is repairing violins and cellos, then head down the street to the left, toward the Seine. Downstairs at **no. 11** is the **Musée de la Curiosité et de la Magie** (museum of curiosities and magic). Normally the museum is open Wednesday, Saturday, and Sunday afternoons. During school vacation periods, children are offered a tour and an introductory lesson in performing magic. The last time we were here during a vacation, the line of children spilled into the street.

Note the façade of **no. 10** and its frieze below the top floor. Check and see if you can go into the very pretty courtyard of **no. 8**. When we visited in the spring, the trees were flowering and a cat picked its way through the little gardens. Notice the wrought-iron stair rails on the left, in the square tower marked ENTRANCE 8D, and the supports for the balconies. Apartment 8D also has a small section of wall that is cantilevered out. This was the privy in the days when apartments did not have private water closets. 8A and 8B have beautiful wrought-iron balconies, in contrast to the cast-iron balconies of 8C.

There are a few more antiques stores as you go. Turn right onto the **rue de l'Avé Maria**. At the corner on the right are two stores selling old lace. **No. 2**, **Fuschia Dentelle**, sells blouses, skirts, and cloth. Next door, **Francine Dentelles** carries dresses remade with lace. She also has a stand at the Marché aux Puces. Other stores on the street carry a number of interesting antiques (if you are not already antiqued-out after your trip through the Village Saint-Paul).

Continue down the street, to the **Hôtel de Sens**, at **no. 1 rue du Figuier**. This striking *hôtel* is one of the oldest nonchurch buildings in Paris, built in an architectural mélange of Gothic and Renaissance, military and civilian. The building was commissioned in 1475 by Tristan de Salazar, the tenth archbishop of Sens, and completed in 1519, the year of his death. Until 1622, Paris had only a bishop, who was under the direction of the archbishop of Sens. This situation called for suitable housing in Paris for the archbishop, although because he had six other bishoprics to manage, he was rarely in residence. This infrequent use protected the building from being renovated over the years by succeeding archbishops.

In 1605, Henri IV asked the current archbishop for the use of the *hôtel* to lodge his ex-wife, Margot, who had been banished from Paris for the preceding eighteen years because of her unseemly behavior. (See Walk 3 for Margot's story.) She did not live there long, but when she did, the sober *hôtel* was transformed into a gambling den while Margot was locked up for days at a time with her very young lovers.

When the Revolution came, the *hôtel* was sold, and a series of commercial tenants defaced and destroyed the original architecture. These included a laundry, a rabbit-skin wholesaler, and a jam factory. The City of Paris finally bought the *hôtel*, in 1911, and restored it in bits and pieces over decades.

The turrets on both sides of the façade, while decorative, served the military purpose of permitting the residents to see down the streets on either side of the *hôtel*. Before you enter the courtyard, stop to appreciate the flamboyant Gothic details of the mansard window flanked by angels, in contrast to the plain façade. Don't miss the gargoyles. Also find the hole above the portal that was intended to permit the residents to drop boiling oil on unwelcome visitors. Enter the courtyard to see the portions of the *hôtel* that are open to the public. On the left is a bookstore selling cards and posters of old advertisements and an exhibition space with changing exhibits. Straight ahead, in the back of the courtyard, is the **Bibliothèque Forney**, a library of art, decorative arts, and art techniques. Take the re-created staircase to the main reading room, on the first floor (our second floor), pausing to look at the photographs of the building before it was restored. The reading room is lovely and light and packed with students hunched over worktables and lined up to wait for books to be fetched from the stacks. In the back left corner, behind the door, is a corkscrew staircase, one of the few original portions of the building to survive. The rest of the building is a re-creation in the style of the period. The library is open from Tuesdays through Fridays, 1:30 P.M. to 8 P.M., and on Saturdays, 10 A.M. to 8 P.M.

Turn right as you leave and take **rue de l'Hôtel de Ville**. This side of the building has beautiful, flamboyant Gothic mansard windows that match the front window. There are also figures of dragons, musicians, and animals, and another turret to allow residents to see in both directions of the curved street. Behind the *hôtel* are formal French gardens and two more beautiful mansard windows.

You are now on the rue Nonnains-d'Hyères and facing you is the **Jardin Albert Schweitzer**, a playground for children. Sit for a moment on the benches and watch the children play table tennis and climb on the equipment. Continue along the edge of the Seine, on **quai de l'Hôtel de Ville**, to the back garden of the **Hôtel d'Aumont**. The *hôtel* was owned by Michel-Antoine Scarron, uncle of the poet Paul Scarron. In 1629, Michel-Antoine's daughter married up socially to the Duc d'Aumont. In 1648, the Duc d'Aumont sold his *hôtel* in the place des Vosges and moved in with his father-in-law. When the father-in-law died, in 1656, the duke enlarged the property by buying four surrounding houses. The architect Mansart was hired to transform the main building, while the interior was turned over to Vouet and Le Brun.

The duke died at sixty-nine of apoplexy. (It apparently ran in his family—his son and grandson both died of it. The third duke was taken ill at his mistress's; she hastened to send him home half dead in his carriage so that he would expire at Aumont rather than in her bed.) When the first duke died, his wife sought consolation in a new marriage, to which her son took offense. He had her confined to a convent, but before she was exiled, she managed to get back at him by burying a large sum of money, which was never recovered.

This second duke apparently did not control his wife as well as he did his mother. His wife, the duchess, lived a gay life that preceded her marriage and did not end with it. The story is told that one lover, surprised by the sudden return of the duke, was forced to hide in an armoire all day before he could make his escape. While the duke's wife collected lovers (including prominent members of the clergy), the duke collected furniture and art. He collected so much that, at his death, the public sale of his possessions took several months.

Today, only the garden façade by Mansart and a ceiling by Le Brun remain. The ceiling survived only because it had been covered over with a false plaster ceiling and forgotten, perhaps for centuries. The garden façade is a classic French construction with *mascarons, oeil-de-boeuf* (bull's-eye) windows, tall windows and French doors on the ground floor, and wrought-iron balconies. The garden is mostly bare, save an inappropriate and rusting modern sculpture that resembles perhaps a broken seesaw. This elegant façade by Mansart is a sharp contrast to the heavy, graceless façade of the *hôtel* on the rue de Jouy. Return at night to see Aumont and Sens dramatically illuminated, rising out of the darkness like a stage set.

Walk along the Seine with the river and the *bouquinistes* (booksellers) (see Walk 2 for information on the bookstalls) on your left and the **Cité Internationale des Arts** on your right. The Cité provides one hundred and eighty apartments for artists from all over the world to come and study in Paris for a year. More than three thousand artists, musicians, and performers have come from seventy countries. Turn right onto the rue Geoffroy-l'Asnier.

Rue Geoffroy-l'Asnier

No. 17 rue Geoffroy-l'Asnier is the **Mémorial du Martyr Juif Inconnu**, memorial to the unknown Jewish martyr, and the archives of contemporary Jewish documentation. When we visited, it was provisionally closed for restoration, until January 2005; however, we did not see any kind of work going on. When it reopens it will be called the Mémorial de la Shoah and will include a wall with the names of all the French Jews who were deported. We don't know if the restored building will still include the crypt, which was a somber, belowground-level room with a large Star of David with an eternal flame burning in the center. Two hundred thousand tiny lights burned in memory of the two hundred thousand French dead in concentration camps. There was also a sculpture, *Despair,* by artist Michael Goldberg, reminiscent of a Virgin Mary with the martyred Jesus across her lap; it represents the universal pain of the loss of a child, a parent, a sibling. It is dedicated to the six million who died in the Shoah.

When we previously visited, the center had a temporary exhibit upstairs on the experience of the French Jews. France was unique during World War II in that it was the only country to deport Jews from territory not yet occupied by the Germans. It is only recently that the French have begun to acknowledge their official collaboration in the Holocaust.

No. 20, directly across the street from the center, has lovely *mascarons* of a lady. **No. 26** is the **Hôtel de Châlons-Luxembourg**, built in the early 1600s. One of the early owners was Antoine Le Fèvre de La Boderie, the French ambassador to England, who returned to Paris with a gift of one hundred and fifty horses. He was unable to stable them and so distributed them to his friends, keeping the best one for himself. Alas, Henri IV heard about the equine gifts and remarked, "Well, pal, am I the only one of your friends not to get one of your horses?" Reluctantly, Le Fèvre was forced to give away his prize horse.

Above the door is the head of a magnificent lion with a luxuriant mane framed by a seashell. The finely carved horses in the door knocker recall Le Fèvre's gift.

Rue François-Miron

Return to the street and continue on to the **rue François-Miron**, turn right, and walk to **no. 68**, the **Hôtel de Beauvais**. There has been a residence here since 1200, and the Gothic remains are still found in the ogival arches of the cellars. The *hôtel's* name, however, is due to its seventeenth-century owner, Catherine Bellier. Known as Cateau, this woman was reportedly ugly and blind in one eye, but she was the confidante and main chambermaid of Anne of Austria, wife of Louis XIII.

As a reward for intimacy (she listened to the details of Anne's romance with Mazarin and administered her enemas), Cateau and her husband, Pierre Beauvais, originally a ribbon

The newly restored courtyard of the Hôtel de Beauvais

seller, were given a baronetcy. Anne was especially thrilled when, after she told her maid her fears for the sexuality of her son, the future Louis XIV, Cateau (forty at the time) relieved the sixteen-year-old of his virginity so that he would not be frigid like his father.

The Baroness de Beauvais received such a large sum of money for her service to the crown that she purchased this piece of property and hired Antoine Lepautre, the king's first architect, to build her *hôtel*. The property was irregularly shaped and required creative use of the space. The resulting building is a polygon with the principal residence in the façade on the street rather than behind the courtyard as, for example, in the Hôtel de Sully. In addition, the architect designed the street level with stores, unheard of for a noble residence but revenue-producing for nobility of humble origins.

One of the building's glories was a magnificent balcony that was topped by a triangular pediment decorated with reclining allegorical figures. On August 26, 1660, the famous balcony was the choice spot to watch Louis XIV and his new bride make their triumphant entry into Paris. Anne of Austria, Queen Henrietta of England, and her daughter shared the Persian-carpeted balcony, shaded from the sun by a red velvet canopy as the royal procession made an honorary stop in front of the Hôtel de Beauvais.

More than a hundred years after Catherine Bellier, Wolfgang Amadeus Mozart, his father, and his sister stayed here for five months. Mozart, only seven, was the breadwinner for the family. Although he was a great success at the court of Versailles, he was apparently unhappy that, after his concert, Mme de Pompadour did not embrace him.

In the last edition of this book, we wrote that the façade was in a mutilated state and we bemoaned the lack of funds to restore this unusual *hôtel*. The interior had been divided into flats, chopping the vast reception rooms into small, featureless rooms. For a dozen years before the restoration, the building was in such bad shape that it was sealed up. Today we are happy to say that the restoration is complete and the gleaming façade lights up the street.

The administrative offices of the Court of Appeals has a seventy-five-year lease, which means that passersby can see the courtyard but cannot get past the security guard at the gates to enter it. Take a moment to appreciate this graceful oval courtyard with its very tall *première étage* (first story) and *mascarons*. Note the frieze under the balcony that alternates intertwined Bs, for "Beauvais" and "Bellier," and the head of a ram (*bélier*).

Because you can't enter the building, some impressive restoration work is inaccessible, including two remarkable staircases. The grand staircase is four ramps of solid carved stone supported by four Corinthian columns. The vaulting is richly decorated with putti, *mascarons,* rams' heads, sphinxes, and so on. In the east wing is the original oval wrought-iron stair rail that once led to the *hôtel*'s private chapel. If you are curious, be sure to visit the Association pour la Sauvegarde et la Mise en Valeur du Paris Historique, down the street at no. 44 rue François-Miron. They have a scale model and photographs of the building.

Continuing on rue François-Miron, **nos. 72** through **78** have nicely restored eighteenth-century façades. **No. 82** is three arcades wide, with a different *mascaron* on each arcade. The center one is the head of a moor with a turban. Notice also the elaborate balcony and the wrought-iron railings. On the window above the center balcony is a pediment with another *mascaron*. Go around the corner on the rue de Fourcy to see the garden and wing of this *hôtel*. In order to widen the street and still have a sidewalk, this side of the building is cantilevered out and held up by pillars.

On François-Miron, cross the rue de Fourcy and continue on the same sidewalk (at this point François-Miron merges into the rue Saint-Antoine) to the second building from the corner. The **Hôtel de Séguier**, at **no. 133**, was built in 1626 and owned by the Séguier family until the Revolution. Note the balcony supported by fantastic chimeras.

Retrace your steps back down the rue François-Miron. At the corner of François-Miron and the rue de Jouy is the restaurant **Au Bourguignon du Marais**, where they serve lunch and dinner Mondays through Fridays. The menu is traditional French and they offer many wines by the glass—the owner comes from a Burgundy grape-growing family, so he knows about wine. In warm weather sit outside for your meal and then buy some wine from their shop to take back to your hotel when you are done.

Continue on to **nos. 44** and **46**, the Maison d'Ourscamp, home of the **Association pour la Sauvegarde et la Mise en Valeur du Paris Historique**, whose official mission is to undertake and lead all action to promote, protect, and make Parisian neighborhoods known in order to preserve their architecture and social harmony. This nonprofit group, which is staffed by dedicated and educated retired volunteers, seeks to promote and protect historical Paris. The offices are open daily, 2–6 P.M.

In the twelfth century, abbeys across France were rich and powerful. They found that they needed a pied-à-terre in the city for the abbot and a dormitory for their students at the school of Notre-Dame. Ourscamp was originally one of these houses, as the vaulted medieval cellars attest. The house owes its name to the Sire de l'Ours, an unfortunate man who lost his head in the early fifteenth century for conspiring against Charles VI's wife.

The building went through many owners and commercial tenants until, in 1941, it was declared insalubrious and was scheduled to be torn down. Almost nothing was left of the original building and the cellars had become a rubbish dump.

The association was founded in 1963, and their first project was to save nos. 44 through 46 rue François-Miron, at their own expense. Work began, with young volunteers who gave their weekends to empty rubbish from the cellars with shovels and buckets. Forming a chain up the stairs, they passed heavy buckets of stones up to the Dumpsters, manually clearing out two thousand tons of gravel. Upstairs, they broke down walls, uncovered walls, and tore out floors. So much dust billowed out the windows that the fire department came several times, called by alarmed neighbors. In 1970 the money ran out, and work stopped for fifteen years. The tarpaulins finally came off in 1987, revealing the beautifully restored façade for the first time in decades.

Take the time to visit the interior, which is like a museum of ancient construction. The floor of no. 44, much lower than that of no. 46, is a thirteenth-century stone floor; the latter's is made of sixteenth-century hexagonal tiles, except where a glass panel reveals a belowground medieval column. The reception area is in the left half (no. 46), where they have a to-scale model of the Hôtel de Beauvais, while most of the artifacts are on the right. On the wall a Gothic window tracery displays items discovered at the bottom of wells that were on the property. No. 44 also displays wrought-iron balconies and a wooden stair rail, a spiraling wooden pillar, and painted beams. The beams in the ceiling and one propped up vertically were recuperated from the Hôtel de Lamoignon. There are two staircases in no. 44. The stairs to the cellar are very steep stone stairs and must be descended cautiously. The cellars are medieval vaulted stone. On one visit, the cellar room was transformed into a Russian nobleman's castle for a movie set.

At the base of the stairs leading to the *première étage* is an exposed wall of chimney tiles marking the site of an old fireplace. If someone is available to accompany you, go up the stairs to look out the window onto the courtyard. The interior façades have been restored with the exposed beams. The rounded protuberances were the privies. Each floor had one privy fitted out with a pot for wastes. Most likely, when the pots were full, they were dumped in the sewers or the river.

The association offers excellent guided tours of historic Paris, conducted in French. However, with advance notice, they can organize an English-speaking tour for a minimum of ten people.

Directly across the street is the café **Chez Raymond**. Here men, mainly from North Africa, spend the day smoking and playing cards or backgammon. When we asked where the women were, one gentleman smiled and joked, "The women are in the cellar." Back on the even-numbered side of the street, **no. 42** has a lovely double balcony and a *mascaron* of a man with lion paws. **Nos. 40** and **36** also have *mascarons,* including the eighteenth-century ladies on no. 36. Across the street, on the odd side, **nos. 11** and **13** have been remodeled to represent how an average house looked in the seventeenth century. The buildings used to be in deplorable shape and were propped up with huge wooden crutches to keep them from crumbling into the street. No. 13, known as "at the sign of the sheep," has a fine fourteenth-century gabled roof. No. 11 is known as "at the sign of the reaper." The researchers at the Association pour la Sauvegarde et la Mise en Valeur du Paris Historique told us that the exposed beams are not full-size, but are thin wooden pieces put on the façade for effect.

Nos. 36, **34**, and **13** are Japanese stores selling pottery, fabrics, and all kinds of sleek, beautifully designed objects. **No. 30** is **Izrael**, **Epicerie du Monde**, a cache of foodstuffs. This is the way stores used to be or perhaps the way we would like to remember them. As you enter, the odor of curry and pickling brine hits you, you begin to salivate, and your stomach begins to grumble. Unlike an American supermarket, where food is carefully packaged to maintain sanitary conditions, here everything is exposed, and the mingled scents are an inspiration to the pleasures of eating. The store is lined floor to ceiling with shelves overflowing with packages, cans, and jars. You have to pick your way around the aromatic barrels of olives and pickled vegetables and bags of beans, nuts, and grains. The store is an excellent source of all kinds of exotic spices that are doled out

at your request into little plastic bags. There is a second room with teas, jams, mustards, and even some American mixes like brownies. They also sell cooking tools, bowls, baskets, posters, and all kinds of treasures.

The shop is owned by a husband and wife. Françoise Izrael's father originally opened the store when he came out of hiding after World War II. He had managed to avoid the Nazis by living in the woods in the Dordogne. M. Izrael, who was from the Balkans, stocked the shop with foods from that region. When Françoise married a man with the first name of Israel, she brought him into the business. She has worked more than forty years in the store, and her husband more than thirty. Now their son helps out. Monsieur, with a big white beard, is the friendlier one, but Madame can be drawn out, and even gave us recipes that use some of the spices she sells. We left with a bag of candied kumquats, Moroccan preserved lemons, and some Hungarian paprika. *Note:* this store keeps traditional French hours—it is closed for a long lunch from 1 to 2:30, except on Saturdays, and is closed all day Sunday and Monday.

When you leave the store, go around the corner to the black glass door of what appears to be a modern building, at **22 bis rue du Pont Louis-Philippe**. Push the door open and, once in the courtyard that lies behind the Izrael store, you will be surprised to see the restored wall to your right. It is of brick and stone and has a wooden mansard at the top.

The interesting and pricey shops on this street include several clothing and paper shops and even a lute maker. Return to François-Miron and turn left. **Nos. 14** to **4** are decorated with elegant wrought-iron balconies that run across the building at the American third-floor level. They are decorated with an elm tree in the center to recall an elm that once stood in the place Saint-Gervais, at the end of the street. From medieval times, people used the huge tree as a meeting point: "*Attendez-moi sous l'orme*" (Wait for me under the elm). The tree was pulled down during the Revolution, and although a new one was planted in 1912, it does not have the significance the ancient

Exotic and abundant groceries at no. 30 rue François-Miron

one had. At no. 4 is a plaque to recall the home of the musical Couperin family, who played the organ in the church next door.

Walk to the **place Saint-Gervais** and pass in front of the church of Saint-Gervais (we will return here shortly) to the **Compagnons du Devoir**, at **no. 1**. This is a training school for twenty-one different trades. Here students follow a five-year course of study to become masters of carpentry and building, shoemaking, ironworking, and *les métiers de la bouche* (the mouth trades) of pastry- and bread-making. The students, who are sixteen to twenty-five years old, live in this building under the watchful eye of a head mother.

To become a *compagnon* you must complete a *chef d'oeuvre* (masterpiece), some of which are displayed here. Go inside, past the wooden model of a cathedral tower and down the stairs with their wrought-iron railing. Go out the door to the courtyard and enter the first door on your right to see a show-room of examples.

Return to the **church of Saint-Gervais**. The history of the church is as old as civilization on the right bank of the river. This spot was one of the few hillocks rising above the marsh and was the first to be settled by fishermen and boatmen. It became a point on the path for the Roman road going northward as well as the site of a pagan cemetery. A chapel was built to serve the cemetery when it became a Christian burial ground dedicated to the twin martyrs Saint Gervais and Saint Protais.

There is little record of this church; it was probably destroyed in the Norman invasion. In 1190, the wall of Philippe Auguste enclosed this plot of land, making it very attractive to the residents. The church became too small to serve its parishioners, and a new one was begun in 1213, not to be completed until 1420. All that remains of this church today are the first two levels of a bell tower that stood outside the body of the building. When the new church became too small, the third (and current) church was begun in 1494. This engulfed the bell tower, whose dimensions set the plan for the size of the whole building. The church was built in the flamboyant Gothic style despite its construction in the Renaissance, but it took so long to complete (sixty-three years) that the façade was built in the

Miséricordes *in the pews at the church of Saint-Gervais*

heavy baroque style that was then current, copied by the church of Saint-Paul.

Paris was so taken with the façade with its three sections in the Ionic, Doric, and Corinthian styles that Voltaire (an anti-Catholic) remarked perhaps sarcastically, "This is a masterpiece, lacking only a square to hold its admirers." The nineteenth-century statue of Saint Gervais is on the left, one of Saint Protais on the right. The evangels, above, date from the early twentieth century. The original statues were demolished during the Revolution.

Saint-Gervais was an important church of the Marais. Mme de Sévigné was married here and innumerable prominent people were buried here. In modern Paris, however, the church has become isolated from its congregants, surrounded as it is on one side by administrative buildings including the city hall (Hôtel de Ville), the non-church-going students from the Cité des Arts on another, and the predominantly Jewish and Arab neighborhood on a third.

On Good Friday, 1918, the church suffered the disaster of being hit by a German shell of the type known as Big Bertha; The shell killed fifty and injured two hundred. As a result of the damage, the stained-glass windows are now all modern.

Enter the church and appreciate the freshly brightened Gothic pillars, especially the flamboyant ones behind the altar. The nave is furnished only with stools because the church's monastic order, the Communion de Jérusalem, believes in simplicity. In contrast, the organ is elaborately carved with garlands, ribbons, and cherubs.

The treasure to discover in this church are the *miséricordes* carved in the pews of the choir, including animals, faces, and scenes representing trades. Find the lion, the man and the woman sharing a bath, and the lady dancing with a jester. These small sculptures were tucked under the brackets on hinged seats that priests could lean against during portions of the service that required prolonged standing. In addition, there are different faces carved on the armrests between the seats. This decoration expresses the humor and vitality of the anonymous tradesmen who built these massive churches.

Leave the church by the back door at the end of the left aisle (an area under construction at the time of our visit). You are now on the **rue des Barres**. To the left and down two doors, at **no. 15**, are the remains of a building and a room with a beamed ceiling. Through the back, the church gardens are visible. Across the street, at the corner of **rue Grenier sur l'Eau** (the street name that inspired the postcard shop mentioned in Walk 5), a building shows its exposed beams and sags from age. This building, **no. 12**, has been beautifully restored as an inexpensive youth hostel. It was once a convent and now houses students from all over the world. Peek into the lobby to see the fine antique furniture.

The rue des Barres offers a dramatic view of the flanks of the church and its attractive roofs and gargoyles. Across from the church is **L'Artisanat Monastique**, which sells products from monasteries all over France—primarily jams, honeys, soaps, candles, and religious articles. The monks and nuns from Saint-Gervais are the salespeople.

In good weather, a small restaurant, **L'Ebouillanté**, serves meals under the wings of the church, in the pedestrian street that dips down to the Seine. The outdoor tables are highly sought after in their peaceful and attractive surroundings. The restaurant is inexpensive and serves generously. It specializes in teas, salads, and hot sandwiches called *brik*.

If you continue to the end of the street you will be at the Seine across from the tip of the Ile Saint-Louis. If you are not too tired, walk over to visit this unique community within Paris. Until the twentieth century, it was not uncommon for residents of the Ile Saint-Louis to be born and die there without ever having left the island. Today it is famous for Berthillon ice cream (at 31 rue Saint-Louis). Pay high prices for precise, small scoops of flavorful ice creams and sorbets.

The bridge to the *île,* the Pont Louis-Philippe, is a meeting place for the French and for tourists. On summer nights and on Sundays, singers, mimes, and all kinds of performers line the pedestrian bridge and pass the hat.

Another option would be to retrace your steps to the front of Saint-Gervais and go from there to the place de l'Hôtel de Ville. The elegant city hall always has interesting free exhibits on some aspect of the City of Paris, and the department store across the street, the Bazaar de l'Hôtel de Ville, commonly referred to as the BHV, has a good stationery department and the best hardware department in Paris. After a fruitless search through antiques stores all over the city, we found a perfect solid brass lion-faced door knocker in the basement of the BHV for a very reasonable price. Stop by their Café Bricolo, a café dedicated to do-it-yourselfers, offering daily workshops on a variety of home-repair projects.

Walk · 7

Les Grandes Trois: Concorde, Madeleine, Vendôme

L'élégance, c'est moi.
—Coco Chanel

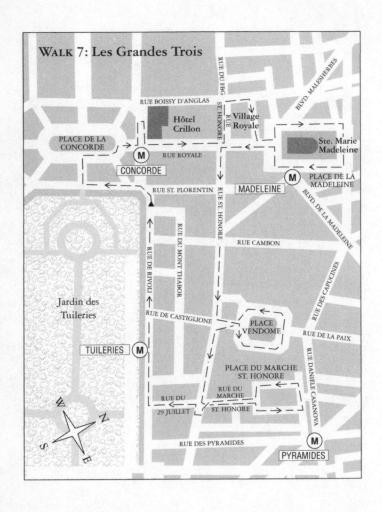

Starting Point: Southeast corner of the place de la Concorde and the rue de Rivoli, Tuileries side of the street, 8th and 1st arrondissements

Métro: Concorde or to Madeleine on the newest *métro* line (14), which is totally automatic. (Sit in the very front and look out the windows as you travel through the tunnel.)

Buses: 24, 42, 52, 76, 84, 94

This walk stretches from the place de la Concorde to the place Vendôme and the rue du Marché Saint-Honoré, and back to the rue de Rivoli. It will take you past some of the most chic jewelry shops, clothing stores, and hotels in Paris. We recommend that you dress conservatively and a little more formally than you might for the other neighborhoods in the book if you want to be welcome in the more elegant shops and hotels on this walk.

This neighborhood, like the Marais, began as an uninhabited marsh. As the water receded, the land was gradually cultivated, providing fresh vegetables and fruit to the fledgling city huddled around the islands in the Seine.

In the seventeenth century, as the wealthy moved west from the Marais they came here, near the Palais du Louvre and Marie de Medicis' Tuileries. Richelieu also built his Palais Cardinale nearby, leaving it to Louis XIII on his deathbed in 1642. The property was renamed the Palais Royale, although the king never lived there. Having royalty nearby was a sure draw for the upper class and while, in the nineteenth century, the wealthiest moved farther west, to the far reaches of the eighth and sixteenth arrondissements, this neighborhood remained the heart of Paris for the well-to-do visitor.

Today we are starting at the place de la Concorde, the largest square or *place* in Europe (84,000 square meters) and considered one of the most beautiful. While it is a major intersection heavily traveled day and night, it is also a must-see sight, making it worth your time to explore and brave the cars. The square is a favorite spot for photographs—we saw two brides posing, in addition to the usual tourists. Early morning, when there is a special natural light, or at night are the best times to see and photograph this busy *place*.

On your way from the rue de Rivoli into the actual square, pause for a moment and look left, at the end of the wall, and note the commemorative plaques that describe the events of August 25, 1944: ten soldiers dead in the battle for the liberation of Paris. At this date every year, wreaths and flowers cover the street. Lest we forget.

At this southeastern corner of the *place* there is a very wide sidewalk where you can take a seat on a pillar between a *lampadaire* (light post) and a *pavillon* (small house). Read the history and figure out the general plan of the square. Then take to the crosswalks with the light and go up to the sights.

The general plan is easy to discern. The octagon is 360 meters long by 210 meters wide. An obelisk stands in the middle surrounded by two fountains. Statues of seated women, representing French cities, are placed at each corner. The Marly horses on the west side mark the entrance to the Champs-Elysées. Twenty lamplights surround the entire square. And, unfortunately, cars pass every which way in a constant need to cross Paris.

The *place* was inaugurated in 1763 with a statue of Louis XV

Place de la Concorde

by Bouchardon, to honor the king's recovery from the pox, which, they say, he got from his loose living. He was depicted in the usual Roman warrior garb, with laurels on his head, and mounted on a horse on a sculpted pedestal. (Why always Roman garb when the French were so anxious to be rid of the Romans?) He was once called the "well-loved" king and, in homage, the pedestal was sculpted with four statues by Pigalle, each representing a virtue: Force, Justice, Prudence, and Peace. By the time of the unveiling, Louis had already bankrupted the country, obviously lost all those virtues, and fallen totally out of favor. After only a few days reigning over the *place,* the statue wore a sign, hanging on his horse's neck: OH, THE BEAUTIFUL STATUE, OH, THE BEAUTIFUL PEDESTAL. VIRTUE LIES IN THE FOOT, VICE IS ON THE HORSE.

The square's early history was not felicitous. In an eerie prefiguring of the violence that the Revolution would bring, disaster hit in 1770 at the celebration of the wedding of the dauphin

Louis and the archduchess of Austria, Marie Antoinette. The square was packed with thousands of eager celebrants and the fountains were flowing with wine when the fireworks were accidentally caused by a misfired gun. The resulting explosions and fire set off a panic, causing the overloaded bleachers to collapse. People were trampled in the struggle to escape, and 133 corpses were collected once the chaos had ended.

Worse was yet to come when the revolutionaries took power, in 1792. They promptly pulled down the statue of Louis XV and renamed the square the place de la Révolution, erecting a new statue, a woman called Liberté. She was cheaply made of bronze-painted plaster, part of which cracked. She wore a red bonnet, carried a sword in her hand, and was seated on Louis' old pedestal. She was enormous.

After centuries of monarchies, now it was the turn of the dispossessed to rule. A guillotine was erected in the square, near where the obelisk now stands, facing east toward the Tuileries. Huge crowds arrived every day, as people always did for hangings. But there was extra fervor for this bloody revolution. The mobs screamed and cheered (and knitted) as the tumbrels rolled by, delivering the aristocracy to their demise.

During the Terror, Mme Roland, a well-known moderate revolutionary, made her death memorable by eyeing the mocking statue and declaring as she mounted the scaffold, "Liberty, Liberty, what crimes have been committed in your name." But on January 21, 1793, no one in the crowd heard Louis XVI, last in the line of the Capetian dynasty, say, "I am innocent," because the tumultuous beating of the drums purposely drowned him out.

Several months later, in October, Marie Antoinette and more than a thousand others' heads rolled—including that of Robespierre, the mastermind of the Reign of Terror. The blood ran so profusely, it is said, that cattle, who know the stench of slaughter, refused to enter the square.

After the cleanup, furious political battles raged about the choice of a new name and a new statue for the square. Louis Philippe, son of the beheaded king, finally chose the calmest way out—an impersonal and foreign monument, an Egyptian obelisk, that has, ironically, become an icon of Paris, and a name, Harmony, that belies the history of the square.

Start by looking at the exquisite *lampadaire* in front of you, one of twenty. This green bronze Corinthian column is bedecked in gold designs, and supports round lamps on either side and a globed one at the top.

At this point, take the major crossing toward the obelisk, which stands in the center of an oval, flanked by two magnificent sculpted fountains created for the monument. A gift from Mahamet-Ali, viceroy of Egypt, the obelisk formerly stood in front of what was once the Temple of Luxor. It is covered in hieroglyphics telling of battles from the reigns of Ramses II and III, more than three thousand years ago. Made of pink granite, it is seventy-five feet high—Paris's greatest phallic symbol after the Eiffel Tower, which can be seen right behind it—and weighs 230 tons (460,000 pounds).

The base of the obelisk tells the story of how the engineers put it up, an event that became a huge public spectacle. Once again, but fortunately for different reasons, a spot in the *place* was as coveted as a ticket to the Super Bowl. Tickets, reservations, grandstands, drama, near catastrophe, were all part of the great event. The obelisk had traveled for three years before sailing down the Seine to Paris in 1836. The architect responsible for the lifting of the obelisk described a sleepless night. What if it fell, killing the workers and breaking into innumerable pieces? One account tells of a crisis when the rope had reached its limit and the obelisk was still not fully upright. A sailor who knew about ropes, and that hemp shrank as it dried, called out, "Moisten the ropes!" Wetting down the ropes would provide the last few degrees to vertical.

This *place* was planned with two spectacular architectural views, so special that they inspired the planning of Washington, D.C. The first is the view from east to west. Look left, through the Tuilerie gardens, and spot the Arc de Titus. The view from the arch goes through the obelisk in front of you, right down the Champs-Elysées, to your right, through the Arc de Triomphe, and continues west through the city to the Arc de la Defense. Three arches are aligned, all visible with the obelisk between them, covering about ten miles.

The second view is shorter and runs south to north. The Assemblée Nationale, across the river, on the Left Bank, marks the southernmost point of the vista. From there, the view travels north through the obelisk and up the rue Royale to the Assemblée's mirror image—the church of La Madeleine.

The huge and imposing twin palaces on the corners of the rue Royale are yet another example of the finest city planning. They were built between 1755 and 1775 by an "angel," Ange-Jacques Gabriel. Observe the wide façade of many arcades, which is topped with a row of Corinthian pillars. To the right is the Ministry of the Navy, not open to the public. To the left is the Hôtel de Crillon, which we will soon visit. These arcades were the setting for the chase and shootout in Hitchcock's *Charade*.

The obelisk is surrounded by fountains. The northern one, closest to the rue de Rivoli, is an impressive scene of Nubian mermaids and mermen, with huge, serpent-like tails. Each one is holding a fish that spouts mighty streams of water. In the center, crowning the entire scene, patriarchs and their ladies sit in boats.

A *pavillon* stands at each of the eight corners of the *place*. A grand dame sits atop each *pavillon,* representing major French cities: Lille, Strasbourg, Brest, etc.

Continue along the crosswalks to get a close look at the Marly horses, another wonder of the square. The trainers are trying to control these wild horses with flying manes. They were originally sculpted for a château in Marly, west of Paris, but when Versailles eclipsed Marly and the latter was destined to be abandoned, the horses were moved to Paris. They announce the entrance to the Champs-Elysées. The Louvre has the originals, if you want a closer look. Continue all the way to the right until you arrive at the Hôtel de Crillon.

The **Hôtel de Crillon** is rich, discreet, and quiet, with its marble floors and walls. There is a serious air to the hotel; perhaps its history as a location for signing treaties hangs in the atmosphere. Louis XVI and Benjamin Franklin signed the treaty of friendship and trade between France and the newly independent thirteen colonies here.

During World War I the hotel was the American political headquarters. The sessions that led to the Treaty of Versailles of 1919 that redesigned Europe and the first agreement of the

Covenant of the League of Nations took place in the Salon des Aigles. President Wilson stayed here in a suite during the negotiations.

The plaque to the left of the entry (facing the building) says:

EN CET HÔTEL

DU 3 FEVRIER AU 11 AVRIL

1919

FUT ELABORÉ

PAR LE PRESIDENT WILSON

ET LES DÉLÉGUES ALLIÉS

LE PACTE

DE LA

SOCIÉTÉ DES NATIONS

During World War II, the Nazis occupied the hotel until the liberation of Paris, when Eisenhower made it the supreme headquarters for the allied expeditionary force, in 1944.

Today ladies come and go with expensive shopping bags. The tearoom (€9 for tea) offers its guests fresh roses, sweet cakes, and sugars as they relax in perfect period armchairs. In the summer you can dine in the elegant courtyard walled with façades adorned with pediments and *mascarons* (mask decorations).

Another way to experience the hotel is through the flower-arranging classes held at the renowned Ecole des Fleurs on most weekdays. The school offers classes taught by some of the hottest names in floral design, and Parisians and admirers from around the world eagerly spend €300 to spend two hours with the artistic director, Christian Tortu.

Go left from the Hôtel de Crillon to the rue Royale and make a left, heading toward the place de la Madeleine. The **rue Royale** was a path (*chemin*) that skirted the walls of the city. The street had several names, reflecting the unfolding history of the city. In the seventeenth century it was called the chemin des Remparts (ramparts); in 1714, chemin des Fossés des Tuileries (ditches); in 1768, rue Royale des Tuileries; in 1792, rue de la Révolution; in 1795, rue de la Concorde; and in 1814, rue Royale Saint-Honoré. In its final incarnation, it was a city planning project designed to match the style of the two palaces built by Gabriel for the place de la Concorde. The façades of the buildings were historically fixed; however, shops have altered the ground and first floors at will. Each building is six windows wide with a *porte cochère* (carriage entrance) in the middle.

At **no. 3** rue Royale, you will find yourself at **Maxim's**. The name may be familiar to you; it is a brand name found in any of the duty-free shops in Paris, on bottles of champagne, truffles, and mustards. But before Maxim's became a brand and spread internationally (there are outposts in New York, Rio, and Beijing), it was the hotspot of Paris nightlife.

Maxim's was opened on April 23, 1893, by a waiter named Maxime, who, in the fashion of the times, anglicized his name by dropping the *e* and adding *'s*. In the late nineteenth and early twentieth centuries, Maxim's was *the* late-night scene in Paris. The richest of Paris society, foreign royalty, and industrial giants made themselves at home at Maxim's tables, of which the regulars had their own. The maître d'hotel, Cornuché, knew all of Paris. He knew the celebrities, the scandals, the political intrigue, and the secrets of the alcove. All these secrets went into his little black book, a guide to the underside of Parisian life. In his book, he made notes about everyone who came to his place—friendships and enmities, where to seat people, dangerous promiscuities, and personal tastes. For instance, when the Baron de Rothschild came with his mistress, you never asked him how he wanted his meat cooked or what brand of champagne he wanted; Cornuché already knew. He established Maxim's as the center of the social world.

Like the Baron de Rothschild, most men came accompanied by women, and also like the baron, their guests were not their wives. Maxim's was a place of lavish pleasure, and no respectable society woman would be found inside. Instead, the men brought courtesans, called *grandes horizontales*. These were educated, witty, and beautiful women whose talents were worth a great price. Their male patrons showered them with money and gifts, and the women were often dripping with furs and jewels. There were three especially well-known courtesans: La Belle Otero, Emilienne d'Alençon, and Liane de Pougy—called "Les Grandes Trois." The three of them often competed for attention, and one night, in a plan to outshine Liane de Pougy, La Belle Otero arrived at Maxim's wearing her entire collection of jewelry and an evening gown cut as low as it could go. Moments later, Liane de Pougy arrived wearing a chaste white gown and only a single diamond (she had been tipped off by a friend)—and behind her, her maid carried her entire jewelry collection piled on a velvet cushion.

Maxim's was a place of excessive indulgence. One night, in an expansive gesture, an American named Mr. Todd threw a fistful of gold coins into the air at Maxim's and let them fall to the ground all over the restaurant. This coin-tossing soon became a tradition at the restaurant, and though the coins that landed on the floor were eagerly picked up by some of the patrons, several hundred of them were found forty years later when the banquettes were removed for reupholstering.

The interior of Maxim's reflects its extravagant past. In 1899, Louis Marnez was commissioned to design the interior, and along with Majorelle, Prouvé, Gallé, and Guimard—some of the biggest names in Art Nouveau design—chose a "return to nature" theme for the restaurant. Inside the restaurant, copper foliage climbs the walls and nymphs dance in forest settings on the murals. Chestnut leaves and their fruits are repeated in stylized patterns throughout the restaurant. The glass ceiling over the main dining room dates from 1893; each piece of its frosted glass was colored with oven-baked enamel. The décor is classified and remains in its original form. A trip inside is like a trip to the glorious past. We visited during the afternoon, between the lunch and dinner crowds, and in the gorgeous, colorful interior of the restaurant, you could almost see the swanky men and women of a century ago.

You are fortunate to be here now that the present owner, designer Pierre Cardin, has opened his museum of Art Nouveau in October 2004. Cardin has been collecting Art Nouveau from around the world for the past sixty years and owns one of the finest collections in existence. He showcases his collection on the American third and fourth floors of the building, including the re-creation of the apartment of a courtesan and her *chambre d'amour*. Guided tours are available Tuesdays through Sundays, 9:30 A.M. to 4 P.M.

Today Maxim's is still popular, though mainly with a touristy crowd.

You are about to walk through a neighborhood with some of the most expensive stores in Paris, and while we have avoided prices in the other walks because they change so often, we are including some here to give you an idea of what luxury can cost.

We hope you are planning to get married or to outfit your mansion when you go to **Christofle**, at **no. 9**. This is the ultimate silver hollow ware store. A family enterprise for six generations, it began with Charles Christofle, who purchased the patents to silver plating and began the first hollow ware factory, in 1842. He became the supplier to Napoléon III. His nephew was next in line and was responsible for introducing electroplating. In fact, the name Christofle has become synonymous with electroplating, the way the terms *Kleenex* and *Xerox* have become synonymous with tissues and photocopies. Later, Christofle became the silverware supplier to the Orient-Express, to the most elegant ocean liners, such as the *Normandie*, and to the Ritz Hotel. Today, Christofle supplies the best homes with elegant, handmade tableware. One place setting in silver, €103; electroplated €40; stainless steel, €17.

René **Lalique**'s eponymous store, at **no. 11**, is a showcase for the handmade crystal objects that are based on designs from the master. A major force in the Art Nouveau movement, Lalique began as a jeweler, achieving renown for designs that were masterpieces of creativity and beauty. Sarah Bernhardt wore many of his creations made especially for her. Lalique's innovation was in blending precious gold and gems with common elements such as horn, ivory, enamel, and glass in designs based on nature. Glass became an art form of its own for Lalique, and he began making perfume bottles. Animals, vases, and other objects joined the repertoire. Unfortunately, none of Lalique's jewelry is being made any longer, but a sensitively expressed animal or an elegant perfume bottle, a lily of the valley or a firebird, might be a perfect gift.

To complete the outfitting of your house, stop in at **Bernardaud**, also at **no. 11**, for the finest Limoges porcelain in the country. The store offers modern and classic designs, as well as your own personalized creations. At the time of our visit, there was a meeting of the distributors, who were seated very cozily at tables in the middle of the store with coffee and small croissants.

Lachaume, no. 10, has been providing fancy flowers to Parisians since 1845. Marcel Proust was a patron of their orchids, which he made famous in *Du Côté de Chez Swann*, the first volume of his opus, *A la Recherche du Temps Perdu* (Remembrance of Things Past). This is the only interesting aspect of the west side of the street, which is in need of repair. We wonder why one side of the street becomes so stylish and the other not.

You are now at the intersection of the rue du Faubourg Saint-Honoré, on the left, and the rue Saint-Honoré, on the right. The name *faubourg* means suburb or, literally, a "false city," indicating that this was the city limit. The wall that was here was built under Louis XIII between 1632 and 1634. Before this, the city limit had been on the rue Saint-Honoré at the level of the Théâtre Français, just west of the Palais Royale, as determined by the wall of Charles V, built in the late 1300s.

The entry to the city was an imposing three-story "door" made of cut stone to resemble a *hôtel particulier* (townhouse). A humpbacked bridge arching over the moat led to a drawbridge before the entry arch.

The whole wall was torn down in 1733 as the city expanded, and the new city boundary was moved out to the level of the Arc de Triomphe, on the Champs-Elysèes. This new wall was known as the Mur des Fermiers Généraux, and it was not a defensive boundary, but a tax collection system. Representatives of the king levied taxes on all goods entering Paris, angering everyone.

At this point we will head to the left on the **rue du Faubourg Saint-Honoré**. When the wall came down there were few private *hôtels* on this street, but gradually, through the eighteenth century, the neighborhood began to rival the elegance of the Faubourg Saint-Germain, on the Left Bank. The street is still one of the most exclusive in Paris.

We are only going one block down the street, but farther west than today's walk is the Palais Elysée (no. 55), the British embassy (no. 39), and the Hôtel le Bristol (no. 112); many fashion designers also have addresses on this street. On another day, experience the pomp of Paris on a walk down the Champs-Elysées and the Faubourg Saint-Honoré.

Note the fairly modern architectural excesses of **nos. 3** and **12** as you head toward **Hermès**, at **no. 24**. Hermès began as a saddlemaker but made its mark in leather handbags and silk scarves, which in the early days of the shop often had equestrian themes. A Kelly bag, named for Grace Kelly (priced in the thousands of euros, depending on the leather and size), and an Hermès scarf (€245) tossed gracefully around the neck are the sure signs of a socially connected French woman.

As you exit Hermès, turn left and left again, onto the rue Boissy-d'Anglas. The street is named for the 1795 president of the Convention (the Revolutionary assembly from 1792 to 1795). A rational thinker, he was known as the enemy of ideologues, and he invented the concept of liberty for one's conscience.

At **no. 23**, on the left, is the service entrance for Hermès. Here is where you bring your worn saddle for repairs. There is also a memorial plaque on this building for an American who was a member of a World War II resistance cell: THE BELLS OF LES HALLES, A RESISTANCE GROUP, TO THE MEMORY OF THEIR REGRETTED COMRADE, ORVILLE J. CUNNINGHAM, AMERICAN CITIZEN, ARRESTED THE 24TH OF SEPTEMBER, 1942, DIED THE 4TH OF DECEMBER, 1943.

Across the street, on your right, is the entrance to the **Village Royale**, aka Cité Berryer. In the mid-eighteenth century, this was a market with butchers, bakers, fishmongers, and produce sellers. This neighborhood could use a street market now, but instead there are chic stores, including British Haviland China and Barbour (the classic shop for hunting clothes), and a trendy café, **Le Village**. If the weather is nice, sit outside in this peaceful spot that feels like a village street in the middle of Paris. This rural impression is mainly due to the low three-story buildings, rare in Paris, with small gable windows on the top floor and flowered balconies and old-style street lamps attached to the façades. The interior of the café is velvety and comfortable, resembling the Café Marly at the Louvre.

The passage connects back to the rue Royale, where you will exit and turn left. You are now about to enter the **place de la Madeleine**.

The *place* as it exists today was designed in 1808 as a frame for the church, which was completed in 1824. Its origins go back to the sixth century, however, when the bishop of Paris had a fiefdom west of Paris named La Ville-l'Evêque. Its chapel was dedicated in 1238 to Sainte Madeleine. Four hundred years later the small village had become a parish, and the old church was inadequate for the needs of the growing *faubourg*. In 1660, La Grande Mademoiselle, Louis XIV's cousin, laid the corner-stone for a new church.

One hundred years later, in 1756, the neighborhood had become so fashionable that plans were again made for a newer, larger church. The construction of the place de la Concorde in-spired the plan for a vista down the rue Royale with the focal point of a magnificent church at the end. The original plan called for a church in the form of a Latin cross capped with a large dome. The architect, Pierre Contant d'Ivry, died before the plans could be achieved, and the new architect, Guillaume Couture, changed the church to the shape of a Greek cross (all four arms of the cross are of equal length), with a Corinthian portico and an even larger dome.

The Revolution put an end to all the construction, and the structure was invaded by small merchants and artisans looking for a sheltered spot to set up shop. Plans were discussed to transform the space into a national library, an opera, the bank of France, and the stock market. Napoléon wanted to make it into a Temple of Glory for those who had died at Ulm, Iéna, and Austerlitz. Louis XVIII wanted it to be a monument to Louis XVI and Marie Antoinette. All the plans came to naught, and in 1845 the space was dedicated simply as a parish church.

In the end, the church ended up looking like a Greek tem-ple surrounded by fifty-two Corinthian pillars on the outside and three domes above the nave—no transept, no side chapels, no bell tower, and, architecturally speaking, no resemblance to a church. Napoleon III wanted the Assemblée Nationale, across the river, to match this Greek temple and had a façade built to create the vista. If you wish to visit the church, enter after you have walked around the perimeter of the *place*, beginning with the left side (when facing the church).

Lucas Carton, at **no. 9** place de la Madeleine, is a Michelin three-star in an authentic Art Nouveau setting. Chef Alain Senderens took over at Lucas Carton in 1985, a place where he had worked before as a young apprentice. Splurge on an inventive, luxurious meal in a room decorated with fabulous wooden panels by Majorelle, the noted Art Nouveau cabinetmaker (see examples of his work in the Musée d'Orsay). Per person, lunch will easily top $100, and dinner $300.

Traffic in the place de la Madeleine is constant and seems to come from all directions, so cross only with the light at the crosswalks as you head across the boulevard Malesherbes, toward **Baccarat**. This is only an outpost of the main store, which is located at no. 11 place des Etats-Unis in the sixteenth arrondissement. Enter here, at **no. 11** place de la Madeleine, to get a taste of the glassware and crystal jewelry made by this classic French luxury company. If you are interested, visit the main address, where there is an elegant restaurant and a museum of the history of crystal production.

The shops that line the perimeter of the *place* are predominately luxury food stores. We can hardly imagine what your food bill must be like if you live in this neighborhood and these stores are your corner groceries.

Now that you have purchased your silverware at Christofle, your dishes at Bernardaud, and your crystal glasses at Baccarat, **Caviar Kaspia**, at **no. 17**, will provide you with the perfect seduction snack—Iranian caviar and iced vodka or champagne, open noon to 1 A.M., Mondays through Saturdays.

Next door, at **no. 19**, is the **Maison de la Truffe**, and next to that is **Hédiard**, at **no. 21**. Ferdinand Hédiard started selling exotic spices and fruits in Paris, in the mid-nineteenth century, from a cart in the place des Victoires, showing astonished Parisians pineapples and mangoes from the tropics. Today, the shop continues the tradition by selling imported foods from the world over, specializing in fruit products such as jams, crystallized fruit, and fruit jellies.

The reigning doyenne of the food shops in the place de la Madeleine, however, is in the northeast corner. **Fauchon**, at **no. 26**, is the most famous food store in Paris, a city known to be passionate about what it eats.

Ironically, Auguste Félix Fauchon began his career employed by Félix Potin, the originator of the first grocery chain in Paris. While Félix Potins are small, utilitarian grocery stores, Fauchon stocks luxury goods to satisfy your every gustatory whim. In our early days in Paris, Fauchon was the only place to get such then-exotic American specialties as cake mixes, corn flakes, and cranberries for that all-important Thanksgiving dinner.

Today, you can shop here for chocolates, teas, fine *pâtisseries* (cakes), wine, out-of-season fruits, and all kinds of classy gifts to bring home. Or pick up ready-made meals and appetizers for a feast in your hotel room.

You will see branches of Fauchon in other parts of Paris and their products in the supermarkets. In a city where nearly every store was a one-of-a-kind business, chain merchandising has become the rule. Many of the once-exclusive Right Bank shops have found it profitable to move into the formerly bohemian Left Bank.

From Fauchon, cross to the side of the church to the flower market, open every Tuesday and Friday. The arrangements are yet another example of French artistry in daily living. In summer, these spectacular flowers are all grown in and around Paris.

Continue toward the façade of the church of the Madeleine. But on the way, stop at the most unlikely and fabulous discovery of the walk. Just to the east of the entry is a sign for public bathrooms, WC. Normally we would not dare go underground to see a public bathroom, but this one is special. It was built in 1905 in the Art Nouveau style. Go downstairs and for less than half a euro get your own stall with a floral carved wooden door. Inside is a clean, private toilet, sink, mirror, and flowering tiled walls. A woman in a small wooden booth monitors the bathrooms and will also shine your shoes, if you desire. Would that all bathrooms in Paris were as charming!

On the other side of the church (the left if you are facing the front) is a discount ticket office for French theater. If you speak French and want to see a play, the **Kiosque Théâtre** is open Tuesdays through Saturdays, 12:30 to 7:45 P.M., and on Sundays, from 12:30 to 3:45 P.M., offering half-price seats.

If you wish to enter the church, do so now.

Cross in the crosswalks to the east side of the rue Royale

(on your left if you have your back to the church and are facing the place de la Concorde).

Ladurée, at **no. 16** rue Royale, is the original site of a very famous pâtisserie and tea salon. We actually now prefer the newer location, at 21 rue Bonaparte (see Walk 3). This is formal, old-fashioned Paris at its best. Enter this cramped space and crowd into the line in front of the display case to purchase *macarons*. For decades we have been making our obligatory pilgrimage here for these treats. Having no relation to macaroons, *macarons* are two hemispheres of ground almond meringue sandwiching rich ganache. They come in an abundance of flavors, such as dark chocolate, bitter orange, lemon, and pistachio. A few miniature *macarons* are a perfect pick-me-up as you walk—they are delicious and rich but don't drip on your clothes. This past summer the special *macaron* was strawberry-poppy, a delicately perfumed marvel of flavor and aroma. You can also perch on a small chair and enjoy a cup of tea with your pastry. This could be a good opportunity to read up on the place Vendôme, coming up, where there are no benches and we have a lot of information for you.

Turn left into the **rue Saint-Honoré**. As in the Marais, the first residents were the religious orders. In the early seventeenth century there were six different convents and monasteries on what is now the rue Saint-Honoré: the Jacobins, the Capucines, and Filles de la Conception on the north; the Feuillants, Capucins, and Couvent de l'Assomption on the south. At that time, the city limits on the rue Saint-Honoré extended to where you are now.

The wealthy began heading west in the early eighteenth century. The Marais to the east was losing its appeal, one reason being that the air was fresher to the west. Prevailing winds brought the foul odors of garbage and waste eastward. Gradually, the wealthy flocked to this westward portion of what is now the first arrondissement. The place Vendôme was the heart of the development, luring the most elegant shops and hotels to the neighborhood. It remains so today. We will cover only a short distance of the rue Saint-Honoré today, but the street stretches all the way to Les Halles by way of the Palais Royale, a neighborhood worth visiting.

Enter the courtyard of **no. 414** to see a re-creation of Gothic architecture. It was built by A. Walwein, architect, and A. Cruchet, sculptor, in 1903. It is interesting to note that this was done at the same time as the flowing, extravagant Art Nouveau style of Maxim's. While the Victorians had a fondness for Gothic revival style, with its caryatids and chubby angels, Art Nouveau and its successor, Art Deco, had a far more lasting impact. The building is a storehouse for antiquities. These doors are never opened, and all the activity happens at the back, on the street behind the building.

Au Nain Bleu (at the blue dwarf), at **no. 408**, is the French equivalent of what F. A. O. Schwartz used to be. Started in 1836, it moved to its present location in 1910. The criteria for the store are elegance and refinement—not common among toy stores.

In 1943 disaster struck the store. A Gestapo agent came in to ask if the store sold flags. A foolish shopgirl offered a French flag, angering the German. She was taken away and interrogated. The Germans returned two days later and rounded up the other shopgirls and the store's director. They were taken to the prison in Fresnes. The salesgirls were held for twelve days, but the director was deported to a prison camp in Germany. He was liberated at the end of the war.

Alison remembers mooning over the luscious stuffed animals as a child, but Sonia never bought her one. Alison, in turn, never bought one for Rebecca, but now Sonia shops for her great-grandchildren. Excellence is not cheap, and the toys here are significantly more expensive than American toys. The doll collection in the front of the store is extraordinary. The dolls are primarily works of art, not playthings.

You are now at the intersection of the rue Saint-Florentin, originally called cul-de-sac de l'Orangerie because it ended at the orange trees of the Tuileries as commemorated in the museum by the same name.

Across the street is **Longchamps**, at **no. 404** rue Saint-Honoré, a famous handbag store. Half of Paris carries the shop's light fabric bags with leather trim. They come in several sizes and styles and many fold into neat packages so you can pack them empty into your suitcase and then fill them with all the goodies you have purchased for the trip home. The building is eighteenth century with a classified wrought-iron balcony and *mascaron*.

No. 281, across the street, is also an eighteenth-century building. In 1859, **no. 265** was the home of the famous actress Sarah Bernhardt, when she was fifteen years old. Today this new building is the home of **Max Mara**, a prominent Italian clothing store specializing in classic yet modern designs.

No. 398 was the home of Robespierre, mastermind of the Terror, from July 7, 1791, until his guillotining on 9 Thermidor (a date under the French Revolutionary calendar), July 27, 1794.

Galerie Schmit, at **no. 396**, is one of the most important art galleries in Paris. It is a three-generation story, beginning with the grandfather, who dealt with old masters but built a catalogue of thirty thousand pieces of eighteenth-century art sales to the present day. Today the gallery shows nineteenth- and twentieth-century art from Ingres to Chagall and Picasso. You are welcome to look for free or buy at the latest exhibition.

No. 390 is yet another famous handbag store. **Hervé Chapelier** makes beautifully colored, machine-washable bags that are immensely popular with young Japanese and American women. Even with a weak dollar, prices here are about half of what they are in the United States.

The **Couvent des Filles de l'Assomption** was installed at **no. 263** in 1622. It was a fashionable retreat for widows, abandoned wives, and penitent women. The daughter of Mme de Pompadour was raised here. She was engaged at age eleven to the Duc de Picquigny, who married her a year later. She died at twenty.

The convent was disbanded during the Revolution, and what remains of the convent's chapel has been the parish for Poles in Paris since 1850. Oddly enough, this elegant oval room has no architectural religious aspect. The altar and angels have been added. The church runs a Polish restaurant in the crypt that is open for lunch and dinner, 12 to 3 P.M. and 7 to 10 P.M. Go downstairs, to the left of the church doors, and eat traditional Polish food under the stone vaulting, surrounded by Polish-speaking diners.

Ironically, across the street, at **no. 261**, was once the famous restaurant Voisin. During the Franco-Prussian War, when

The menu at Voisin on Christmas Day, 1870

Paris was under siege, food became very scarce. Parisians ate anything, and according to an English journalist of the period, the price of rats rose to 80¢ and dogs or cats cost $4 a pound. On Christmas Day 1870 (the ninety-ninth day of the siege), the restaurant served an elaborate meal with meat obtained primarily from the zoo—elephant consommé, stuffed donkey head, kangaroo stew, roasted camel *à l'anglaise*, and cat accompanied by rat. Yum.

No. 382 was another convent. The Couvent des Filles de la Conception was founded in 1635 by thirteen religious women. Paul de Gondi, future cardinal of Retz, wrote about his first visit to the convent, in 1650: "I was not ignorant of the fact that in this ministry there were more than 24 young women, many beautiful and coquettes, and I was at pains not to test my virtue. I never spoke to them when their veils weren't lowered. After six weeks of this, I had given my chastity a marvelous luster."

Perhaps by the time you get to **nos. 368–74**, the restoration will be complete. At the time of our writing, however, a construction fence masked most of the façade of these eighteenth-century buildings. The peeks we could get hinted at beautiful architecture and historically certified doorways and balconies. Except for the façades, these four buildings to the corner are being gutted to build a shopping area, which will be called 9 cour Vendôme. The corner building gives it the desired address.

No. 374 was the salon of Mme Geoffrin, known as the "minister of society" and hostess to the intellectual heavyweights of the late eighteenth century. These included philosopher Diderot, architect Soufflot, society and later salon mistress Mlle de Lespinasse, writer Montesquieu, writer-philosopher Voltaire, painter Quentin Latour, one of the brothers Grimm, and painter Boucher. Mme Geoffrin had married a wealthy but boring man who was forty-seven years old to her fourteen. She, however, was intelligent and generous, gathering artists on Monday nights and writers and foreigners on Wednesday nights. She died here at age seventy-eight. The building has been remodeled, and the grand staircase that the famous climbed to reach Mme Geoffrin's salon no longer exists.

Look up at the façade of **no. 366**, **Christian Lacroix**. A lovely *enseigne* (sign) from a previous shop owner—a book-

Enseigne *on 366 rue Saint-Honoré*

seller, new and antique—still hangs over the door. The main door is beautifully carved and topped with a *mascaron* and a lovely wrought-iron balcony. On the wall are the elegant initials *CF,* but we don't know their historical significance.

In 1576, Catherine de Médicis installed a monastery of Capuchin monks at what is now **nos. 239–51**. When the community reached one hundred and twenty monks, the building was expanded. The church was built 1601–1610, although it was very austere, unlike the convents of the Jacobins or Feuillants. The Capuchin vows of austerity and poverty were too much for some: two monks fled to England with two sixteen-year-old girls. Could the young ladies have come perhaps from the convent of the Capucines, right across the street?

The convent closed in 1790, and its church became a book depot until it was demolished in 1802. Nos. 247–51 went through many changes: first it was a hippodrome; then the Cirque Olympique in 1807; a riding school in 1817; and a department store in 1828. In 1841 it was a concert hall and *bal dansant* (dance hall), where it cost 2 francs to come and dance. In the 1880s, it became the Thermes Saint-Honoré, but bathing was not a successful venture because there were already competing baths nearby, on the Seine. The winter circus that shared the space, however, was a hit. It had its last show in 1926.

Across the street was the Couvent des Capucines, at **nos. 360–64**. In 1601, the widow of Henri III left 60,000 *livres* in her will for the establishment of a convent for the Capucines. The monastery was completed in 1606, with high walls to protect the nuns from the "lubricious" eyes on the ramparts of the city walls. On June 18, eighty Capucines, wearing crowns of thorns and escorted by eighty Capuchins, paraded down the rue Saint-Honoré to their new home. The Capucines lived entirely from alms, always walked barefoot, and never ate meat or fish. Their privations must not have appealed to French women: this convent was the only order of Capucines in France. In 1688, Louis XIV moved them out in order to take over the property in preparation for the construction of the place Vendôme.

The **Hôtel de Costes**, at **no. 239**, was once the cemetery for the Capuchins. Today it is a very trendy hotel. The entrance is flanked by security men in black shirts and pants, but they won't stop you from entering. Instead, the hostess for the lovely tented restaurant in the courtyard may be the one who cuts you short. The diners are all *très chic*. We were amused to watch a much older gentleman fawn over a young thing who couldn't be bothered to put down her cell phone.

The hotel has no brochure, and we did not see a hotel room, but the salons are decorated in "Empire bordello," in dark velvets and romantic intrigue. In the basement are a sybaritic swimming pool and spa decorated like a Moroccan palace. Book a room here just so you can indulge in a pedicure on a chaise longue while your partner swims in the turquoise-tiled pool.

You are now at the corner of the rue de Castiglione and the **place Vendôme**. Because there are no benches in the place

Vendôme, you might take a break at **Le Castiglione**, a café diagonally across the street, where you can read the history of the *place* before walking through it. Once there, your only option for a seat is one of the large parking stanchions that surround the area.

Turn right into the *place*. In 1686, Minister Louvois persuaded Louis XIV that he needed a grand square that would be an ornament in the city, would improve circulation, and would provide a location for academies, the royal library, and embassies. Louis envisaged that this square would be anchored by a pedestrian statue of his royal self, and he would create a new street to open a vista between this *place* and the place des Victoires, where his equestrian statue stands.

But, in the end, the project was too expensive, and it was finally completed as a series of private residences with funds from the city and six speculators who took ownership of the buildings.

Jules Hardouin-Mansart and Boffrand designed the square in a smaller octagon, fittingly shaped like a perfect emerald-cut diamond, considering that the *place* is now home to the most expensive jewelry stores in Paris. The architects moved the buildings forward twenty meters, at great expense; it cost half as much to demolish them as it had to build them (labor must have been cheap). This allowed for larger residences behind the impressive façades to appeal to private investors. And yet the square still feels vast and, while architecturally beautiful, lacks any human dimension.

The square's décor is a series of arcades separated by horizontally ridged stones and topped with *mascarons,* each one different. Above the ground floor is a double row of windows divided by Corinthian pillar caps. At the angled corners and in the middle of the long sides, the windows are divided with Corinthian columns with triangular pediments. The windows are fronted with wrought-iron balconies decorated with a sun (Louis XIV was the Sun King). The whole is topped with a typical mansard roof of blue slate and mansard windows.

The monument in the center of the square has had several transformations. The original equestrian statue of Louis XIV was, like everything else, destroyed during the Revolution. In

1803, Napoléon decided that he wanted to re-create the Roman column of Trajan. This was a monumental one-hundred-foot-tall column of marble that was decorated with a continuous sculpted frieze that wound itself to the top, where it was crowned by a gilded statue of the emperor. The column was hollowed out inside and fitted with a spiral staircase rising to a viewing platform at the top.

Napoléon's plan was completed as a forty-four-meter column of bronze with seventy-six bas-reliefs of the campaigns of 1805 mounted on the base that had once held Louis. The bronze was obtained from 1,250 cannons captured from the Russians and Austrians. This column was topped by a statue of Napoléon decked out in the garb of a Roman emperor.

In 1814, Napoléon was pulled down and recast into a new statue, of Henry IV, for the Pont Neuf. Instead, an enormous fleur-de-lis spent a few years atop the column only to be replaced in 1833 by another statue of Napoléon, this time in military coat and tricorne hat. Napoléon III replaced that statue with another of Napoléon as Roman emperor.

This one came to a spectacular end under the Commune. The painter Courbet organized a pull-the-column-down party on May 16, 1871. Half a dozen men sawed away at the base of the column and pulled on ropes attached to pulleys. Progress was slow, and the crowd was restless. The band played "La Marseillaise" until finally, late in the day, the column came crashing down.

Maxime Vuillaume, a chronicler of the time, described it thus: "I will never forget that huge shadow that crossed my eye! . . . A cloud of dust . . . All is over . . . The Column is brought down, smashed, its stone entrails in the wind . . . Caesar is on his back, decapitated. The head, crowned with laurel leaves, rolled like a pumpkin all the way to the edge of the sidewalk."

Courbet payed dearly for his crime. He tried to convince the judge that he did it to improve circulation in the square and that the artistic quality of the carving was poor, "It was sculpture like a child would have done. No perspective. None. The figures are completely grotesque." The judge didn't buy it. Courbet had to fund the new column at a cost of 350,000 francs. The debt crushed him, leaving him destitute, and probably shortened his life.

The new column used the same molds to re-create the bas-reliefs, and Napoléon dressed in Roman emperor attire was replaced on the top. There is a staircase inside the column, but no one is permitted to climb to the top.

Today, the *place* doesn't feel Parisian. There are no cafés (in fact, nowhere to sit at all) and the traffic is strictly controlled by metal stanchions and underground parking. Tourists gawk, but no one lingers.

The place Vendôme has been described as the heart of fashionable Paris because it is home to the world's most expensive jewelry and watch stores and to the Ritz Hotel. The number of exclusive names adorning the shop fronts is astonishing. Stand and read the shop awnings, from the south side moving counterclockwise from six o'clock: **Buccellati** is at **no. 4**; **Repossi** at **no. 6**; **Mikimoto** and **Dior** at **no. 8**; **Bulgari** and **Patek Philippe** at **no. 10**; **Chaumet** at **no. 12**; **Piaget**, at **no. 16**, ironically shares an address with **Swatch**—watches for the elite and watches for the plebeians; **Chanel** jewelry at **no. 18**, **Breguet**

Buccellati's silver animals in the window on the place Vendôme

Chanel storefront with mascarons

and **Mauboussin** at **no. 20**; **Van Cleef & Arpels** at **no. 22–24**. The west side of the square houses **Cartier** at **no. 23**, and **Fred** at **no. 7**, but it is dominated by the **Ritz**, at **no. 15–17**.

The customer list of Van Cleef & Arpels is representative of the fashionable clientele of this neighborhood: Prince Ranier for Grace Kelly, the shahs of Iran, Eva Perón, Sophia Loren, Liz Taylor, Audrey Hepburn, Maria Callas, Marlene Dietrich, Joan Fontaine, Gloria Swanson, Queen Noor, Lady Diana, and many others. A company motto is that a jewel from Van Cleef & Arpels is, above all, a promise of happiness. (Not quite true for all of these women.)

Window-shop and dream to your heart's delight. If you wish to enter any of the jewelry stores you must be buzzed in, and security is tight. In any store other than Swatch, casual browsing is not encouraged.

Now tour the *place* counterclockwise from right to left.

At **no. 8**, in the courtyard, is **Stoklux**, a second-hand clothing store. Live in the tradition of the *place* and pick up a Chanel suit for €1,500. Frédéric Chopin briefly lived at **no. 12**. He moved in in July 1849 and died there on the seventeenth of October of tuberculosis. His funeral was thirteen days later, at the church of the Madeleine, and his body was buried at Père-Lachaise cemetery, while his heart was sent to the Church of the Holy Cross in Warsaw, Poland.

No. 16 was rented to one of the greatest con men of all times, the German doctor Franz Mesmer (the origin of our word *mesmerize*). In October 1778, Mesmer moved in with his famous electromagnetic basin and started offering sessions in "animal magnetism." Mesmer claimed that the stars produced a fluid that had an effect on live beings that could be reproduced by the laying-on of hands, and that he could heal illness. After a few happy cures, he was inundated with desperate patients. He saw fifteen patients at a time seated around a basin filled with water, metal filings, and ground glass. A patient would grasp an iron blade that rose out of a hole in the basin's cover and hold it to the afflicted part of his body. A long cord connected all the other patients to the basin in order not to dissipate the energy.

Mesmer would walk behind the patients, touching them and driving illness out of them as if by enchantment. His reputation spread, and he began to offer cures for the wealthy that he personally saw to and cures for the poor administered by his valet. A visit to Dr. Mesmer became all the rage, and society folk asked one another if they would be meeting over the doctor's basin in the same way that today people arrange to meet after work at a bar.

Perhaps greed got the better of Mesmer, but when he tried to use a tree instead of the basin, his success suffered. In response, he demanded that the government offer him land and a château. Instead, they offered him a salary of 30,000 *livres*, which he refused. He sold the secrets of his cure to the Masons for 340,000 *livres*. This was fortunate timing because a government commission had just determined that Mesmer's marvelous cures were due to the patients' imaginations. Descredited, but 340,000 *livres* richer, he fled to London, where he died in 1815, forgotten—although his name lives on.

In 1878, the Countess Castiglione, known as the crazy woman of the place Vendôme, came to live at **no. 26**. At forty-one years old, she was obsessed with her mortality and the loss of her beauty. She covered all her mirrors and draped the walls in black. Her shutters were closed, and she received no one. She had a special side entrance to her apartment built so she could slip out under cover of darkness and wander the neighborhood like a black wraith.

No. 21, on the west side of the square, was the showroom for designer **Elsa Schiaparelli**. Unlike Coco Chanel, Schiaparelli was born into a privileged and wealthy Italian family. Schiaparelli distanced herself from her family as a young adult when she married a count, William de Wendt de Kerlor, and moved to the United States, where her husband left her for Isadora Duncan.

Schiaparelli's brief marriage produced a daughter, and left the two of them all alone in America. Legend, spread by Schiaparelli herself, has it that she lived in poverty and survived only on oysters and ice cream, but her daughter, nicknamed Gogo, says that her mother loved to be dramatic about finances, and in fact they continually received money from the family in Italy. It was with this money that Schiaparelli eventually returned to Europe, but not to Rome—this time it was to Paris.

In Paris, Schiaparelli began her career as a designer. She opened her first shop in 1927, at 4 rue de la Paix, a street leading into the place Vendôme. Her popularity increased, and in 1935 she opened her store permanently at 21 place Vendôme and started to compete with Chanel. In contrast to Coco Chanel's knowledge of the intricacies of design and sewing, Schiaparelli knew nothing about how to construct clothing. She was an artist who drew what she wanted and simply supervised the manufacture. This annoyed Chanel, who called Schiaparelli "that Italian artist who makes dresses."

Schiaparelli's first design was a sweater with a trompe l'oeil bow in the front. The idea for this design was considered shocking then, and the word *shocking* is still used to describe Schiaparelli's designs and colors. Her fashion had a tremendous sense of humor. There were hats made to look like anything else—shoes, lamb cutlets, fabric whose pattern made it look torn, handbags in the shape of telephones, and other designs that played on the trends of the time and other cultures. Schiaparelli was friends with the major artists of the time and used the genius of Cocteau and Dalí to design daring and clever clothing.

"Shocking" also became the name of her perfume. Her Shocking perfume came in a bottle shaped like the torso of a woman—a bottle designed by Dalí based on the curves of actress Mae West.

There is still an office to represent Schiaparelli products in the building, although, regrettably, none of her clothing is still being made.

The jewel of the place Vendôme is **no. 15**, the **Hôtel Ritz**. The name is so associated with luxury it has come into the vernacular in common expressions, such as "ritzy" or "puttin' on the ritz." Ritz crackers were invented during the Depression to create an impression of luxury. F. Scott Fitzgerald, a fan of the hotel, titled one of his short stories "The Diamond as Big as the Ritz."

At the end of the nineteenth century, César Ritz had the brilliant idea to start a luxury hotel at a time when the wealthy rarely stayed in hotels; they visited at one another's estates. His concept was to create a princely house where the wealthy would feel at home. He paid close attention to detail: when he saw a horse-drawn wagon dragging a cauldron of hot water to the Hôtel le Bristol for the Prince of Wales's bath, he knew then that his hotel would have private bathrooms with hot and cold water for every room. The bathrooms at the Ritz were so extraordinary, Parisians came to view the marvels "like visitors to a museum," Mme Ritz wrote in her memoirs.

Ritz didn't stop at the baths. His rooms were the first to be electrically lighted, but with the precaution of peach-colored shades to flatter the women's complexions. He also offered telephones in every room.

Today the Ritz is owned by Mohammed Al Fayed, who has invested more than $250 million in renovations. There were rumors that he wanted to sell the property after his son, Dodi, died in the Paris car crash that also killed Princess Diana in 1997.

One of Ritz's best moves was to hire Auguste Escoffier as his chef. "Good food is the basis of true happiness," Escoffier would often say. In our opinion, Escoffier's version of happiness is truer than Van Cleef & Arpels', and we are not alone. In response to the question "Would you like a jewel from Cartier?" famed hostess Elsa Maxwell is reputed to have said, "No, I'd prefer a party at the Ritz."

Today the chef at the Ritz restaurant, **L'Espadon** (swordfish), is Michel Roth, winner of the Bocuse d'Or and Best Craftsman in France, 1991. Enjoy a meal in the elegant dining room with trompe l'oeil ceilings and red velvet banquettes or on the quiet flowered terrace. In 2004, the prix fixe menus were €68 for lunch and €160 for dinner.

One of the most famous residents of the Ritz was Coco Chanel, who lived here for thirty-five years. Today the name Chanel is synonymous with wealth, style, and class, but Chanel herself was not born into the upper class. An illegitimate and unwanted daughter named Gabrielle, she earned the name Coco in her career prior to fashion—as a *cocotte* (high-class courtesan). It was through a wealthy lover, an English nobleman named Boy Capel, that Chanel got her start in designing. Capel gave her the gift of a small millinery boutique in the place Vendôme, a place chic enough to distance Chanel from her shabby beginnings.

From the small shop, Chanel grew an empire. She opened her studio nearby, on the rue Cambon, while still maintaining a storefront in the place Vendôme. The back entrance of the Ritz opened to the front entrance of her studio. Chanel's goal, which was revolutionary at the time, was to dress the women of Paris "simply, and in black." Her designs—graceful and modern, austere and independent—challenged Poiret, the reigning fashion designer at the time. In response to them, he said, "Until now women were beautiful and architectural, like the prow of a ship. Now they all resemble undernourished telephone operators."

Chanel's place in the fashion world allowed her access to high society, a place where she would never have belonged on her own. Chanel linked herself to the wealthiest members of society and to the most influential artists, such as Salvador Dalí, all of whom influenced her designs. Coco Chanel was the epitome of French fashion and style, which at the time set the tone for the rest of the world. Her role and styles remained unchallenged until 1935, when Elsa Schiaparelli moved in to the place Vendôme.

The Ritz has restored Chanel's apartments at great expense and effort. Sixty people worked seven days a week for two months to re-create her personal décor. You can experience the two-bedroom, two-bath suite for €6,600 a night.

The Ritz has always been a draw for American authors. In the late twenties, F. Scott Fitzgerald and his wife, Zelda, enjoyed the glamour of the hotel and introduced Ernest Hemingway to its pleasures. Hemingway was still far too poor to pay for his own drinks, but soon he began saving his money and betting on horses to finance a once-a-week indulgence. After the financial success of *The Sun Also Rises,* he was finally able to afford a room at the Ritz, saying "When you're in Paris, the only good reason for not staying at the Ritz is lack of money." Small detail.

On June 14, 1940, German officers marched into the Ritz with an official order of requisition, and the Nazis began a four-year occupation of the hotel. The managing director of the Ritz ordered his remaining staff (all those who wished to leave at the Germans' arrival were given permission to go) to provide service but nothing more. In fact, a mini resistance cell was organized to send out information on the comings and goings of the German high command—disguised as fictitious food orders from the Ritz kitchens.

A stay at the Ritz was the prize for high-ranking officers. Goering stayed here. Ostensibly stationed in Paris to command the bombing of England, Goering apparently spent most of his time pillaging French art.

On August 25, 1944, Hemingway "liberated" the Ritz. He arrived in a jeep with a group of armed allied soldiers ready to capture the Germans. Discharging their weapons at nothing more than linen sheets drying on the rooftop during their sweep of the hotel that turned up no one—the Germans had already left—Hemingway and the other soldiers all repaired to the bar to celebrate their victory with martinis.

Relive the era with a drink at the Hemingway Bar, open to the public from 6:30 P.M. to 2 A.M., Mondays through Saturdays, or in the Vendôme and Cambon bars (jackets required).

The basement of the Ritz houses an elegant health club and the largest private swimming pool in Paris. While the hotel prefers to focus on the elegance and luxury of its facilities, the pool has received the most attention as the location where the British-born American ambassador to France, Pamela Harriman, died of a stroke. An elegant and colorful person in Paris society, she was a great devotée of the pool. For you, an annual subscription will cost €3,400.

Another way to experience the Ritz tradition is to enroll in the Ecole Ritz Escoffier. This cooking school offers a variety of options, from amateur to professional. Most classes, including children's classes, are in French, so for many Americans the most convenient is the Monday-afternoon demonstration class offered in English for €47.

Entering the Ritz can be daunting. You will be scrutinized by security and doormen, and we were told that the "typical American tourist in shorts with a camera around his neck" is not permitted to enter. We recommend that you be well dressed and walk with purpose if you wish to see the inside of the hotel. Ask where the shops are. They are always willing to sell.

At **no. 13**, to the left of the entry to the Ministry of Justice, is a marble stone engraved with an official meter measure. It was put here in 1795 under the Convention, along with fifteen others in public places in the city, to familiarize the citizenry with the new measure. This is one of two remaining meter measures in Paris.

The Emir of Dubai owns the southwestern corner of the *place*. He has reportedly initiated renovations that are not in keeping with the original style of the building and yet has never actually lived in the *hôtel*. You can identify his property by the blank look of the tinted windows and the empty feeling of the building.

Leave the *place* from the south side and turn left onto the **rue Saint-Honoré**. Across the street, **Goyard, Malletier**, at **no. 233**, is one of those old-fashioned shops that make us wish we led the kind of lifestyle that required its services. A custom trunkmaker since 1853, Goyard has supplied luggage to a list of prominent customers, including the Duchess of Windsor and members of the British royal family, presidents of the United

States, the Grand Duke of Russia, Sarah Bernhardt, Catherine Deneuve, John D. Rockefeller, and César Ritz.

Goyard's trunks are made of mahogany and covered with a custom waterproof fabric of linen, hemp, and cotton. The only change that has been made over time is that new dyes are being used to create the bright colors for the contemporary trunks.

Goyard's forte is specialized cases, such as a trunk for thirty-five pairs of shoes made for the Duchess of Windsor. Go upstairs to see the trunks made for chef Alain Ducasse. One is designed to hold all Ducasse's important cooking tools and his favorite pots and pans. A second is lined with shelves to transport his cookbooks. The conference table in the center of the room is used by clients and the Goyard designers to plan the requirements for personalized trunks.

Not being very savvy, Alison asked the representative how one could check these trunks with an airline. He politely explained that the people who ordered these masterpieces usually traveled by private plane. The shop does sell small pieces of luggage, handbags, and wallets that we average Joes can indulge in.

At **no. 231** is one of the several excellent chocolate shops in Paris, **Jean-Paul Hévin**. Buy chocolate bars from different countries in Africa and South America to appreciate the different flavors chocolate can have. The finest chocolate is always bittersweet, and the higher the cocoa content, the more intense and less sweet the flavor. Anything over 70 percent is too strong for most Americans. You can also buy mixed chocolates in gift boxes. Choose from the selection of poems printed on cards in a box by the door to include with your gift. On the second floor have a light lunch or, even better, afternoon tea featuring an indulgent chocolate pastry made by Hévin, a master *pâtissier* (pastry chef).

No. 352 is restored; its monumental door and balcony are classified.

Nos. 235–229 were the site of the **Couvent des Feuillants**. The buildings on the rue Saint-Honoré were added in 1782 to offer apartments for rent to raise revenues for the convent. Unfortunately, this was a short-lived enterprise. The Revolution soon followed, and in 1790 the convent was closed and a Revolutionary group, the Club des Feuillants, took over the property.

Louis XVI and his family spent three nights here before being transferred into imprisonment in the Temple. In 1804, the buildings were razed to make way for new streets, leaving only this piece. Enter the courtyard of no. 229 to see the remains of the back of the nave of the convent's church. Today, the tower-like structure, plastered over in white, supports the building on the other side of the wall.

The convent got its start in 1587 when sixty-two Bernadine monks and their abbot settled here in a ruined house, dedicating themselves to an ascetic life. Henry III hired an architect to build a proper convent, and it was Henry IV who placed the first stone in 1601. That same year, Marie de Médicis came to the still-primitive church to pray for the birth of a son. A few months later, Louis XIII was born. Anne of Austria tried the same technique in 1637 and gave birth to Louis XIV a year later.

La Fontaine, famous for his moral fables, lived in a flat above the entrance to the convent. For twenty years he was the guest of Mme de la Sablière, the flat's owner. He moved in, in 1673, after the death of his first patroness, the wealthy, widowed Duchesse d'Orléans.

No. 350 has an extraordinary history. Originally it was two houses, and in 1746 the eastern half was occupied by Charles de Savalette, a guard of the royal treasury, while the western half was owned by Gilbert de Nozières, who left it to his daughter, the wife of Savalette. In 1774, the two houses and the house next door, at no. 348, became one under the ownership of Charles-Pierre de Savalette de Langes, a former royal magistrate and guard of the treasury. Very wealthy, in 1791 he loaned seven million *livres* to the counts of Artois and Provence to enable them to emigrate and escape the Revolution. But being a cautious man, he hedged his bets and rallied to the Revolution, taking as a lodger Barrère, a member of the Committee of Public Safety. This smart move saved Savalette's head when the Commune came after him for the royalist loan.

Savalette died in 1798. During the Restoration, a young woman named Jenny Savalette came to Paris complaining bitterly about her financial ruin as a result of the outstanding loan her father had made to the brothers of Louis XVI. She was welcomed with open arms and a government pension, a political posting to the head of the post office of Villejuif, and an apartment in the Château de Versailles. She socialized in the highest ranks of society for many years, until her death, in 1858, when she left a fortune of more than 200,000 francs. Imagine the neighbors' shock when they came to prepare her for burial and discovered that not only was she no relation to Savalette but she was also a man who had conned them all for years!

Enter the courtyard of **no. 350** to see a charming statue of a naked lady.

Nos. 350–334 date from the late 1700s and early 1800s. **No. 334** was known as the petit Hôtel de Noailles because the Duchesse de Noailles gave it to her son in 1723. See page 268 for the Hôtel de Noailles proper.

No. 223, a splendid house eleven windows wide, decorated with vermicelli stones, a shell above the door, and a *mascaron,* was the home of Mlle George, a classical actress in the mid-nineteenth century. She was the kept woman of the Polish prince Boleslas Sapieha, who reportedly paid her 5,000 francs a night. *Pas mal.*

Turn left into the **rue du Marché Saint-Honoré**. **No. 1** (up a little from the corner) is **Styl Honoré**, a pen and ink store. They are known for the inks made in special colors, such as cassis and kiwi. They have a pen for every requirement. Open only on weekdays.

At **no. 5** is **WK**, a second-hand store. Always shop for second-hand clothes in a neighborhood where the women are better dressed than you. At WK you can pick up Chanel, YSL, Prada, Dior, and much more at prices that start around €100.

This short street is a rare food street in this neighborhood, although it is not really adequate—there is no bakery to be seen. However, across the street is **L'Ecume**, at **no. 6**, a serious fish store with an oyster and raw bar in the back. The shop does not have a restaurant license, so all the fish is uncooked, but their sushi and oysters have a loyal following, including a mention by Patricia Wells in the *International Herald Tribune*. A tape of seagulls plays in the background.

The top of the street is dotted with restaurants. But we must warn you that the *place* you see opening before you is also packed with restaurants where you may fare better. The ones on the street are popular local hangouts, and their customers probably find the trendy restaurants in the *place* too chi-chi for their taste. Try the traditional **Au Bistro**, at **no. 8**, **Le Rubis**, at **no. 10**, or **La Table du Marché**, at **no. 12**. As proof of their adherence to tradition, Le Rubis still has Turkish toilets—a ceramic square with "footprints" for you to crouch over a hole. (In contrast, the ultra-sleek bathrooms of Nomad's, at the corner in the *place,* are sheathed in black stone so shiny you can watch yourself using the toilet.)

Enter the **place du Marché Saint-Honoré**. In good weather, come here to see and/or participate in the very popular outdoor lunch scene far from car traffic. The eastern half of the *place,* on your right, is lined with restaurants, their tables spilling onto the sidewalk, every seat claimed.

The *place* was originally the Couvent des Jacobins. It was founded by Marie de Médicis in 1613 for the Dominicans, called "Jacobins" because they came from the rue Saint-Jacques. Although there are no longer any traces of the convent, it was once extensive.

The main entrance to the convent was at the present rue du Marché Saint-Honoré and the rue Saint-Honoré, and the monumental entry portal was three arcades topped with statues. The central arcade was large enough for carriages, the sides for pedestrians. The courtyard was fifty meters long, the church fifty-five, and behind that, convent buildings surrounding a vast garden extended back past the rue Gomboust. The convent was so extravagant, that a writer of the period sourly remarked that Queens Marie de Médicis and Anne of Austria, and Marquis Jean du Tillet de la Bussière, "did the convent a lot of [financial] good."

In 1792 the convent, with its sixty monks and twenty novices, was eliminated and replaced with the Revolutionary Club des Jacobins, with Robespierre in command. As the Revolution turned on itself, a decree of 28 Floréal (eighth month of the French Revolutionary calendar), an III (May 18, 1795) declared that the establishment of the Jacobins of the rue Saint-Honoré would be given over to a public market that would be named the Market of the Ninth of Thermidor (the date of

Robespierre's execution). Completed in 1810, the market was four very large slate-roofed sheds surrounding a fountain. The plan was to build elegant apartments in the style of the rue de Rivoli, but it was thought that no one would rent so far from the center of Paris. Sober, somewhat boring buildings were built instead. We think that high-rent apartments were impossible not because of location but because of the neighbors. Why would a wealthy person choose to live on top of a dirty, noisy market that included several butchers, with their carcasses, stench, and attendant flies?

Unfortunately, in 1960, the market was torn down and replaced with a charmless cement building providing parking, a gas station, and a firehouse. This in turn came down in the 1990s, to be replaced with the present glass structure. The architect, Ricardo Bofill, chose glass to reflect the buildings surrounding the square. There is a small food market here on Wednesday afternoons and Saturday mornings, until 1:30 P.M., and an occasional antiques fair in the *place*.

Before you settle in for lunch, walk all around the *place* to assess your options. At **no. 18**, on the south side of the square, is **Le Pain Quotidien**, an extremely popular breakfast and lunch spot appreciated for its earthy breads and fresh, light food. This is a small chain with outposts in New York City. At **no. 24** is **L'Absinthe**, a bistro owned by Michel Rostang and run by his daughter, Caroline. In winter, dine in the comfortable, smoke-free rooms, and in summer, eat on the terrace. All the restaurants here will serve you a good meal, ranging from traditional French to Italian or Asian—just be sure to arrive before 1 P.M. in the summer if you want a coveted outdoor table.

In the northwest corner, at **no. 33** place du Marché Saint-Honoré, be sure to check out **Philippe Model**'s fabulous hat shop. The multipaned exterior looks charmingly old-fashioned, while the bright blue paint hints at the sense of humor found inside. Philippe Model is well known as the provider of hats for the social *gratin* (upper crust) who attend events such as the Royal Ascot horse races or the French equivalent, Le Prix de Diane.

Straw hats in fabulous shapes and in all colors of the rainbow are topped with extravagant flowers and ribbons. Some resemble an entire garden poised delicately on your head. While

Philippe Model's hat shop

we were there, women arrived carrying their dresses to match to a hat for their special occasions.

Philippe Model also sells fabulous gloves with fur and embroidery in lush colors. Hats start at €150 for a plain straw hat and go up into the thousands. Gloves range from €70 to €900. The shop opens at 11 A.M.

At **no. 23**, on the east side, note the round tower in the façade. Perhaps this was a staircase.

Cotélac, at **no. 19**, in the southwest corner, is a French women's clothing chain with four boutiques in Paris. Designer Raphaelle Cavalli makes easy-to-wear, casual clothes with panache. Her family comes from Lyon, the heart of the French

The courtyard of the Hôtel de Noailles

textile business, and she buys her cloth there. She says, "I know how to make fabric live, not really how to make clothes."

Leave the square on the rue du Marché Saint-Honoré, in the center of the south side, and retrace your steps back to the rue Saint-Honoré. We will be heading down to the rue de Rivoli, but before we do, let's make a brief detour to the left, on the south side of the rue Saint-Honoré.

No. 209 has an ironic history. Following the Revolution, it was the home of Dr. Guillotin, the inventor of the guillotine. Dr. Guillotin's infamous creation was originally a humane effort to make death swift and painless, and he could not have imagined the ways in which it would be abused. We don't know if he ever

An old-fashioned pharmacy

watched the tumbrels lumber down this street with their human cargos, but he could surely have heard their echoes once he moved here.

The decorated shop fronts at **no. 211** are wonderfully evocative of an earlier century. Originally, no. 211 was the **Hôtel de Noailles**, which was an extensive property that stretched almost to the place des Pyramides, to the south, and the present no. 229 rue Saint-Honoré, to the west. Originally built in 1687, the property came into the hands of Count Adrien-Maurice de Noailles, later Duc de Ayen in 1711. He was married to a niece of Mme de Maintenon, first the tutor of Louis XIV's children and then the king's wife. Noailles was named *maréchal*, ambassador, state minister, and *pair de France* (peer of the realm). He was known for his intelligence and work ethic.

He made his home into a veritable museum and installed a barrier in front of the entry, a privilege reserved only for the royal family and the very highest dignitaries.

In 1774, Noailles's daughter married the Marquis de LaFayette. We know him as the French hero of the American Revolution, but few know more than that. He was orphaned at twelve, a very wealthy eligible young man; he joined the army at fourteen and married Noailles's daughter in 1774, at age sixteen. She was fifteen. When he sailed to the American colonies in 1777 (at only nineteen years old) to fight the British, his wife remained in Paris, in the family *hôtel*. Marie Antoinette paid them an honorary visit here in 1779, upon LaFayette's return to Paris.

The *hôtel* was confiscated during the French Revolution and used by different committees. It was finally restored to the Noailles family under the Restoration. The huge property was divided in 1830 and cut up by the creation of new streets in the neighborhood.

Today what remains is the property of the Clarion Hôtel Saint-James et Albany. The front door is on the rue de Rivoli, but you can enter the beautiful courtyard through the *porte cochère* (carriage entrance) between the lovely shop façades. The courtyard behind the iron gate is used by the hotel as an outdoor restaurant in the warm weather. Go in. Note the wrought-iron balconies, *mascarons,* and Louis XV décor.

At **213** rue Saint-Honoré is **Colette**, a busy center for modern design and trendy accessories. Young people come here to get the latest watch or electronic must-have. The lower level has a sleek restaurant open for lunch.

Return to the corner and make a left onto the rue du 29 Juillet, named for the third day of the 1830 revolution, and walk south to the rue de Rivoli. Named for Napoléon's success at Rivoli in January 1797, this street is a relative newcomer for the heart of Paris. This western half of the street was built from 1800 to 1835 with strict zoning regulations. There were to be no artisans, no workers who used a hammer, no food sellers, and no shopkeepers who needed to use an oven. The façades had to be uniform with arcades and could not be decorated with writing or shop signs. To encourage businesses to agree to these strict rules, all owners were exempted from taxes for thirty years.

Shop signs are obviously now permitted, and many of the stores are tourist oriented, spilling scarves, T-shirts, and postcards into the arcades. There are, however, a few holdovers from the elegant 1800s, when this neighborhood was the center for wealthy English visitors who stayed in the expensive hotels and shopped in the British-style clothing stores and English bookstores.

Galignani, at **no. 224**, was begun in 1802 to foster friendship between France and England. It was the first English bookshop on the Continent and was a home for Englishmen to read the papers and find English-language books. Today the excellent selection includes both languages.

Next door, **Angelina**, at **no. 226**, is another traditional spot for the denizens of the neighborhood. Established in 1903, it was originally called Rumpelmayer for the Austrian owner, Antoine Rumpelmayer. But Antoine had a brother in the same neighborhood, and when they had a falling out he renamed his tea shop after his wife, Angelina.

The décor of painted panels and mirrors has not changed and, despite being a little faded, has its charm. Generations of Parisians have come here to enjoy their rich hot chocolate and a pastry known as a Mont Blanc, made with mounds of chestnut cream piled high to represent the alp for which it is named.

The winter is the shop's busy season, when writers, designers and their models, actors, and French society grandmothers bring their grandchildren here for a treat. Coco Chanel and Marcel Proust were frequent patrons.

The next two addresses on the street belong to luxury hotels, the **Meurice**, at **no. 228** rue de Rivoli, and the **InterContinental**, with its address around the corner, at **3 rue de Castiglione**. The InterContinental has a decidedly sober and masculine décor; however, their courtyard restaurant is a delight, surrounded by elegant building façades and a greenhouse back wall. For a peek at the traditional luxury within the hotel, dine at night at the small restaurant **L'Ardoise**, at **28 rue du**

Mont Thabor. From their windows you will be impressed by one of the hotel's ornate ballrooms. The restaurant is also reasonably priced and serves good food. The menu is written each day on the slate board (*ardoise*).

WH Smith is the other English bookstore in the neighborhood, at **no. 248**, the corner of rue de Rivoli and rue Cambon. Smith's is part of a large worldwide chain, and while it provides an excellent selection of books, it does not have that same old-world bookstore atmosphere that you find at Galignani's.

The building was occupied during the war by the Germans, who used it as an officer's club for the Luftwaffe. Maybe this was the hangout for the officers whom Goering didn't want in the Ritz. After the liberation, German propaganda and graffiti were found on a door in the basement.

You are almost back to the place de la Concorde. As you go, note the plaques to commemorate the Marshall Plan of World War II, at the corner of rues de Rivoli and Saint-Florentin.

IN COMMEMORATION OF

THE 50TH ANNIVERSARY OF

THE MARSHALL PLAN

ADMINISTERED HERE

AT THE HOTEL TALLEYRAND

1947–1952

"AGAINST HUNGER, POVERTY,

DESPERATION, AND CHAOS"

THE AMERICAN CLUB OF PARIS

DECEMBER 12, 1997

The Marshall Plan was a huge American financial effort to aid Europe's post–World War II recovery. According to the official statement of purpose, it was a "rational effort by the United States aimed at reducing the hunger, homelessness, sickness, unemployment, and political restlessness of the 270 million people in sixteen nations in West Europe." More than $13 billion was spent to help Europe, $2.7 billion of which went to France.

You are now at the place de la Concorde. From here you can

take the *métro* or bus anywhere in Paris. But you are in the heart of the city and within easy walking distance of the Louvre via a stroll through the lovely Tuileries Gardens, at the foot of the Champs-Elysées, or a romantic walk across the Seine from the Musée d'Orsay.

Cafés, Restaurants, and Hotels

Cafés and Restaurants

The following is a list of restaurants and cafés in or near the area of the walks. Each group is arranged in order of expense. Meals cost 40 to 50 percent more in Paris, but we hope you will find that the quality is worth it. These are the places we have frequented, but there are many more for you to discover. If we have not included the phone number, the restaurant is casual and you can just stop in. We have listed restaurants as inexpensive, moderate, or expensive just as a general guideline. Keep in mind that $50 can feel much more expensive at a café than in a tablecloth restaurant. You can modify the price of your meal, however, by how you order. Appetizers can be as expensive as the main course, and aperitifs, wine, and bottled water can easily send the bill in a modest restaurant into the expensive category. To save money in a café, eat standing at the counter. It's much cheaper, but lacks the advantage of permitting you to sit and rest your feet.

Saint-Julien-le-Pauvre and Saint-Séverin

Allard, 4 rue Saint-André-des-Arts, tel. 01 43 26 48 23. A famous classic French restaurant with delicious food and generous portions. Expensive.

Atelier Maître Albert, 1 rue Maître Albert, tel. 01 56 81 30 01; ateliermaitrealbert@guysavoy.com. Excellent rotisserie cooking in a restaurant owned by the famous chef Guy Savoy. Moderate/expensive.

Les Bouchons de François Clerc, 12 rue de l'Hôtel Colbert, tel. 01 43 54 15 34. Excellent food. The wine is sold at cost. Moderate/expensive.

Le Reminet, 3 rue des Grands Degrès, tel. 01 44 07 04 24. Charming and small, with delicious traditional French cooking. Closed Tuesday and Wednesday. Moderate/expensive.

Fogón Saint-Julien, 10 rue Saint-Julien-le-Pauvre, tel. 01 43 54 31 33. Spanish tapas and paella. Moderate/expensive.

La Rôtisserie Galande, 57 rue Galande, tel. 01 46 34 70 96. Roasted meats and fish, simple and good. Moderate.

Chieng Mai, 12 rue Frédéric-Sauton, tel. 01 43 25 45 45. Authentic Thai food. Pleasant service and tasty meals. Moderate.

La Fourmi Ailée, 8 rue du Fouarre. *Salon de thé* with a limited menu of real food. Popular for Sunday brunch. Moderate/inexpensive.

Hippopotamus, 9 rue Lagrange. The French version of a hamburger joint. Don't expect much. Inexpensive.

Latin Mandarin, 4 rue Saint-Séverin. Small, good, and inexpensive Chinese.

The Tea Caddy, 14 rue Saint-Julien-le-Pauvre, tel. 01 43 54 15 56. Light lunch, afternoon tea, and cake. Inexpensive.

Le Départ, place Saint-Michel. A large, busy café good for people-watching. Inexpensive.

Man'Ouché, 21 rue Saint-Jacques. Mostly take-out or eat-in-the-street Lebanese food. Try the pancakes cooked on a *tannour*. Very inexpensive.

Dammann's Glacier, 1 rue des Grands Degrès. Homemade ice cream and some prepared sandwiches and salads. Very inexpensive.

Saint-Germain-des-Prés

Brasserie Lipp, 151 boulevard Saint-Germain, tel. 01 45 48 53 91. Alsatian food. Reserve ahead as it is popular with writers and publishers in the area. The regulars are seated downstairs; tourists, upstairs. Moderate/expensive.

Le Petit Zinc, 11 rue Saint-Benoît, tel. 01 42 86 61 00. Flowing Art Nouveau décor. Decent food and service. Moderate/expensive.

Armani Café, 149 boulevard Saint-Germain. Modern; inside the Armani boutique. Italian food, but be well dressed for better service. Moderate.

Le Bélier, L'Hôtel, 13 rue des Beaux-Arts, tel. 01 44 41 99 01. Very small, high-style restaurant with updated traditional recipes in a famous boutique hotel. Moderate.

Fish à la Boissonnerie, 69 rue de Seine, tel. 01 43 54 33 47. An American/Kiwi-owned wine bar/restaurant. An atmospheric hangout for expats and neighborhood characters. Good food and good wine. Moderate.

Les Deux Magots, 170 boulevard Saint-Germain. Busy, popular, historic café. Get a drink and people-watch. Moderate.

Café de Flore, 172 boulevard Saint-Germain. Same as the Deux Magots. Moderate.

Ladurée, 21 rue Bonaparte, tel. 01 44 07 64 87. *Salon de thé* and restaurant. Chic and classy spot for a light meal or tea and pastry. Don't leave without some *macarons*. Moderate.

La Palette, 43 rue de Seine. Arty and popular casual café and restaurant. A limited menu of so-so food. Inexpensive.

Così, 54 rue de Seine. This is the original, owned by the New Zealander who is co-owner of Fish (above). A great inexpensive, quick lunch.

Guenmai, corner of the rue Cardinale and the rue de l'Abbaye. One of the oldest macrobiotic restaurants in Paris. Lunch only. Inexpensive.

The Marais

Place des Vosges

L'Ambroisie, 9 place des Vosges, tel. 01 42 78 51 45. The only three-star restaurant in the Marais. Exquisite food. Reserve months ahead. Very expensive.

Coconnas, 2 bis place des Vosges, tel. 01 42 78 58 16. Set menu specializing in stews. Moderate to expensive.

La Guirlande de Julie, 25 place des Vosges, tel. 01 48 87 94 07. A bower of flowers and fine food. Eat outdoors in the summer. Moderate to expensive.

Café Hugo, 22 place des Vosges. A popular café with free Internet. The connection was so slow, however, we gave up. Moderate.

Ma Bourgogne, 19 place des Vosges. A popular café in a great location. Meat plates and wines. The cost adds up quickly for a café meal. Moderate.

Nectarine, 16 place des Vosges. A light lunch of salads and vegetable pies. Try the dense chocolate cake. Inexpensive.

Salon Victor Hugo, 8 place des Vosges. Another light lunch spot. Inexpensive.

Francs-Bourgeois to the Centre Pompidou

Benoît, 20 rue Saint-Martin, tel. 01 42 72 25 76. Michelin one-star restaurant. A classy bistro with excellent food. Expensive.

Le Dôme du Marais, 53 bis rue des Francs-Bourgeois, tel. 01 42 74 54 17. A beautiful dining room worth seeing, with food to match. Live music. Moderate to expensive.

Georges, Centre Pompidou, tel. 01 44 78 47 99. Go for the spectacular view from the top of the Centre Pompidou, not the food. Moderate/expensive.

Ambassade d'Auvergne, 22 rue du Grenier Saint-Lazare, tel. 01 42 72 31 22; www.ambassade-auvergne.com. Traditional Auvergnat food. Try the *aligot,* fabulous creamed potatoes and cheese. Moderate.

Marriage Frères, 30 rue du Bourg Tibourg, tel. 01 42 72 23 11. The finest tea store in Paris. Hundreds of teas from all over the world weighed out from large black tins for a line of customers.

Tea shop in the back specializing in food made with tea. Expensive for a lunch/tea shop. Tea museum upstairs.

Le Hangar, 12 impasse Berthaud, tel. 01 42 74 55 44. A hidden restaurant on a dead-end street, with delicious food and reasonable prices. No credit cards. Moderate.

Camille, 24 rue des Francs-Bourgeois, tel. 01 42 72 20 50. A busy, moderately priced neighborhood bistro. Classic French food and nice service.

Au Gamin de Paris, 49 rue Vieille-du-Temple, tel. 01 42 73 97 24. Good classic French food. Don't miss the chocolate cake. Moderate.

Le Dos de la Baleine, 40 rue des Blancs-Manteaux, tel. 01 42 72 38 98. A typical neighborhood bistro with reasonable prices and good food. Moderate.

Georget Louise, 64 rue Vieille-du-Temple, tel. 01 42 78 55 89. An old-fashioned restaurant with long wooden tables and a big fireplace. No credit cards. Moderate.

Goldenberg, 7 rue des Rosiers, tel. 01 48 87 20 16. Jewish, but not kosher, Eastern European food. Meals and deli takeout. Moderate.

Le Grizzli, 7 rue Saint-Martin, tel. 01 48 87 77 56. Good French bistro food. Eat outside in good weather. Moderate.

Un Piano sur le Trottoir, 7 rue des Francs-Bourgeois, tel. 01 42 77 91 91. Live music. Moderate. Closed Mondays.

Korcarz, 29 rue des Rosiers. A bakery and restaurant. Tasty and kosher. Buy your bagels and strudel here. Inexpensive to moderate.

L'As du Fellafel, 34 rue des Rosiers. Street food with the best falafel. Inexpensive.

Villa Marais, 20 rue des Francs-Bourgeois. Crêperie with rooftop dining in good weather. Inexpensive.

Bastille to Saint-Gervais

Bofinger, 7 rue de la Bastille, tel. 01 42 72 87 82. Beautiful Art Nouveau décor. Alsatian food and shellfish are specialties. Reserve. Expensive.

Les Grandes Marches, 6 place de la Bastille, tel. 01 43 42 90 32. Large traditional restaurant serving the Opéra. Comfortable setting. Expensive.

Le Bistrot du Dôme, 2 rue de la Bastille, tel. 01 43 35 32 00. Fresh fish. Friendly service and serious food. Moderate to expensive.

Le Petit Bofinger, 6 rue de la Bastille, tel. 01 42 72 05 23. Less formal and less expensive than Bofinger. Traditional, quality food.

Pitchi Poï, place du Marché-Sainte-Catherine, tel. 01 42 77 46 15. Kosher Polish food and blinis. Eat on the terrace. Moderate.

Ariang, place du Marché-Sainte-Catherine. Korean barbecue. Moderate.

Bistrot de la Place, place du Marché-Sainte-Catherine, tel. 01 42 78 21 32. Moderately priced. Eat outside if you can.

L'Enoteca, 25 rue Charles V, tel. 01 42 78 91 44. An Italian wine bar with weekly menus. Very good food at moderate prices and an extensive wine list.

L'Excuse, 14 rue Charles V, tel. 01 42 77 98 97. New French food in a romantic, intimate setting. Moderate.

Thanksgiving, 20 rue Saint-Paul, tel. 01 42 77 68 28. When you need an American food fix with Creole emphasis. Reserve for weekend brunches. Moderate.

Au Bourguignon du Marais, 52 rue François-Miron, tel. 01 48 87 15 40. A wine bar owned by Burgundians with wines by the glass and traditional food. Sit outside in the summer. Moderate.

Le Coude Fou, 12 rue du Bourg-Tibourg. A small, eccentric restaurant with painted murals. Inexpensive.

L'Ebouillianté, 6 rue des Barres. Light lunches, teas. When the weather is good get a table outside. Generous servings and inexpensive.

Café des Phares, place de la Bastille, near the rue Saint-Antoine. Popular café with a philosophy debate every Sunday morning. Inexpensive.

Le Brisemiche, 10 rue Brisemiche, on the place Igor Stravinsky. A good spot for people-watching. Inexpensive.

Concorde/Madeleine/Vendôme/ Marché Saint-Honoré

Lucas Carton, 9 place de la Madeleine, tel. 01 42 65 22 90; lucas.carton@lucascarton.com. A Michelin three-star restaurant in a fabulous Art Nouveau décor. An experience you will never forget. Very expensive.

Carré des Feuillants, 14 rue de Castiglione, tel. 01 42 86 82 82. Updated southwestern French by Alain Dutournier. Two Michelin stars. Very expensive.

Le Meurice, Hotel Meurice, 228 rue de Rivoli, tel. 01 44 58 10 50. Cherubs dance on ceilings dripping with chandeliers, and sumptuous food is served. Michelin two stars. Very expensive.

Les Ambassadeurs, Hôtel de Crillon, 10 place de la Concorde, tel. 01 44 71 16 16. In the formal Duc d'Aumont's ballroom, the restaurant offers continually changing, elegant modern French cooking. A Michelin one-star restaurant. Very expensive.

L'Espadon, Hôtel Ritz, 15 place Vendôme, tel. 01 43 16 30 80. One of the most romantic restaurants in Paris, with sophisticated food. One Michelin star. Very expensive.

Maxim's, 3 rue Royale, tel. 01 42 65 27 94. A step into the past, except that the colorful participants are no longer. Amazing décor and moderately good food. Expensive.

Buddha Bar, 8 rue Boissy-d'Anglas, tel. 01 53 05 90 00. A swanky bar scene with good music. Go for a drink—the food is pricey (drinks are, too, for that matter). Expensive.

Pinxo, Hôtel Plaza Paris Vendôme, 9 rue d'Alger, tel. 01 40 20 72 00. Trendy and minimalist, with an open kitchen. Go for small bites of modern, inventive food meant to be shared. An Alain Dutournier creation. Expensive.

Ladurée, 16 rue Royale, tel. 01 42 60 21 79. The original location for this patisserie/tea shop is very old-fashioned; we prefer the fresher décor of the branch on rue Bonaparte (see page 275). Moderate.

L'Ardoise, 28 rue du Mont Thabor, tel. 01 42 96 28 18. Daily specials are posted on the chalkboard. Tasty and crowded; a good deal for this neighborhood. Moderate.

L'Absinthe, 24 place du Marché Saint-Honoré, tel. 01 49 26 90 04. Modernized traditional bistro food in a restaurant owned by Michel Rostang. Eat outside in summer. Moderate.

Le Soufflé, 36 rue du Mont Thabor, tel. 01 42 60 27 19. Traditional and tasty soufflés for every course, if you desire. (Two out of three might be a better choice.) Moderate.

Le Rubis, 10 rue du Marché Saint-Honoré, tel. 01 42 61 03 34. Order the *plat du jour* and enjoy the wine at this traditional wine bar. Moderate.

La Crypte Polska, place Maurice Barres (corner of rue Saint-Honoré and rue Cambon), tel. 01 42 60 43 33. A Polish restaurant in the crypt of the church of l'Assomption. Moderate/inexpensive.

Le Pain Quotidien, 18 place du Marché Saint-Honoré. Popular for brunch and fresh, light lunches. Good bread. Inexpensive.

L'Ecume Saint-Honoré, 6 rue du Marché Saint-Honoré. Raw bar only for fresh fish at lunchtime.

Angelina, 226 rue de Rivoli. Go for hot chocolate, a Mont Blanc, and the atmosphere in this old-fashioned Parisian *salon de thé*. Inexpensive.

Jean-Paul Hévin, 231 rue Saint-Honoré. Tea shop and light lunch restaurant. Go for the chocolate pastries. Inexpensive.

Hotels

Saint-Julien-le-Pauvre and Saint-Séverin

Les Rives de Notre-Dame, 15 quai Saint-Michel, tel. 01 43 54 31 16. Elegant, especially for this neighborhood. Expensive.

Hôtel Colbert, 7 rue de l'Hôtel Colbert, tel. 01 40 46 79 50. Elegant small hotel, recently redone. Moderate to expensive.

Hôtel Parc Saint-Séverin, 22 rue de la Parcheminerie, tel. 01 43 54 32 17. Nice hotel tucked away in this neighborhood. Great view from top floor. Moderate.

Hôtel Henri IV Rive Gauche, 9–11 rue Saint-Jacques, tel. 01 46 33 20 20. A charming new hotel with sound-proofing. Friendly. Moderate.

Hôtel Esmeralda, 4 rue Saint-Julien-le-Pauvre, tel. 01 43 59 19 20. Very small but cozy. Great location. Inexpensive.

Hôtel du Mont Blanc, 28 rue de la Huchette, tel. 01 43 54 49 44. Recently redone; noisy street. Inexpensive.

Saint-Germain-des-Prés

This neighborhood has many charming, moderately priced hotels. You are safe booking a room in any of them.

L'Hôtel, 13 rue des Beaux-Arts, tel. 01 43 25 27 22. Highly decorated, with fabulous atrium. Some rooms are very small. Expensive.

La Villa, 29 rue Jacob, tel. 01 43 26 60 00. Sleek, modern hotel with a popular jazz club. Moderately expensive.

Hôtel des Deux Continents, 25 rue Jacob, tel. 01 43 26 72 46. Popular. Moderately priced.

Hôtel des Maronniers, 21 rue Jacob, tel. 01 43 25 30 60. Nice courtyard. Moderately priced.

Hôtel Millisime, 15 rue Jacob, tel. 01 44 07 97 97. Nicely decorated and friendly. Moderate.

Hôtel Saint-Germain-des-Prés, 36 rue Bonaparte, tel. 01 43 26 00 19. Charming lobby, updated rooms. Moderate.

Hôtel de Seine, 52 rue de Seine, tel. 01 46 34 22 80. Up-to-date. Moderate.

The Marais

Hôtel Pavillon de la Reine, 28 place des Vosges, tel. 01 42 77 96 40. Elegant, charming hotel tucked away in the *place*. Expensive.

Hôtel Caron de Beaumarchais, 12 rue Vieille-du-Temple, tel. 01 42 72 34 12. Eighteenth-century décor, modern amenities. Friendly service. Moderate.

Hôtel Jeanne d'Arc, 3 rue Jarente, tel. 01 48 87 62 11; information@hoteljeannedarc.com. Eclectic, charming furnishings in a very reasonably priced hotel. Inexpensive.

Les Trois Places

Hôtel Ritz, 15 place Vendôme, tel. 01 43 16 30 30; for reservations 01 43 16 30 70; resa@ritzparis.com. The ultimate elegance with prices to match. Very expensive.

Hôtel Meurice, 228 rue de Rivoli, tel. 01 44 58 10 10; meuricehotel .com. Marble and gilding and high-fashion red velvet chairs with flower-shaped backs. Luxurious and very expensive.

Hôtel InterContinental, 3 rue de Castiglione, tel. 01 44 77 11 11; paris@interconti.com. Luxurious and very expensive.

Hôtel de Crillon, 10 place de la Concorde, tel. 01 44 71 15 00;

crillon@crillon.com. Historic palace, refined, and very expensive.

Hôtel de Costes, 239 rue Saint-Honoré, tel. 01 42 44 50 00. Trendy and dramatically decorated in style Napoléon III. Expensive.

Plaza Paris Vendôme, 4 rue du Mont Thabor, tel. 01 40 20 20 00. A luxury hotel a notch less expensive than some of the others in the area. Expensive.

Relais Saint-Honoré, 308 rue Saint-Honoré, tel. 01 42 96 06 06; saint.honore@escapade-paris. A comfortable seventeenth-century building with exposed beams and free Internet access. Moderate.

Acknowledgments

We would like to thank all of our friends who came to visit and were dragged willingly or unwillingly into the streets of Paris to test our walks. Also, we thank all those who read the manuscript, for their encouragement and helpful advice. We have received many wonderful letters from readers and walkers, with valuable information and suggestions. We are most indebted to Jacques Hillairet, author of *Dictionnaire Historique des Rues de Paris,* the foundation work for the history of the streets of Paris.

Thank-you to Daniel Reid, who was eager to publish yet another edition of *Pariswalks* and who helped us with pleasure and enthusiasm. Thank-you to Anne Peretz, the original photographer, and in later editions to photographers Myrna Paterson, Templeton Peck, Carol Shapiro, Noa Landes, and Ellen Reeves.

Un grand merci to our spouses: to Nicholas, for saving us from computer disasters, and to David, for reading almost every word with a discerning eye.

Index

Index

About the Authors

SONIA, ALISON, and REBECCA LANDES own an apartment in the Marais for their frequent visits to Paris. Sonia is most often in Cambridge, Massachusetts, and Alison, a freelance writer, and Rebecca, a doctoral student in clinical psychology, live near Philadelphia.